Human Development,
Learning and Teaching

By the Same Author:

EDUCATIONAL PHILOSOPHY OF HERMAN BAVINCK
FUNDAMENTALS IN CHRISTIAN EDUCATION

HUMAN DEVELOPMENT, LEARNING & TEACHING

A Christian Approach to Educational Psychology

by Cornelius Jaarsma, *Professor of Education, Calvin College Grand Rapids, Michigan*

Wm. B. Eerdmans Publishing Company, Grand Rapids, Michigan

Library of Congress Catalog Card Number, 60-12644

PRINTED IN THE UNITED STATES OF AMERICA

To: *Geraldine* • *Raymond* • *Helen*

Preface

IN THIS VOLUME WE STUDY HUMAN DEVELOPMENT, LEARNING, AND teaching with a view to developing a Christian approach to educational psychology. The title of the book conveys the thought that a Christian approach to educational psychology requires the study of these three areas, not in any way exhaustively, but with reference to the central task of educational psychology as a science, namely, to help teachers understand the learning process.

Teaching is the artistic skill of helping others learn. One cannot keep children from learning. They are indefatigable learners. The question is whether they learn the things that are best for them. Parents, pastors, and teachers should understand not only what things are best for them, but also how these best things may be realized in their lives and personalities. How to realize these aims is determined by what we observe in child behavior in the light of what we know a child to be. Educational psychology is the science that studies child development systematically.

For its broad perspective educational psychology looks to other areas of learning, namely, theology, philosophy, ethics, logic, and aesthetics. These are often spoken of as normative sciences, for they concern themselves primarily with human standards. Education likewise is normative, for, informed by these sciences, education seeks to formulate its goals for human development. (Learning is essentially problem-solving in the course of goal-seeking.) In order that ultimate goals of child development may be realized, they must be broken down into graduated goals according to pupil readiness; thus they may challenge the learner as a goal-seeker. Educational psychology informs itself of right goals in order to ascertain the best way for pupils to realize them.

Educational psychology is also informed by other sciences, especially psychology and sociology. Psychotherapy, more art than science, likewise has much to contribute to educational psychology in trying to understand child development.

Educational psychology is a science, and teaching is an art. William James, in his *Talks to Teachers*, correctly makes the observation that no science directly generates an art out of itself. It can call a teacher's attention to what to avoid and what to pursue. But the doing is a peculiarly personal matter. As an art, teaching is the fruit of sound judgment of a competent teacher based on sound knowledge, including a scientific knowledge of educational psychology. But the same psychological principles may find various expressions in competent teaching.

Furthermore, we should give these related areas of study a scriptural perspective. As Christians we are constantly at work making the scriptural mandate relevant to Christian living. The teacher as artist faces this task in a special way. We know that God has spoken infallibly in the recorded Word which has been preserved for us through the ages by the Holy Spirit through the work of the Church. This Word is to us first of all the good news of salvation in Christ for those who believe in him. But to those who believe, it is likewise the light entering vertically into the horizontal areas of life. This record tells who man is and what God intends him to be. This record points to the thought and purpose of God in the natural world about us and in the course of history. This record tells us how to value all things in their right relationships. When we divorce the light of the Word of God from the data of our observation and from the principles of interpretation, we cut ourselves off from the truth in the light of which all other truths are clearly discerned.

By accepting God's self-revelation in his Word and in his work we deviate from most current discussions in educational psychology. The man who does not accept the Bible as God's Word to man, but accepts it as a human account of religious experience that at best has historical validity among other documents of this kind, will call us biased, authoritarian, sectarian, or perhaps say that we are consciously or unconsciously preoccupied with metaphysical concepts instead of addressing ourselves to the facts at hand. We would challenge those who so judge us to examine their own presuppositions, chief among which is that man has received no authoritative declaration of truth and that man has nothing but his own reason with which to judge and value things. We say with Joshua of old, "but as for me and my house, we will serve the Lord." Paraphrasing this challenge in the setting of our discussion, we might say, as Christian teachers, we ask first of all what the Lord has to say to us, for in his light only do we see light.

The attempt to have the light of God's Word fall upon the areas of human development, learning, and teaching is a difficult undertaking. The student should look upon this study as an initial attempt. Very little has been done in this field. The difficulties are several. There is first of all the fact that the study of education as such is very recent. Until comparatively recently, theories of learning and teaching were deduced from certain concepts of theology and philosophy as, for example, cultivating the intellect or training the mind. Furthermore, the sciences to which education looks for help today, namely, psychology and sociology, are themselves nearly as recent in their first-hand explorations. One can expect that in such new areas of research many conflicting interpretations often struggle for supremacy. It is often extremely difficult to distinguish fact from fancy, dependable data from personal opinion or dogma. It is human nature to become dogmatic about things we understand least.

Another difficulty concerns the proper use of Bible facts and pronouncements. While we hold the Bible to be authoritative in its message and reliable in its historical account, we do not mean that its terminology is scientific. How to use the Bible and not to abuse it when we seek to understand the relevance of *the* truth to the truths we observe about us, this is indeed a very difficult task. And yet, this must be done if we would acknowledge the Christ of God as King in all domains of life.

So it behooves us, always, but especially now, to approach our study in the deepest humility and with a prayer that God may direct our steps. We have the promise in Proverbs 3:6, "In all thy ways acknowledge him and he shall direct thy paths." May the Lord inspire us and equip us as teachers for the responsible task to which he in his providence has called us. May we ever take example from Jesus Christ, the master teacher, as he taught, meeting the true needs of those who came under his hearing.

When the findings of educational psychology are presented and the principles of teaching based thereon are expounded, one is apt to hear teachers or students say, "That sounds just like plain common sense." Sometimes one may hear the statement added, "What's new about that?"

If psychological principles of education were not in accord with daily experience, they would certainly be suspect, for psychology and the learning process seek to explain the behavior of normal people. The formal science of educational psychology, with its special vocabulary, seeks to conceptualize what is perceptually often evident in daily experience and thus to clarify and verify experience. When we do so, however, we find "common sense" as often wrong as right.

Only by careful investigation can we determine whether "common sense" should be accepted and propagated.

The material in this text has been used in class as a syllabus for several years, and has been revised in the light of that use. Students have made valuable suggestions for improvement, as have several colleagues. These are acknowledged with thanks.

The author acknowledges his indebtedness to several other sources and persons, too many to enumerate. The following among them merit special mention: L. E. Cole and W. F. Bruce, authors, and the World Book Company, publishers of the text *Educational Psychology,* for ideas of organization and for several quotations used by permission; L. J. Cronbach, author, and Harcourt, Brace and Company, publishers of the text, *Educational Psychology,* for suggestions of a chart on developmental tasks, and for several quotations used by permission; A. A. Hoekema, Professor of Systematic Theology at Calvin Seminary, for suggestions on the word "heart" in the Scriptures; Mrs. Ethel DeLeeuw for typing a large part of the manuscript; and the author's wife for typing and especially for her constant support and inspiration. Special mention too must be made of Dr. J. Waterink of the Free University, Amsterdam, the Netherlands, and his associates Drs. A. Kuypers, L. Vander Horst, and H. R. Wyngaarden. The writings of these men have been valuable sources for a Christian orientation in psychology.

A preface is written, or at least completed, when the volume is ready to go to the printer. As this book is presented for reading and study, the author feels that he would like to rewrite several parts, for new ideas have occurred to him since. But revisions will have to wait. In the meantime those using the text will make their own revisions. Suggestions for further improvement of the text will be gratefully received.

— CORNELIUS JAARSMA

Contents

PART FOUR: WHAT IS TEACHING?

LIST OF FIGURES AND TABLES

Introduction

1

The Person and Learning

JACKIE AT CHURCH

The story is told about a pastor who preached a mission sermon one Sunday on the text, "For the zeal of Thine house hath eaten me up" (Ps. 69:9a; recalled in the reflection of Jesus' disciples in John 2:17). On the Monday following, the pastor made a brief trip to the church shortly before noon to pick up something in the church office. He took his five-year-old son, Jackie, along, as he was wont to do on such short trips. As they approached the church building, Jackie began to hang back and loosen himself from his father's grip. Finally he stopped completely. The pastor was puzzled at his son's unusual behavior. At other times he had been eager to go along, and had even entered the church ahead of his father.

"Aren't you going in with me, Jackie?" inquired the father. "You always do."

With this challenge Jackie proceeded to enter, but he held tightly to his father's hand, even huddling close to him. He took a few more steps, but then turned and ran out.

Altogether confounded by Jackie's unusual actions, which so clearly betrayed fear, the pastor asked, "What's the trouble, Jackie? What are you afraid of? You never acted like this before."

Jackie looked at his father, started to speak, but just as quickly stopped.

The pastor, having become a bit impatient by this time, commanded rather firmly, "Come on, son, we must hurry, for mother will be waiting for dinner."

Under pressure of the pastor's urging Jackie began to speak tremblingly: "But . . . but the . . . the seal, daddy, the seal."

The father was filled with consternation; he could not understand his son's problem. It never occurred to him that yesterday's sermon text was the occasion of Jackie's fear.

17

But it was. His mother had recently read him stories about seals which lived by the sea and jumped up and down in the water as they caught fish. The picture in the book portrayed vividly how these victorious seals went about it. And then not long ago his father and mother had taken him to a zoo where he saw live seals and watched the caretaker feed seals with little fish.

Jackie had learned something from his father's sermon. But not zeal for the work of the Lord, as the pastor had intended. Jackie had learned to fear the seal in the church building.

Interpretation of Jackie's mistake

Though this is only a story, it has important implications for the psychology of learning. Jackie's mistake is repeated many times, in diverse ways, by children at home, at play, and in school.

Superficially considered, the mistake was in hearing. The sound of "zeal" actually had no meaning for him, but he confused it with another sound which did have meaning, namely "seal." In this respect Jackie was like the primary school child who repeated this oath of allegiance to the flag: "I pledge a legion to the flag to the republic of Richard Sands; one nation and a vegetable with liberty and justice to all"; and the child who sang lustily, "The grandpas we watched were so gallantly screaming."

But we must inquire further into the reason for this confusion. Jackie, we have said, did not understand his father's message. Why not? Because he lacked a *perceptual basis* for comprehending its meaning. On the other hand, he did have this perceptual basis for understanding talk about seals eating things up. The picture-book illustrations and zoo experiences were still fresh in his imagination; furthermore, on that same day his Sunday School teacher had related Pharaoh's dream of the seven lean cows eating seven fat cows. Animals eating other animals seemed familiar to him; and now — horrible thought! — wasn't his father talking about predatory seals in church?

Jackie's mistake illustrates a general principle: we understand symbols only to the extent that our perceptual history fits them into a meaningful context. Other examples of this truth may be taken from Christian doctrine. We would not understand "our Father who art in heaven" if we had no earthly fathers; we would not understand the eternity of God if we had no experience of time. The "new birth" and the Trinity are meaningful to us only through inadequate analogies.

As succeeding cases will show, perceptual experience is only one of many individual limitations which condition understanding. The point to be derived from them all is that teaching and learning must be related to *each* student in terms of his peculiar gifts and handicaps, and furthermore, that each student enters the learning situation with his *total* personality. Learning is not the same as training of the intellect; as we saw with Jackie, feeling-tones and behavior resulted from his misunderstanding. The whole person makes a difference in learning, and learning makes a difference in the whole person.

OTHER CASES OF LEARNING DIFFICULTY

Susan. "Until Susan was 3 years of age she advanced in weight, height, and other physical characteristics in fair accordance with the norms. At 3, however, she suddenly began to grow fat; at 6 she was 35% overweight. Discussion of the problem with the family physician merely confirmed the belief of the mother that the cause lay in some physiological factor. Susan's behavior in the family became so obstreporous, however, that her mother finally brought her to a psychological clinic. As a result of the analysis of the staff, the mother, at the request of the director, kept a daily detailed record of Susan's behavior over a period of several weeks. This included records of weight, kinds and amounts of all food eaten, and all signs of aggressive behavior. The amount of food eaten astounded even the clinical staff; in one week of unusually aggressive behavior Susan ate voraciously, gaining six pounds.

"Studying the data, the clinic's staff centered attention on a social factor which they said was the key to the enormous overeating — namely, Susan's attitude toward a baby brother who had been born when she was three years old. The records of growth showed that the sharp increase in weight and overeating began at the time of the birth of the baby. They learned from the mother that Susan had not been prepared in advance for the coming of the baby brother. That Susan had resented the newcomer was clear from the beginning, and it is not uncommon to find an older child reacting thus toward a new baby, a competitor for the love and affection of the parents. Scrutiny of the complete story of growth pointed inescapably to this social and emotional factor as the cause of overeating, of resentment for the new baby and a distinctively aggressive attitude toward him. Although the mother was loath to accept this explanation the psychologist insisted that the basic factor was psychological and social. Thwarted from attacking the baby by the mother's protection, and resenting the shift in her mother's interest and attention, Susan turned to overeating as a substitute. Needs that had been suddenly left unfulfilled were thus compensated.

"But, added the clinicians, physiological factors played a part also. Susan would not have gained so greatly in weight if she had not been of the easily fattening type. In fact, Dr. Bruch's study led her to the conclusion that most obese children possess a physiological constitution which lays on fat easily. Thus, in stressing the importance of social factors in explaining such physical conditions as obesity, one must not ignore the fact that physiological factors play an important part also. The case of Susan is especially illuminating in showing that for a susceptible child to lay on fat, appropriate social conditions must be at hand. In this case they were provided by a home in which food was abundant and parents were indulgent, and by the motivating conditions created by what the child felt as neglect at the time of her brother's birth."[1]

The school may or may not be able to meet Susan's unfulfilled need, but it should be clear that whatever the teacher says and does, Susan's learning will be colored by the presence of that need.

Bill. "Bill Chelton is well toward the top of the group in tested intelligence. His record in school is mediocre, all his grades being B or C. His file from previous years — he is now a high school sophomore — shows that many teachers have complained of his indifference or his ability to concentrate. Bill shows several consistent patterns of behavior which are represented in the following incidents reported by an observer.

(1) Bill is belligerent and out of step. His German teacher opens class with a comment on the deadline for an assignment. Bill calls out, 'But you said that wasn't due till Thursday.' The other pupils turn on him and squelch him with polite and impolite comments that it was due Tuesday and everyone else knew it. Bill subsides, mumbling to himself. Minutes later, pupils are reading orally in turn from the prepared assignment. No one else has trouble, but when Bill's turn comes, he falters repeatedly, knowing much of the passage but requiring help on several words. When helped, he says petulantly, 'I can *translate* it, but it still doesn't make sense.' Two minutes later when he is again called on, he has no idea of the place to be read next. As soon as the oral work is done, Bill reopens the matter of the assignment with, 'We voted for *Thursday* last week.' The class again squelches him in chorus: 'We voted for Tuesday.' Bill, 'Well, let's vote again.' The teacher firmly ends the debate and introduces a new activity. (Fifteen minutes of class time are covered by these incidents.)

(2) Bill volunteers occasionally, seemingly with real interest. In English, he follows up the teacher's comment on Sweden with a long story about smörgasbord. Another time he offers to run a

1. L. E. Cole and W. F. Bruce, *Educational Psychology* (Yonkers-on-Hudson, N.Y.: World Book Co., 1950), pp. 5, 6. Quoted by permission.

motion picture projector . . . . He volunteers to the German class about the book he has been reading.

(3) Bill does not work seriously on group activities. When the class is discussing ways to improve the school, five or six of the boys offer facetious comments, and Bill, among them, says they should put in an elevator. . . . When the boys are practicing basketball, Bill tosses the ball in a perfunctory manner, seeming not to try or care. . . . 'On one occasion,' the observer comments, 'he astonished me by offering to answer three questions in regular geometry work. The only reason I could see was that, because the rest of the class was stumped, he found it a chance to show off.' "[2]

Some teachers will think Bill a first-class nuisance in the classroom and pounce on him, perhaps send him to the principal's office as an arch-disturber. Others will be challenged by Bill's aggressiveness and give him opportunity to use his ability. Why the difference?

Bertram. "Then there was Bertram — IQ 87. He spent two years in grade one, three years in grade two, two years in grade three, threatening all the time: 'The day I get to be fourteen I'll leave this school flat.' He did. On the morning of his fourteenth birthday he joined his fourth-grade class as usual, and in the middle of the session rose, pushed his books on the floor, and said, 'Miss Brown, this is the day. I'm fourteen, and I am getting out now. No more school for me.' He left, became a handy boy in a barber shop, and went from one unskilled manual job to another. One day, some years later, the neighbors heard that Bertram had passed the civil service examination for school engineer. He became the assistant superintendent of the building at the junior high school, and for forty years cleaned the building successfully, helped run the heating plant, guarded the children in all sort of emergencies, and handled the practical chores of the job efficiently.

"As the years passed, the neighbors began to notice references to something Bertram was doing — especially his "investments" and "business deals." He had bought a house on Highland Avenue. He had acquired a farm in Townsend. It was rumored that he was always looking into properties put up for sale because of unpaid taxes. "Personals" in the *Sentinel* recorded his progress through the offices of the town civic organizations. He was an officer in his Community Club. When the Camp marched on Memorial Day, Bertram in full regalia of plumed hat, Sam Browne belt, and sword was at its head. The announcement of the mayor's appointment of citizens' committees frequently included Bertram's name. The artisan family of his married sister got a new automobile every three or

2. L. J. Cronbach, *Educational Psychology* (New York: Harcourt, Brace & Co., 1954), pp. 127-128. Quoted by permission.

four years — Bertram paid for it. Bertram put a new bathroom and oil heater into the old homestead.

"Thus Bertram, low in aptitude for those tasks the school provided, but equipped with a good supply of personal shrewdness, industriousness and dogged persistence, became one of the town's accepted citizens and even held small positions of leadership."[3]

There are many Bertrams in school who push themselves to positions of effective leadership in church and society upon entering later vocational activities. Their latent abilities lie in certain directions. Their development follows a course laid out by their latent capacities. They come to understanding of life in the framework of the talents they possess. Unless schools and teachers understand this, they will fail in making a vital contribution to boys and girls of the kind that Bertram presents.

SUMMARY

The key to right learning is meaning and understanding. Every one of these children has the ability to understand God, man, and the world. But each comes to school with his own peculiar personality.

For this reason, there is no single formula to describe the process of understanding. Each student forms his personality in relation to a community with a common environment, and the good teacher will so arrange the school environment that each student profits maximally from it.

THE IMPORTANCE OF UNDERSTANDING

It is a truth of general psychology that understanding is essential to personal well-being. We must understand our world, our fellows, and ourselves in order to live a full and well-ordered life. Ignorance breeds suspicion and fear, whereas knowledge leads to confidence, levels prejudice, calls forth sympathy and co-operation, and creates the conditions for effective communication and self-examination. Human understanding can never be complete; but within its limits, it is a goal to be sought by all.

Within the Christian context, understanding is a necessary condition for the effective service of God. Education, therefore, which has as one of its chief goals the development of understanding, ought to proceed under the guidance of the Spirit of God. To return to Jackie for a moment, understanding as a function in his soul-life must open up to him the abundant life in Christ as the goal for all his striving. In the words of Paul, "I press toward the mark

3. Cole and Bruce, *op. cit.,* pp. 7, 8.

for the prize of the high calling of God in Christ Jesus" (Phil. 3:14). The child of God who has the new life in Christ Jesus is capable of understanding his world, his fellows, and himself in relation to the supreme goal held forth by the Apostle.

BROAD CONCEPTS UNDERLYING THIS STUDY

THE SELF

The self, I, or subject is that which is given most immediately in consciousness. The self cannot be observed with sense organs, but its real and continuous existence is more certain than that of the externally perceived world.

Though the meaning of "self" varies according to the school of psychology using it (a subject to be discussed in detail later), we will follow Holy Scripture in identifying it as the human spirit. The spirit recognizes itself to be individual, unique, and distinct; but it also recognizes itself to be a part of God's world, needing fellowship and companionship. The human self is a creature of God; it is the source of direction and vitality for every aspect of the human being, and the focus around which is organized all of man's knowledge, experience, and behavior.

THE PERSON

The second basic concept is *person*. In everyday conversation, and even in scientific psychology, this term is often used very vaguely. The word (Latin *persona*) originally meant mask, a face that one puts on. Gradually the word *persona* and *person* in various European modern languages pointed to characteristics of an individual as they were observed by others. In modern usage the word generally designates the total subject. You are a person. I am a person. There are many persons. In our daily language we often make person and self synonymous. In our study, however, we distinguish between them.

In order to function in the world, the self manifests itself in two distinguishable but not separable ways. It manifests itself *psychically*, in the soul-life, and *physiologically*, in the life of the body. To show the intimate unity of this manifestation, we often say that it functions *psycho-physically*. The person, then, is the single psycho-physical life of the self.

We may illustrate both the unity and the complexity of the person as follows. Suppose that you see a house. The *you* that does the seeing is your person as a psycho-physical unity. Yet we may distinguish the various processes that go on: light rays act physically and chemically on your retina; other physical and chemical processes carry an electrical message through your body to your brain; the image is perceived and related to your memories, concepts, and feelings; and all the while you recognize that this is an activity of your own peculiar self. Seeing a house is, in a sense, one act performed by one individual. Yet its complexity can be shown by noticing that one can *look* without *seeing,* and one can *see* without *taking conscious notice of.* The process may be interrupted at any "level."

PERSONALITY

The third main concept used in our study, *personality,* is also widely but ambiguously used in ordinary speech. Originally as the term *person* came to denote a particular individual, his qualities as they affected others and were noticed by them (such as having a heavy gait, a friendly demeanor, an incisive manner of thought and speech, etc.) came to be known as personal qualities. Finally, all of these qualities taken together acquired the name *personality.* Personality, then, is that unique group of characteristics which describes the individual *in relation to other people.*

We may speak of personality characteristics as extensions or dimensions of the person. Four such dimensions may be distinguished: the physiological, the emotional, the social, and the intellectual. But as we noted about the "levels" of functioning in the person, these dimensions are not to be taken as separable entities. Together they constitute *a single pattern* by which the individual relates himself to others. For instance, we call a person *well-poised* who is not physically awkward, who keeps his temper, is gracious in company, and coherent in conversation.

COMMUNITY

As we have been suggesting all along, a man is not a thing apart. Though every person has his integrity, his being-himself, he is nevertheless set by God into a cosmos which surrounds him and affords him a *field* for his knowledge and activity.

It is important that we understand the nature of this environment and our relationship to it. Though it is a truism that men are somehow related to each other and to the world as a whole, many naturalistic philosophers have assumed that these can be understood by a "scientific" procedure which ignores the basic insights of divine revelation. They suppose, for instance, that scientific psychology can explain man as wholly the product of heredity and environment where these are considered strictly as natural phenomena.

If we use the term "environment," we must be careful to remember that according to the Word of God it means the universe as created by the divine wisdom for divine purposes. Man is not a digit in an impersonal nature, but a being created in God's image to have vital *communion* with all His works. The world is an organic whole and we are organic persons in that world. Society and nature are not merely our environment, but our *community;* and similarly, our proper relationship to them can well be described as one of *community.*

PROBLEMS FOR STUDY IN THIS BOOK

With these concepts clearly in mind we are ready to begin our main task, which will be to understand how a person develops as he comes to grip with his community. He meets the demand for learning, for coming to understand the truth; and as he learns, he submits himself to the truth and orders all the dimensions of his personality in accordance with it. He obeys the truth; he becomes formed by the truth; and to the degree that he does these, he becomes properly related to God. Jesus said, "I am the truth."

To pursue this study we consider three major areas:

(1) Development. What is personality, and how is it developed?
(2) Learning. How does a person come to understand truth in such a way that he commits his entire personality to it?
(3) Teaching. How can the school best direct learning?

QUESTIONS FOR FURTHER STUDY

1. Try to recall in what areas of your past learning rote memory rather than understanding was largely prevalent. When, if at all, did a measure of understanding enter your experience? How?

2. Is habit formation based on understanding? Illustrate your answer from early and later human development.

3. Try to secure a textbook in elementary arithmetic published about thirty years or more ago and compare it with a recent text as to the attempt to give meaning to the number work.

4. Sunday school lessons generally have memory selections associated with them. Appraise this practice.

5. Perhaps you have attended catechetical classes in your church. In the past it has often been the practice to assign a group of questions and answers for memorization to be recited at the next session of the class. Then a brief explanation of each answer followed. Appraise this practice.

6. Why do we have a better understanding of the Fatherhood of God than of the triune nature of God's being? Does the difference in understanding make any difference in our behavior?

QUESTIONS ABOUT THE CASE HISTORIES

1. How does Susan's case show that physiological, emotional, and social factors depend upon one another for balanced development?

2. What need in Susan's life was suddenly left unfulfilled?

3. Why did Susan follow this way out?

4. Supposing that Susan came to school at the age of 5 or 6 without her need having been met in a constructive way, what problems would she present to the teacher?

5. How does Bill seem to interpret every school activity?

6. What difficulties does he encounter?

7. How are these difficulties interpreted? Why?

8. By what standards was Bertram a failure?

9. How might we account for his success upon leaving school?

10. How could the school have discovered Bertram's latent talent?

11. Suppose one or more of these children would enter your classroom, what information concerning their development would you seek in order to help them?

12. Why would each one of them have to be approached differently?

13. What prospect has each of these children of becoming a person who can serve the Lord as a faithful steward?

SELECTIONS FOR FURTHER REFERENCE*

At this point in his study the student may find the reading of a few selected cases profitable. It introduces him to some of the problems he will face in understanding development, learning, and teaching. As the student proceeds in his study it is well to return to these cases for further analysis and illustration.

Cronbach: Clark, who has a physical handicap (pp. 117-123); Olive, with low academic ability (pp. 123-127); Margaret, who felt unloved (pp. 145-149).

Havighurst: Jed, a boy who failed and what the school might have done to help him (Chapter XIII); Roberts, a girl who succeeded and how the school helped her (Chapter XIV); Elsie, a girl who failed and what the school might have done to help her (Chapter XV).

Jenkins *et. al.*

Rothney

*References here are cited by author's name. See Bibliography for title and complete publication data.

Part One:

Foundations of Educational Psychology

2

Person and Personality

HOW PSYCHOLOGY AFFECTS EDUCATIONAL THEORY

In the introductory chapter we pointed out that because a child is a person who in the process of development forms personality, the way to effective learning is by understanding. We should now consider further the meaning of these concepts.

We use the concept education with reference to persons, not animals. Animals can be trained to perform. Humans are educable. And they are educable because they are persons. Education is the process by which we direct an immature person, a child, in the development of his resources so that he is formed into a mature personality. We are now engaged in the study of that phase of education which is psychological in character. We must understand the psychology of the developing personality in order to know how learning takes place and how to teach.

Psychology as a science, that is as an area of learning and investigation, focuses its attention upon the soul life of the person in distinction from the physiological life. The soul life is the area of thinking, feeling, willing, purposing, judging, valuing, etc. of the person. We speak of these as mental functions in distinction from physical functions. Both mental and physical functions are functions of the person. For example, passions as experiences of the person may originate in physical stimuli such as "lust of the eye" and generate physiological changes which are experienced by the person as feeling tone and drive to action. Physical and mental functions combine in the consciousness of the person as an organic unity.

Psychology as the science of the soul life, mental life, or mental functions of the person, therefore, makes a major contribution to the understanding of the process of education. It is especially in recent years that amazing insights in the ways of human behavior and its motivation have brought psychology and education into

29

closer relationship. What is actually happening is that while education until comparatively recently received its main directives from such areas of learning as theology, philosophy, and ethics, today it is growing much closer to psychology and psychotherapy.

In Christian education as well as in education in general we should seek to profit from these new insights. But we may not permit psychology, as a science that describes the processes of the soul life, to interpret their meaning for us. The meaning of these processes depends on who the person is in his very being. For an authentic account of the person who experiences the soul life we must turn to the Scriptures, for only they contain the record of man's origin and being.

THEORIES OF THE PERSON

We first ask the question, Who or what is the person that we seek to form into a personality?

MODERN SECULAR THEORIES

When we speak of secular or humanistic psychologies, we mean psychologies that do not make the Bible normative for their thinking. They will grant that the record as contained in the Bible may contribute data for psychology, both of a factual and interpretative character, but the Bible is no infallible rule for thought and discernment either in psychology or in any other scientific field. What the Bible says about the nature of man is to be taken as an idea among ideas the validity of which must be established by the facts, they say. They claim to be unbiased when they reason thus. Have then would-be unbiased psychologies anything to say about the nature of the human person? One might expect not. But this is not the case. In fact they have very much to say about who the person is. It is rarely stated in so many words, but the answer is clearly implied. For one capable of critical appraisal it is soon evident on what assumptions their discourse is based.

It is well, then, that at the outset we take a good look at the humanistic psychologies. On the one hand, we wish to be on our guard lest we fall into gross error without proper discernment. On the other hand, we do not want to brand as error what is well-established fact and reasonably sound interpretation.

When one surveys the field of psychology today for some kind of convenient and functional classification, he is hard put to it. As an area of scientific investigation psychology is very much a newcomer among such established areas of research as philosophy, ethics, physics, chemistry, anthropology, etc. To bring some kind of order out of the welter of ideas and theories floating about today is wellnigh impossible. Yet for our purpose it is possible to make a functional classification. Any kind of earmarking will perhaps do a measure of injustice to certain views and groups, but classify we must in order to do some talking about them.

We will classify the current psychologies, then, into three kinds: the mechanistic psychologies, the dynamic or psychogenic psychologies, and the organismic or biosocial psychologies; the first is physiologically-oriented, the second psyche-oriented, and the third society-oriented.

The Mechanistic Psychologies. The mechanistic psychologies would have us see the study of psychology as a natural science like physics and chemistry. The data of psychology are the data of the objective world of fact to the mechanist. All human experience can be interpreted as something that can be analyzed, observed, and measured like any other object present to the senses.

Though they share this basic point of view, mechanistic psychologists disagree among themselves about certain subsidiary issues. One such issue is this: can psychological concepts and theories be *reduced* to the level of physiology? Depending on whether their answer to this question is yes or no, mechanistic psychologists are called either *reductionists* or *non-reductionists* (sometimes: *mentalists*).

Reductionism is obviously the more radical kind of mechanism. It holds that all behavior is physiologically determined, and that all human experience is nothing but reactions to stimuli. There is no essential difference, no qualitative difference, no difference in kind between thinking and cerebral activity, between living and physical energy-exchanges. What we call consciousness and self-consciousness are forms of activity or functions of the body. All behavior is of one kind, and can be studied objectively like the data of physics, chemistry, astronomy, and other natural sciences.

Other psychologists of the same basic persuasion try to avoid the crudely materialistic flavor of reductionism by calling themselves behaviorists. Psychology, they say, is the science of human behavior, and behavior is physiologically-oriented activity. The student will also meet the appellation *connectionist*. This term emphasizes the view that experience is to be explained as a linking together of stimuli and responses in a complex neural system. The reductionist, the behaviorist, and the connectionist are sub-classifications of the more radical psychologists among the mechanistic school. Their designation may vary according to where they place the emphasis in their interpretation of human experience.

But not all mechanistic psychologists want human experience reduced to physiological terms or concepts. They recognize that mental phenomena cannot be reduced to physiological structure and function. These psychologists are very likely to resent being called mechanists, and especially materialists. They do, however, treat their data as objective facts subject to the methods of the natural sciences. Though they make a qualitative distinction among data, they deal with them in a like manner.

Mechanistic psychologists can also be divided into *atomists* and *configurationists,* according to whether they view human experience and behavior as aggregations of separate parts, or as elements of a unified field or pattern. Atomists characteristically use the language of "chain reflexes," "connection systems," or "conduction units"; they believe that the various units are externally related, much like bodies in a physical system. Configurationists, on the other hand, have come to recognize that wholeness of experience is more basic to human behavior than the distinctness of the parts.

Whether these labels have been fairly applied or not, the theories of psychology called mechanistic do have a view of the person. They hold that the person is the totality of his observed behavior, the coalescence of all his functions, and that the term "person" is a collective noun designating the functional unity of an aggregation of parts, as in a herd of sheep or a flock of birds. As a mnemonic device one might speak of this group as third person psychologists. The person is an objective aggregate of factual things.

In general psychology this theory still has prominent adherents, but in educational psychology it is fast losing ground. This will become clear as we proceed.

The Dynamic or Psychogenic Psychologies. Not all psychologists who claim to be scientific limit their methods and conceptual tools to those of the natural sciences. The *dynamic* psychologists, for instance, though they take full account of physiological structure and functions, claim to have discovered other, more potent sources of human behavior. Their view is very complex and difficult to summarize; nevertheless, something must be said for the sake of our purposes.

According to this view, the key to human nature lies in an analysis of its *development.* At birth the organism is the locus of various forces which arise out of the dim past of its ancestry and become individuated as the organism encounters its environment. Among these forces are impulses, urges, drives, and passions of varied descriptions. As these forces interact with the environment awareness or consciousness arises, including the awareness of being a self. This self as area of conscious forces constitutes the *ego.* The forces that do not enter into the conscious constitute the area of the *unconscious.* This great mass of unconscious force is much larger in scope than the conscious area.

In addition to this large unconscious mass that constantly prompts the organism to action, the ego or self encounters the demands of culture and civilization. Often these demands conflict with those of the unconscious, in which case the ego represses the unconscious desires in an attempt to maintain social acceptability. Normally the ego maintains a harmony among the various forces acting upon it, so that the person's behavior at any given time may be viewed as the mediated product of subconscious and cultural demands. But when the ego's guard is down, strange behavior may result.

Our mysterious dreams, for instance, are held to be distorted revelations of the subconscious. And even in our conscious life we do things whose motivation is difficult to trace. There are times when we say, "I wonder why I did this! There seems to be no rhyme or reason to it." The writing of an ordinary letter to a friend may combine accepted standards of thought and action with urges and passions that barely remain concealed from conscious awareness.

How these psychologists conceive of the person can best be expressed in terms of three concepts: the unconscious, the ego, and the super-ego. These three, the area of the unconscious drives, the ego as the regulator of action, and the super-ego as the accepted standards of conduct interact and in their interaction constitute the person. Many of a person's motivations are desires that arise in the interaction of the ego with his environment. They constitute standards of conduct or criteria for behavior. But there is also a hidden source of motivation in the unconscious, which threatens at any moment to drive the ego almost unawares into actions difficult to explain. When he reflects on his actions, he judges himself according to accepted standards and develops a sense of guilt.

We have called this emphasis in psychology the dynamic or psychogenic theory. From our brief description of it the reason should be clear. This is not a physiologically-oriented psychology, though physiological processes are recognized. This is not a scientific psychology in the sense that scientific tools of the laboratory of the natural sciences can be employed. This is a psychology that aims to plumb the depths of human motivation. For this reason some of its adherents are known as depth psychologists and their psychology as depth psychology. Human behavior is viewed in its dynamics as it arises in the substance of the organism. The appellation "psychogenic" suggests that the organism gives birth to psychic phenomena in behavior and experience.

Much of clinical psychology and psychotherapy are either dominated or influenced greatly by this view of the person. Both seek to penetrate to motivations beneath the surface of perceived behavior. While they do not discredit the validity of laboratory data of human behavior, they feel that adequate self-understanding and understanding of others demands a careful analysis of the dynamics of action. The mnemonic device we can use to remember this group of psychologists is the first person psychology. The ego is the central concept here.

As educational theory develops, it gives more and more of a hearing to this view of the person. First the dynamic theory was confined to one or more chapters on mental hygiene. But in many recent texts on educational psychology the psychogenic theory dominates the whole discussion. The student will notice that this book, too, owes a great debt to this school of thought.

The Organismic or Biosocial Psychology. The mnemonic term that best fits this theory is the second person or *you* psychology, for it emphasizes the self-other relationship. Here we call it the organismic or biosocial view. Other names for it are the perceptual theory, the field theory, and the phenomenological theory.

By this time the student may be lost in technical terminology. Upon careful consideration, however, these designations are not as confusing as they seem. These psychologies hold uniformly that if the proper study of mankind is man, then man must be studied among men. There is not only a relationship within man, but also a relationship among men which determines what the person shall be. Behavior is viewed as a function of perception. The phenomenal field, or universe of experience, opens to the individual at the moment of his behavior. The perception of self and perception of reality constitute a field of inner relationships. It can be seen, therefore, that all these appellations refer to a single theory.

The self-other process may be described something like this. Man is a biological organism whose structure is essentially that of all living beings. This structure cannot be explained in purely physical terms, so we speak of it as biological. In the evolutionary ascent, however, man has reached a level at which distinctively human potentials come into being. He walks erect, manipulates objects with consciously chosen purpose, communicates in articulated sounds that spell out a language to those who grasp their meanings, produces a culture, and the like. As he develops his human resources and brings them to expression in interrelationship with his environment he becomes a person. The perceiving self interrelates reality about him into a perceptual whole with reference to himself. The word "person" designates the organism in his inner and outer relationships.

Human potential develops out of a biopolar tension. On the one hand there is a biological drive toward individuality or discreteness. But man cannot exist wholly in isolation from others; he is dependent socially as well as physically. As the perceiving self needs the perception of reality about him to complete his person, so the individual needs the group to constitute his person. The consciousness of self and of others emerges at the same time. It is in equilibrium or balance of inner and outer relations that the person emerges.

This view is called organismic because it holds that one organic structure is formed by the dynamic interaction of the biological being with its environment. It is called biosocial because of the two poles so indicated. And it is called phenomenological because it maintains that perception is the substance of human experience.

A CHRISTIAN CRITICISM OF THE SECULAR APPROACH

When we compare these psychologies with one another we are struck by two noteworthy facts, namely, there is a battle royal between the first two though they are not mutually exclusive, and the third is inclined to borrow heavily from the others.

First a word about the battle royal. It may be viewed as a battle between Pavlov and Freud, who were contemporaries. The first was a physiologically-oriented experimental psychologist, the second a clinically-oriented analytic psychologist. Both were geniuses. The former worked in the laboratory; the latter in his office. How exponents of these two views have attacked one another's theories and practices! Yet in a sense the two masters approached each other. In his latter years Pavlov became interested in problems of psychiatry and wrote broadly on the implications of his early work with experimental neurosis. Freud, who was an associationist, emphasized the role of learning in the development of behavior disorders. Efforts have been made to bring the two giants together, but the first development of their psychologies kept them far apart. Ernest Jones, a biographer of Freud, writes that Freud is reported to have said that in time to come it should be possible to cure hysteria and nervous disease by merely administering a drug. Apparently Freud, if this report is correct, saw a close relationship between the first two views we have discussed.

The student may have read that many new drugs are now being used successfully in connection with psychotherapy. But it should be borne in mind that as a rule they only prepare the patient for psychotherapy and are not substitutes for it. In addition, we read that experimental psychologists admit that they have given very little help in solving clinical problems.

Why mention this in connection with our discussion of schools or systems of psychology? In order that the student may be very discerning as he studies sources setting forth one or more of the views in psychology today.

The third group, as we said, borrows heavily from the first two. But it is more socially oriented. It looks for the explanation of the person in the phenomenological, in the perceptual relationships of life. While it profits from both groups and avails itself of both when needed, it carries on its own experiments, observations, social services, and the like. So the student should look for much overlapping of the three views, though each represents a distinct interpretation of the person.

The contribution of these psychologies to education has been comparatively limited. Not that psychologists have not been interested in the study of education, but their efforts have not been too rewarding. Most of the contributions so far are by inference. But the psychologist and the psychotherapist, like the sociologist, have turned up data that the educator needs to incorporate into his own study. The insights achieved through these new data are no less amazing than those gained in nuclear physics. Because of this new achievement, education is growing closer to psychology and psychotherapy. It is well, then, that as Christian teachers we understand these views in psychology in order that we may properly appraise and avail ourselves of the best insights achieved.

What concerns us more than the differences between these psychologies is the fact that their theories of the person are uniformly anti-theistic; that is, they actively deny or conveniently ignore the scriptural anthropology (doctrine of man). In spite of their disagreements, these psychologies are all *immanentistic*: they all hold that man is essentially a part of the natural world. This is a one-level view. God, man, and nature constitute a single real order. Christian theism, on the other hand, teaches that there are two levels of reality, God the Creator and the creation he called into being and holds "in the hollow of His hand." Man is a *creature* — that is the first answer to the question concerning the human person.

Presuppositions. In order to understand the chief issue between Christianity and secular psychology it is necessary to discuss briefly the philosophy of *knowledge*. All of us recognize that the scientific method, in psychology as well as in other fields of inquiry, has discovered many new facts. But the scientific method is not an absolute thing for at least two reasons: it cannot give us answers about value, about what *ought* to be; and it rests upon certain deeper assumptions which it cannot justify.

These assumptions, sometimes called *presuppositions* or prescientific commitments, constitute the basic issue between Christianity and secularism. The secularist, as we said, has an *immanentistic* point of view; he holds that everything in the universe, including man, is of basically the same sort and therefore is to be studied with the same method. If science cannot answer certain questions, then there is *no* reliable answer to these questions. Thus secular man absolutizes his own reason, refusing to consult divine revelation where his own methods of research fail him.

The non-Christian thinker cannot remedy his plight simply by reading the Bible. The root of his mistake lies deeper than a mere absence of data; even if he read the Bible, he could not genuinely apply its insights to his scientific work unless the Spirit of God removed the blinding effects of sin in his intellect. Ultimately, as Paul says (Rom. 1:18-23), the natural man *holds down* his knowledge in unrighteousness.

The characteristic fault of secular theories is their *partiality*. This can be understood in two ways: (1) the *overall tendency* of these theories is oriented toward ("is partial to") a total view of the universe which does not leave room for the God of Christian revelation; and (2) the *truths* contained in these theories are always *partial* truths. Though they may contain correct information about some of the trees (so to speak), they never give us a true perspective of the forest.

The question of facts versus presuppositions is controversial, and we will not take sides in it. This much must suffice: Facts are objective realities, as are relationships among facts. For example, we observe a thyroid gland in the neck of the human body. This is a fact. We see that it secretes a hormone. This is a fact. We call it thyroxin according to its origin in the thyroid gland. We find too that this gland can impede or stimulate growth according to the absence or presence of thyroxin. This is a fact. The nervous system can stimulate the thyroid gland. This is a fact. We observe that human behavior involves glandular-neural-muscular activity. This too is a fact. Suppose, now, I make the statement that human behavior is nothing but glandular-neural-muscular activity. This is *not* an observed fact. It is a conclusion following from a prescientific commitment that human behavior can be described wholly in terms of the phenomena we observe. The conclusion does not follow from observed fact, but facts are interpreted according to the assumptions that say who or what man is.

We stand to profit from the contributions of current psychologies when we view the findings in the light of scriptural truth concerning man. Who or what is the person, must first be answered scripturally before we can view the soul life of man, which is the field of psychology as a science, in its true context. Because as Christians we listen first of all to what God has to say and make His Word normative for thought and action, we turn to the Word for the beginning of all knowledge, including psychology and educational theory.

A Scriptural Approach. Before we develop the elements of a Christian theory of the person, we should look further at the biblical approach to human knowledge. One way to begin is to ask the question Why? Why is a biblical approach necessary, and what purpose does it serve?

There are essentially two reasons for such an approach. In the first place to have the true view of any part we must have the true view of the whole. We are in this world as part of it. In our seeing the parts we are apt to lose sight of the forest for the trees. The significance of the forest for the entire landscape and the relative importance of the individual trees remain unknown. Even the right view of each individual tree may be obscured. Where do we turn for the right view of the whole? We had it in ourselves, in our understanding, by creation. God so created us. Adam named the animals according to their nature. The psalmist sings of man's original glory in Psalm 8, "Thou makest him to have dominion over the works of Thy hands." But man lost this supremacy. This is the second reason for our need of the Word as recorded in the Bible. The Word gives us the perspective for true insight into the nature of things. Man's vision is blurred. What little remains in him by God's grace is altogether insufficient for adequate and true knowledge. And God's own children, the born again, the saints, have only a small beginning of genuine knowledge.

We need true self-knowledge to know what a person is. But this self-knowledge cannot be gained merely from observation or introspection. Only the Bible gives us true knowledge of self. John Calvin has stated this truth as follows: ". . . man never arrives at true knowledge of himself unless first he has contemplated the character of God and then descended from that contemplation to the consideration of himself" (*Institutes* I, 1, ii).

What is a scriptural approach like? It is like stepping outside of this world and getting the view of all things in one glance, in one act of thought, and with a penetrating understanding of every part. It is obvious that man cannot attain to such a transcendent view. Only God has this all-comprehensive view. But he can and does share it with us to the extent that our finite and sinful nature allows. He gives us — not the fullness of divine knowledge — but the divine *perspective* on the universe.

Consequently we must not expect the Bible to give us a detailed, scientific account of human personality or of any other subject. Such insights man gains by his inquiry into the world itself. But the Bible does provide the right framework or perspective which allows us to fit particular bits of knowledge into a meaningful whole.

The natural man of sin, in his search for knowledge, is like the proverbial five blind men who were asked what an elephant in reach of them was like. One touched the elephant's legs and said, "He is like a tree trunk." Another explored the ears and said, "He is like a fan." The third leaned against the beast and made the observation, "He is like a wall." A fourth felt the tusks and judged the elephant to be like a rake. The last one felt of the trunk and thought the elephant to resemble a snake. The limited perspective of each made the elephant a stranger to them. Each part was generalized as an account of the whole. But the parts cannot be known as parts except in relation to the whole.

It follows that non-Christian psychologists and educators cannot have an adequate perspective on the nature of man, and therefore cannot understand the child adequately either. In the blindness of their immanence they raise one phase of their observation to a general perspective and judge the whole thereby. The inadequate definitions of psychology which the student meets in current readings and texts have their source in this limited perspective. The same is true for distorted views and malpractices in education.

So that the student may understand the reasoning of secular educators a bit better, he should be alerted to two distinguishable non-Christian approaches in the study of education.

(1) The first approach takes the erroneous view that no assumptions or presuppositions are necessary at all. It is believed that theories of learning can be formulated objectively, that is, based wholly on observation and experimentation. Let observed facts speak for themselves. Discern carefully between opinion and fact. Observe how a child behaves under certain conditions. Record your observations. Compare with similar observations. Interpret your findings according to related studies. This is the road to understanding the educative process, it is said.

In comment, we should note that although observation is undoubtedly necessary in scientific procedure, it is equally true that experimenters cannot even observe meaningfully unless they do so in the light of assumptions or hypotheses. The basic criticism of this approach is that it naively confuses a part of the truth (the need for observed facts) with the whole truth about human knowledge (including its dependence upon presuppositions and assumptions).

(2) The second approach rests upon a partial recognition of our first criticism. Those who follow it assert that the experimenter first accepts certain propositions that seem reasonable to him, and then uses these propositions to help interpret the observed data.

For example, he accepts the proposition that man is a rational animal, an evolved form of animal life that developed the ability to think. The child he observes trying to work out a solution to a problem is understood as a problem-solving, thinking organism who seeks to establish his way with satisfaction to himself. Everything else the observer sees in the child's behavior he views in the light of his accepted proposition. Should his proposition, which is a hypothesis or theory to him, prove inadequate for the data he observes, he goes back to re-examine the validity of his theory.

Up to a point this approach is correct. But its fault lies in the assumption that human reason *alone* can be the source of all hypotheses and presuppositions necessary for scientific work. Here we see man proclaiming his independence of God, declaring himself to be autonomous in directing his own thinking. As St. Paul observed long ago, the self-declared autonomy of human reason is as old as sin itself (cf. Romans 1:18-23). The natural man knows God, but he holds down his knowledge in unrighteousness. Being without righteousness, the natural man of sin turns his creaturely knowledge of God into self-ordained knowledge that corrupts his entire perspective.

When we, therefore, seek a biblical ground for our study of how Jackie may become a mature person who is challenged and directed by his father's sermon text to form his life for the service of God, we do not expect to find there detailed scientific concepts. Rather, we seek light pertaining to the correct perspective on who Jackie is as a person and what God expects him to become. This perspective human science cannot give us, but without it the truths of science lose their meaning.

A CHRISTIAN THEORY OF THE PERSON

The Bible seems to give us three groups of references that direct us to an understanding of the person. One group deals with man's creation, another with the term "heart," and a third points to a varied use of concepts to designate the person.

Creation. The first group, dealing with man's creation, includes the following:

> And God said, "Let us make man in our image, after our likeness, and let them have dominion over the fish of the sea, and over the birds of the heavens, and over all the earth, and over every creeping thing that creeps upon the earth."
> So God created man in his own image, in the image of God created he them; male and female created he them (Gen. 1:26-27, RSV).

. . . . . then the Lord God formed man of the dust of the ground, and breathed into his nostrils the breath of life; and man became a living being (Gen. 2:7, RSV).

For similar passages, see also: Job 33:4; Job 27:3; Psalm 104:29a; Psalm 8:4-8; Hebrews 2:7; and I Corinthians 15:27.

Five truths about man as a person are revealed in these passages:

(1) God fashioned man from the substance of creation that preceded him.

(2) Man's life-giving essence is the breath of God, or spirit.

(3) He became a living being, an organic unity.

(4) He is made in God's likeness.

(5) He was made lord of creation.

Let us take a closer look at each of these important truths about man.

(1) God took of the materials of the natural world of creation that preceded man and shaped or formed him. These materials need not have been only the things we call matter, though the Bible uses the expression "dust of the ground." Vegetative life and animal life, structure and function, preceded man. There is soul life in the animal world. But even if materials must refer to matter, the very nature of matter is under scientific scrutiny today. And we are told that ninety percent of the human body consists of oxygen, carbon, nitrogen, and hydrogen.

(2) We learn further that God took the human form so constructed by his hand and breathed into him the breath of life. God, not himself being a human form, cannot exhale carbon dioxide or even oxygen and breathe it into man. No, we recognize that we have here an anthropomorphic expression (a truth set forth in language perceptible to man). God's "breathing into" has reference to his creative act of making the human form a living being in whom the spirit (breath of God) is the life-giving essence, the life principle. Human life is the living spirit. Man is of vertical origin, from God. He is spirit. Horizontally he is linked to creation in the form he takes from creation about him. God infuses spirit in man's earthly form so that he becomes an organic whole.

(3) Because man is an organic whole, it is incorrect to teach that soul and body, or spirit, soul, and body are separate parts of a man. The Bible uses all these terms, but in such a way that they are distinguished (not separated) as different functioning structures in the organic unity we call a person. The Bible clearly indicates the unity of man.[1]

1. A. Kuypers, *Inleiding in de Zielkunde* ("Introduction to Psychology") (Kampen, the Netherlands: J. H. Kok, 1953), p. 24.

Let us develop this concept of organic unity a bit further. We have said that, on the basis of Scripture, we must think of the person as an organic unity in whom the ego, self, or I is the life principle. Every function, both mental and physical — to use a common distinction among functions — is an activity of the self. The light waves upon the retina, the sound waves upon the ear drum, etc. set up a physiological activity in the nervous system. These are experienced by the person as a part of himself and are translated into personal experience. In the activity of seeing, I identify a house as my residence. As person I call it my home. All that home stands for, love, security, rest, good food, etc. enters into the total activity of the person. The whole person is involved in the process from the first stimuli to the final self-conscious act of identification and acceptance.

We have become accustomed to grouping the functions of a person as mental and physical. The distinction is helpful as long as we do not sharply differentiate the two. We do not know where the one ends and the other begins. The morning grapefruit has a bitter taste about it which one has come to like. Because of the taste, the grapefruit has acquired personal value as a breakfast food. When the season for good grapefruit is past, mother inspects the grapefruit at the market carefully, knowing that at this time they can be nearly tasteless. Mother's act of selecting grapefruit with careful discrimination is based upon the experience of tasting and valuing grapefruit according to the symptoms that suggest this taste. Psychic functions and body functions interact, flow into one another, but one cannot point out the point of transition. What common factor have they to give rise to the unity of experience as mother selects her grapefruit? It is very evident that mental function is based on physiological structure and function. Without the sense of taste no such selective experience could take place. A blind person must find suitable sensory substitutes to function meaningfully in his mental life. Cerebral activity is necessary for thinking. But the cerebrum is not the thinker. *I* think. William James said thoughts are our thinkers. No, thoughts are mental, psychic functions. The person is the thinker. The center of activity, whether it be tasting or thinking, is the I or self. The very spirit, breath of God, is the explanation of all function, psychic and physiological. The life of man is the life of the spirit.

Once we see the limitations of talking about "parts" of an organic unity, we should also recognize that because man is a *complex* unity we cannot begin to understand him without *some* sort of analysis or "breaking-up." The following diagram is an attempt to reveal both the complexity and the unity of the person:

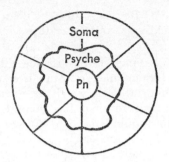

Figure I

ORGANIC UNITY OF THE PERSON

Recalling our previous discussion (Chapter I) of the self and the person, we proceed to signify the self or ego with the Greek term *pneuma,* meaning breath, standing for the self-conscious center of all experience. The mental processes and functions, such as thinking, feeling, willing, and perceiving, we designate by the Greek term *psyche,* meaning soul. The Greek word *soma* is conveniently used for body structure and function. All of these words are also used in Scripture with approximately these meanings.

The center circle represents the pneuma. The lines extending from it to the periphery indicate the life-giving and directing activity, the infusion of the pneuma into the psyche and soma. It penetrates the entire organism as the life-giving spirit. Human life is the life of the spirit. The psyche or soul life is represented by a very irregular line indicating the difficulty with which we distinguish between mental and physical activity in human behavior. Where does the conscious feeling of a toothache begin and nerve action leave off? I feel, not the nerves. Feeling is the soul action of the person. The soma, or physiological structure and function, is represented by the outer area. These are three facets of the unity of a person. The actual unity in the spirit eludes our grasp. We cannot describe the interrelationship of these three facets other than to say that they constitute an organic unity.

(4) Man is made in God's likeness. In a sense this is true of the whole creation, because it displays the power and wisdom of God. But man is uniquely the image of God because he is a spirit. Only of man is it said that God's breathing into him made him a living being.

What, precisely, does it mean to have the image of God? From their classes in Christian doctrine students learn that there are at least two answers to this question. One is principally Roman Catholic, though some Protestants also hold it; the other is Protestant, or more specifically, Reformed. Because this theological disagreement has implications for psychology and education as well, we will discuss it here.

According to the Roman Catholic view, the image of God is something added to human nature. Man is a unity composed of an immortal soul and a mortal body which together constitute the whole of his humanity. By nature man has mental and physical powers by which he lives harmoniously with himself and the world, but which by themselves do not make him religious. The image of God, on the other hand, is an added gift (*donum superadditum*) given to man over and above his natural gifts; this is a gift of grace by which man becomes godlike and hence religious. Having the image of God, therefore, is not essential to being a human being; according to the Roman Catholic man is not *intrinsically* a religious being.

The Reformed view, in contrast, holds that the image of God is essential to man's humanity. Man is a religious being in very essence. He is of God, a son of God. He can never cease to be a son of God. But as son of God he can turn from God. In the fellowship of God he has knowledge, righteousness, and holiness. Apart from God, he is still image of God, he is still a religious being, but without knowledge, righteousness, and holiness. Man is either a worshipper of the true God or an idolater. And this is because man is a religious being. This conception of the person as religious being will keep recurring in our study.

The disagreement between Roman Catholic and Reformed theology at this point is relevant to our study in at least two ways: in the first place, according to the Roman Catholic view it is possible to describe human nature and its processes apart from any reference to man's religious nature, so long as we restrict ourselves to the "natural level." This thesis is contrary to the approach we have adopted in this book. In the second place our Scripture passages, our immediate self-consciousness, and the best insights of modern psychology alike testify that there is a basic unity in human experience which is hard to reconcile with the Roman Catholic scheme of body-soul-*donum superadditum*.

We should say more about the image of God in man since it is foundational to our thinking in psychology and education. The following may prove helpful to see the relationship of this truth to our study.

a. In the primary sense, man is the image of God *collectively*. That is, the whole human race with all its potentials and expressions manifests the personal being of God, just as creation as a whole manifests the wisdom and power of God.

b. How, then, can we say that a single individual is the image of God? Because he partakes of the qualities of the human race. The human race is an organic unity; hence each man has the image of God, and hence, too, each man has Adam's sin imputed to him.

c. Because the individual partakes of the image of God, he has certain native capabilities and tendencies which express his godlikeness. In particular, every man has an urge toward *unity* and *freedom* — two important concepts in psychology and education. Unity and freedom, to the degree that they are achieved by the individual or the race, are possible because God has made them possible. They are not merely products of development, but are progressively realized in learning and development.

d. Man is free, not to be something else than man, but as man to give expression to God's likeness or not to do so. Man cannot change his being. Metaphysically, as we say in philosophy, he is man. This is his created being. But in his humanity he can choose to give expression to the image of God which he is in essence or can choose not to do so. He is given dominion over all creation beneath him, but he can neglect or violate his created right and become a victim to and slave of the forces he was destined to control.

e. As a free being man is responsible to God as his Creator to realize the purpose for which God created him. As a religious being made in the image of God, he is obliged to *fulfill, express,* and *realize* this being. In this setting the modern concepts of self-realization, self-expression, and self-fulfillment state the goal of all education.

(5) Man was made lord of creation. He was created to have dominion, to be viceroy of God's handiwork. He is appointed to be nature's master, under God, to order and develop it to God's glory. What a task! Notice, not adjustment, the term of modern psychology and education, but dominion is the charge given man by his Creator. No praise is returned to God by a mute creation. Only a person can bring God genuine praise, for he can do so consciously and voluntarily. Man was created to be the mediator of nature's praise to God. And he was created to mediate the work of God in nature. As the acme of God's creation he is called upon to mediate between God and nature as the one who is given dominion over all things.

The Heart. A second group of Scripture passages, this time dealing with the "heart," give us another clue to the nature of the person. Among the many possible instances we cite the following:[2]

2. The word "heart" is in every instance a translation either of the Hebrew *lebh* or *lebhabh,* or of the Greek *kardia.* This fact, along with the Scripture references here cited, derive from an (unpublished) study by the author's colleague, Dr. A. A. Hoekema, Professor of Systematic Theology at Calvin Seminary.

Heart as center of feeling: Ex. 4:14; Lev. 26:36; Ps. 4:7; Ps. 119:11; Luke 24:32; John 14:1; Rom. 9:2.

Heart as seat of willing: Ex. 25:2; Ex. 35:5; Jos. 24:23; II Chron. 19:3; Is. 29:13; Luke 21:14; Acts 11:23.

Heart as the seat of thinking or memory: Gen. 6:5; Deut. 29:4; Ps. 19:14; Prov. 2:2; Is. 6:10; Matt. 9:4; Matt. 15:19; Luke 2:19; Rom. 10:6; Heb. 4:12.

Heart as the seat of sin: Gen. 6:5; Ps. 95:10; Luke 6:45; Deut. 15:7; Prov. 28:14; Eph. 4:17, 18.

Heart as the seat of the regenerated life: Deut. 30:6; Ps. 51:10; Ezek. 11:19-20; Acts 16:14; Rom. 2:28, 29.

Heart as the seat of processes that invlove man's spiritual renewal, faith, and the practice of Christian virtues: Ps. 28:7; Luke 8:12; Acts 15:9; Eph. 3:17; II Thess. 3:5; I Peter 1:22; Matt. 18:35; Jas. 4:8.

What do all these passages indicate to us? They help us to answer the question, what, according to Scripture, is the primary or directing center in man. The Greeks thought it to be the intellect. Medieval and early modern philosophy and psychology thought it to be mind or soul, some non-physical entity or force. The Bible says the heart. But what can the Bible mean by heart? Surely, we should relate all these and similar passages to the passages we quoted from Genesis which tell us that man is an organic unity in whom the spirit is the life principle and that in the organic unity of the race man individually and collectively is the image of God.

Variety of Biblical Concepts. Not only does the Bible ascribe properties of soul life to the heart, but to other parts of the body as well:

Attributes of soul life are ascribed to the blood: Ps. 94:21; Is. 59:7; Luke 22:20; Rom. 3:25; Ps. 20:9.

We read of "eyes of the heart": Eph. 1:18.

In I Cor. 3:17 we read, "Ye are the temple of God"; and in I Cor. 6:19, ". . . your body is the temple of the Holy Spirit."

Body is used to represent all the faculties of man in Romans 12:1.

We are to love God with heart, soul, and mind. Matt. 22:7; Deut. 6:5.

From these Bible passages we may, it seems, infer some important truths concerning the human person.

(1) Every man has something of the miraculous in him.[3] The Scriptures recognize that we inherit certain aptitudes, powers, poten-

---

3. Kuypers, *op. cit.,* pp. 24-25.

tialities, and dispositions from our ancestors, but over and above these, they point to a kernel or essence that is new in each person.

This kernel or essence is the life principle in man, the directive center of his total being. It infuses the whole. It gives the whole organic unity. According to Kuypers, it is this center (in psychological terms, the self or ego) that the Scriptures speak of as breath of God, spirit, and heart. It is this center, moreover, that is said to live, die, and put on immortality.[4]

(2) The Bible clearly indicates the unity of the person. He is a living being of whom the Bible speaks as heart, soul, mind, body, blood, and the like. In each concept the whole is represented. These are not technical terms to label parts in an analytic fashion, as we do in science. Each points to the whole in its functional relationship. The organic unity of the person is clearly established in Scripture. The Bible does not confront us with man in his component parts, nor with a comparison of human existence over against that of animals. Rather, it gives us the compelling aspect of man's existence in his relationship to God.

(3) The Scriptures clearly distinguish between the essence of man which lives, dies, and puts on immortality and the functions in man as represented in his soul life and body life. In the language of A. Kuypers it is the distinction between the moral and the functional, man in the essence of being and his mental and physical activities. Since modern psychology regards the totality of man's functions to exhaust his being, this distinction in Scripture is especially significant for us as we face our study.

(4) The Bible clearly teaches a functional neutrality.[5] Functional neutrality means two things: (a) there is no hierarchy of function in man, and (b) no function is the seat of evil. One function cannot be thought to be superior to another. Under Greek influence human reason or the intellect has for a long time been regarded as supreme in man. We read much of the supremacy of the intellect, and, in the nineteenth century, as a reaction to a one-sided emphasis, of the supremacy of desire or will. We have seen that the Bible points to the very core of man, the essence of his being of which intellect, desire, will, etc. are functions. Any optimism or supremacy of the intellect is excluded.

Neither is any function the seat of evil. Evil proceeds not from man's functions, according to the Scriptures, but from the center of his being, the I, the self. Functions are good in themselves. Every gift of God is good.

4. *Ibid.*, p. 7.
5. *Ibid.*, pp. 24-25.

(5) The Scriptures present man as a religious being. The image of God, as we have been trying to understand it, is of the very essence of man. It is infused in the totality of man's person. The Scripture do not present man as an organism who attains to religious values among other values of life. "Religious" describes his very being. This too is important in our approach to psychology and learning. Motivation in man is basically religious and all human seeking is to be interpreted accordingly. So is learning. So is teaching.

(6) The Scriptures instructed us in the unconscious life of man long before psychology turned to it for scientific exploration. The psalmist, wearied of self-examination and feeling that the depths of his soul life have not been reached, opens himself to God in the words of Psalm 139:23, 24, "Search me, O God, and know my heart, try me and know my thought, and see if there be any wicked way in me, and lead me in the way everlasting." Psalms 16 and 26 likewise point to a depth in the soul life which wields a mighty power in the behavior of a person. Nowhere, however, do the Scriptures assign indigenous motivation to the unconscious. It too is a manifestation of the self, the ego, the I. It is inherent in the organic unity of which the I is the essence or life principle.

(7) The Bible also teaches us that man is adapted to the natural world about him. He needs interaction with the natural world for self-realization and self-fulfillment in body life and soul life. And the natural world is amenable to his powers. Man has dominion over a world whose resources he needs for the full realization of what he is, the image of God.

PERSONALITY THEORY

The student will recall from Chapter I that personality is that unique group of characteristics which describes the individual in relation to other people. Hence infants, for example, can hardly be said to have personality even though they are clearly persons. They are persons by creation: each is an organic unity of spirit, soul life, and body life. But they must *become* personalities: they must acquire and develop those traits which identify them as individuals in the social sense.

Obviously this distinction is tied very closely to the Christian view of the person. Hence we should not be surprised to discover that secular psychologies obliterate it. The three psychologies discussed earlier, for instance, view man as originally a biological (not a spiritual) entity who *becomes* a person (or personality). Everything distinctively human about a person is acquired, not innate.

Hence these psychologies have no real basis for distinguishing person from personality.

THE DIMENSIONS OF PERSONALITY

When we describe personality we describe how a person affects others. When we describe how a person affects others we characterize, so to speak, extensions of that person into his community. Assuming a posture or facial expression in public is, for instance, to "extend one's person into the community"; so is being irritable, or congenial, or uncomprehending.

It is convenient to classify these extensions of oneself into four "dimensions" of personality. They are the physiological, the emotional, the social, and the intellectual. Of course these are not separate entities; as dimensions of a single personality they are always involved in one another. Take a hearty laugh, for instance; this is physiological, but its concomitants are understanding the joke (intellectual), being pleased (emotional), and joining in the festivities of the party (social). The qualities that constitute one's personality are like a constellation or cluster that reflect a larger whole.

In Figure II (below) the unity of personality as integrated in the pneuma or spirit is diagrammed analogously to the unity of the person in Figure I. The student will notice that the social and emotional dimensions have been conjoined, for reasons which are intuitively evident (see also Chapter VII).

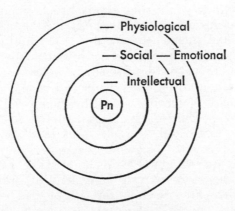

Figure II
DIMENSIONS OF PERSONALITY

THE WHOLE-PERSON-IN-LIFE

Personality is obviously the most *inclusive* concept that we can apply to an individual. Within its scope fall not only what we have called pneuma, psyche, and soma, but also the various dimensions of the person's social expression. Personality is also the most *concrete* concept we have used so far; it applies to the individual as we actually observe him living his life. Personality traits are not theoretical abstractions, but revelations of the person in action. Therefore it is useful at this point to introduce a term that suggests this concreteness and inclusiveness: the "whole-person-in-life."

There is a competitive term, the "whole-person-in-*action*," which is used by some psychologists operating within the secular perspective. These psychologists reason this way: We begin with an organism in an environment. Events occur in the environment, called stimuli; other events occur within the organism, called experience. The events within and outside the organism form patterns of response and action in the organism. The elements of these patterns we call personality traits, and their aggregate we call personality. The essence of personality, then, is to engage in *actions*.

The implications of this view of personality for education are not easily overstated. As a matter of fact they are among the determining factors in educational theories today. Our further studies should disclose to the student what this means for education. Just this much for the present. It is held that as a biological organism man is in constant tension with his environment. Events from within and events from without must find equilibrium, balance to relieve the tension. In the interaction the organism develops modes of adjustment in which conflicting events are brought into balance. The various patterns of adjustment constitute the acquired traits of behavior. It is the sum of these traits that constitute personality. When well-integrated for effective adjustment, they constitute a positive, wholesome, balanced personality. When poorly integrated, they constitute a maladjusted personality.

But this is unacceptable from the Christian point of view. The person is not the personality, and personality is not identical with actions. Activity is derived from *life* and that life is not merely biological but spiritual. Therefore when we contrast the term "whole-person-in-life" with "whole-person-in-action" we mean to point out that personality as a concrete unity has its ultimate genesis in the divinely-created life principle, the ego or spirit. The person is the ego operative in psychosomatic functioning. The person, in turn, expresses himself in life through his three dimensions of personality.

When a person communicates in the dimensions of life according to consciously accepted ends, he is a personality. When ends and the direction of communication of a person fail to constitute a field of related activity, he is without personality. An infant, comparatively speaking, is without personality. Likewise a person has lost contact with his in-life relationship when end and relationship fail to constitute a field of meaning. The latter is true of extreme forms of abnormality in the mentally ill. Personality is strong when the in-life relationship is well established, weak when it lacks adequate field relationship. Personality is bad when the in-life relationship of the dimensions of life violate standards of righteousness, good when they are valued as right. A person communicates in the dimensions of life, and it is in the in-life relationship that these dimensions are formed according to consciously chosen direction of the person. We speak, therefore, of the whole-person-in-life.

QUESTIONS FOR FURTHER STUDY

1. Appraise the following statement: "The person you are to be you are now becoming."

2. The following definition of personality was given to a group of Christian teachers as a basis for effective teaching. "Personality is the habit structure formed as the ego-centric impulses in tension with the environment achieve recognition, satisfaction, and security." How would you appraise the definition?

3. Do you think we can have a Christian psychology? If so, what makes it Christian?

4. Education is said by some Christians to seek to restore the image of God in man. Do you agree?

5. Psychology tends toward a wholistic rather than an atomistic view of the person today. Do you think this a sound trend from a Christian point of view?

6. You have read of the primacy of the intellect. Can you see how a belief in this theory affects education? Can you find evidence of this theory in education today? Do you agree with this theory?

SELECTIONS FOR FURTHER REFERENCE*

Hall and Lindzey. A very helpful attempt to bring together in survey existing theories of personality.

Kuypers. A Christian interpretation of psychological data.

Overstreet. An account of human development based on the maturity concept.

Waterink. A Christian interpretation of psychological data.

*References here are referred to by author's name only. See Bibliography for title and complete publication data.

3

Personal Disunity and Its Remedy

THE TRAGEDY OF DISUNITY

What we have already said about the organic unity of the person and the dimensions of his personality is fundamental to the theory of education. The aim of education is to form personality, and to understand this forming process we employ the concept of the whole-person-in-life.

But to speak of the unity and wholeness of man, when we consult actual experience, seems hardly to be realistic. Existentially we find conflict and disharmony, not unity and integration. There is constant tension within every person and among persons, and whatever balance that exists is only temporary and partial. There are physiological tensions, emotional tensions, social tensions, intellectual tensions, and tensions of the spirit. So, too, in the structure of personality: more often than not one dimension will conflict with another, or one quality with another within the same dimension. How shall this disunity be diagnosed, and what shall be prescribed for it? This, again, is a major issue between Christian and secular psychology.

DISUNITY AS VIEWED BY SECULAR PSYCHOLOGIES

Tension and conflict in life are not ignored or denied by secular psychologies. On the contrary, much study and experimental work has been directed toward a better understanding of them. Tension and conflict are the very essence of things, it is said. They are a given in human experience. But the secular psychologist has a ready explanation. It is simply this, that they are ultimate facts about the nature of things. Philosophers and theologians may speculate about their origin, but the only realistic course to follow with our conflicts is to adjust. Some adjust well, and live reasonably happy and effective lives. Others cannot adjust, and lose all meaningful contact with reality. They "go to pieces"; that is, they lose balance completely. The value of all human functioning is measured by its contribution to successful living, wholesome adjustment, in the kind of world that we happen to live in.

This view of the secular psychologies ignores and thereby denies another basic teaching of Scripture concerning man. Because they fail to accept the scriptural doctrine of man as a living being created in the likeness of God, and fail to view man as a religious being in his very essence, they must likewise set aside the plain teaching of the Bible that man fell in sin, that he rebelled against the God who created him. They view man as what he existentially appears to be, a struggling organism in a world more or less antagonistic or at least indifferent to his needs. And they call this situation natural, or native, to man. Freud saw in this struggle what he called a reversion *in utero,* a longing to return to the security of prenatal life. They fail to see that the completely harmonious life in every dimension, physiological, social-emotional, and intellectual is natural or original to man, and that his present state of conflict and confusion is that of a man who is lost, away from his Father's house and feeding on husks. The nostalgia within him he fails to recognize as a longing to return to his Father. This very longing the man of sin holds down in unrighteousness,[1] and consequently he has neither the desire nor the ability to return home.

DISUNITY AS EXPLAINED BY SCRIPTURE

God clearly tells us that the plight of man results from his voluntary disobedience. In the beginning God created nothing but beauty and harmony. Man was whole; organic unity in his person and personality were his natural state. But on the prompting of Satan, man chose to be like God, that is, independent of God and relying on his own resources. He rejected the place God had given him in creation, and instead vied with God for absolute supremacy.

God pronounced the curse of death upon this choice. And so it must be, for man had voluntarily severed his own lifeline, which is the loving fellowship of God. Lacking their true orientation, his functions became fragmented and disordered; lacking peace with God, man came to be at war with himself and with his fellows. In religious terms we say that man is now in the state of *unrighteousness,* which in the perspective of creation is an *un*natural state. Man is a sinner who now suffers the catastrophic consequences of his sin; this is the biblical explanation of human disunity.

When we attempt to translate biblical language into psychological language, we must take care not to confuse the *moral* with the

1. Romans 1:18-23.

functional in man. Unrighteousness is a moral term which denotes a serious disruption of the human condition, but it does not imply that man has ceased to be the image of God. Man, in other words, is still man; he has lost none of his being and none of his functions. He is functionally intact, but morally perverted.

The student will recall from the preceding chapter that human functions are neutral. This means that physiological functions, e.g., are neither superior nor inferior to psychic functions, and that no function is inherently evil. The *use* of any function is in itself good, but its *abuse* is evil. Seeing is not evil, but lusting with the eyes is; desiring is not evil, but coveting is; and so we could continue. The point is this: in the state of righteousness all of man's capabilities find wholesome and harmonious expression, but in the state of unrighteousness they become abused and distorted by a disintegrated personality.

Dr. H. R. Wyngaarden, psychologist at the Free University in Amsterdam, has portrayed this contrast graphically as shown in Figures III and IV.[2]

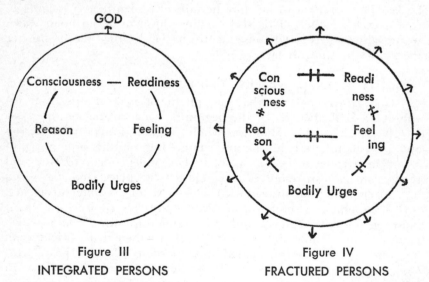

Figure III
INTEGRATED PERSONS

Figure IV
FRACTURED PERSONS

In Figure III the functions are shown in orderly interrelation, as indicated by unbroken lines, and their totality focused upon God. In Figure IV we see the focal point removed. Orientation becomes scattered, as shown by the many arrows. Functions become detached

2. *Hoofdproblemen der Volwassenheid* ("Major Problems of Adulthood") (Utrecht, the Netherlands: Erven J. Byleveld, 1950), p. 47. Diagrams reprinted with permission of the publisher.

and disordered, as shown by broken lines. No *functions* have been lost as a result of sin, but their focus and organization *have* been lost.

Not only man suffers the curse of sin. Nature, too, is distorted and disarrayed because of it. And this aggravates the human problem. Man without righteousness tries to create some semblance of order in a disordered world, but being broken within he can hardly succeed. The whole-person-in-life is merely the name of an impossible ideal, a lost dream — except for the fact that God has graciously intervened to restore it.

THE REMEDY FOR DISUNITY

ACCORDING TO SECULAR PSYCHOLOGY

Before we discuss God's revealed remedy for man's calamitous condition, we should note that according to secular psychology the only available remedy is human adjustment. Like all other elements of nature, man as a biological being is amoral. Either he adjusts himself to function effectively in his environment or he does not. When this adjustment conforms to accepted social ideals, he is said to act morally, and when it does not, he acts immorally. Generally speaking, this view holds that the most successful adjustments are made when the person conforms to social standards of practice.

ACCORDING TO SCRIPTURE

As we have seen, Scripture clearly teaches that the source of conflict lies in the spirit's revolt against God. Not only the body and the soul are sources of energy, but the spirit as well. The body is a source of energy in its physiological process. The soul is a source of energy in its psychic structure, and the spirit is the life principle involved in the psychosomatic. The spirit acts in the self-conscious choices and motivations of life.

In the anxiety of his lost existence man turns his functions into channels of evil. Morals and morality refer primarily to the person as I, ego, and to his function and personality field only as they express the moral or immoral person. Hence, morals and mores must not be confused. No degree of adjustment makes a good man. Who we are determines our righteousness, and what we do must be viewed in the light of who we are. The son of God, the restored man, may still do immoral deeds, but he is righteous. He follows evil deeds with penitence of heart and firm resolve to live righteously. Christ lives in him. The unregenerate may function in a given situation according to accepted form, but he is immoral, unrighteous.

It follows that the doctrine of redemption by grace is anathema to the secular psychologist. Having denied man's creation and his subsequent fall into sin, the secular psychologist believes the doctrine of grace to be wholly superfluous and based on a pessimistic view of man. He is of the opinion that the doctrines of grace and sin paralyze all genuine human aspiration. The words of Paul in Ephesians 2:1-10 deflate man's rightful dignity. In the blindness of his immanence he fails to understand that man can be seen in his true dignity when he is viewed as a son of God, fallen into sin but saved in the restoration of sonship in Jesus Christ. To the secular psychologist, the humanist, redemption consists of readjustment and reintegration of functions in line with changing conditions. The gospel of the Lord Jesus Christ is for him one religious-social message among many, showing a way to bring functions of the human organism into line with the demands of the mores.

To the Christian, however, the doctrine of redemption by grace in Christ Jesus is as essential as the doctrine of creation, for the former is the doctrine of re-creation, of restoring the lost creation. It calls our attention to two great divine acts. First, God extends the fellowship of His love to a race of His own choosing. This is the race restored to a living unity in Christ, as we read, "I am the vine, ye are the branches" (John 15:5). Second, in order to maintain a fit environment for the gathering of His own, God restrains the disintegrating effect of sin in the human race at large. Though man is dead in trespasses and sins, God enables him to integrate his functions well enough to achieve a measure of goodness and a degree of truth. The world continues for the sake of the church of Christ. When the ingathering of the saints of God is completed, time has run out for grace in the world outside of Christ.

We read in Ephesians 2:10, "For we are his workmanship, created in Christ Jesus for good works, which God afore prepared that we should walk in them." In Jesus Christ as the vine God grafts into organic union men and women of His own choosing restored to the fellowship of His love. They have righteousness restored to them in Him (cf. Romans 7:15-25). In principle harmony of will and purpose are restored, but the remnants of the disharmony of sin remain. Alive in Christ, the Christian is not fully delivered from the drives that would once again estrange him from God. But to those in Christ is the promise, I will be "a God unto thee and thy seed after thee" (Gen. 17:7b). The restoration of the lifeline of God's love in God's people does not automatically change functions in the person, nor the qualities of personality. The restored lifeline brings with it the desire and ability to restore unity of purpose and to direct functions toward ultimate harmony, for it is Christ who now lives in the new man. Conversion does not change a man's temperament but it does establish the basis for integration that can overcome the conflict of which temperament is a part.

IMPLICATIONS FOR EDUCATION

Two kinds of education

According to the Christian view, every child comes to the educational process suffering from the disharmonious effects of sin. Even if God chooses to restore a child to the fellowship of His love, thus establishing his essential righteousness, that child must still struggle with the remnants of his sinful nature. Nevertheless the fact that there are both regenerated and unregenerated children means that two kinds of education are possible.

Roland Allen expresses this fact well when he says that Christian education is more the education *of* Christians than *by* Christians. In his book on missions entitled *The Spontaneous Expansion of the Church,* he makes this noteworthy statement, "Christian education is education *in* Christ, and presupposes a certain relationship of the person who receives it to Christ. Eliminate that relationship and the education ceases at once to be Christian for him who receives it."[3] In another of his works, *Education and the Native Church,* Allen makes the following observation: "Teaching received by a Christian from a non-Christian is made Christian in the Christian mind; teaching received by a non-Christian from a Christian is non-Christian in the non Christian mind."[4] Exactly so. Education is what it is first of all because of one's relationship to Christ. If *in* Christ, the personality is being formed by education according to the inner motivation of the new life. If *outside* of Christ, the personality is being formed according to the inner motivation of the man of sin.

It does not follow that the objective content of education is unimportant. It does matter whether one teaches what is true or what is false. But subject matter, however accurate, cannot effect the restoration of a human spirit any more than biological generation can create it. Both are the work exclusively of God — to be sure, as He acts through the processes of human life. Hence, although the content of education can assist or hamper the development of life in Christ, it cannot by itself determine the nature of that education.

We cannot escape the fact that there are two kinds of education

3. Roland Allen, *The Spontaneous Expansion of the Church* (London: World Dominion Press, 1956), p. 122.
4. Roland Allen, *Education and the Native Church* (London: World Dominion Press, 1928), p. 24.

going on in this world: the education of Christians and the education of non-Christians. Both may be found in the most distinctive Christian school, and similarly both may be found in a school founded on secular principles. The Christian school seeks to establish an educational program appropriate to the child *in* Christ, and because God chooses to work through human agencies, that program may also be used to work in a child the restoration of the life *in* Christ.

EDUCATION AS DEVELOPMENT

We have seen that education is a process in which the whole person proceeds from immaturity to maturity. How to define maturity, that is, the *goal* of education, is properly the concern of normative sciences such as ethics, philosophy, and theology. Educational psychology, on the other hand, has as its task to *describe* accurately the process of child development and learning, especially as these relate to so-called "formal" education.

Two principles have already emerged from the foregoing discussion. The first is that the formation of *personality* is a key consideration for our study. At birth the infant is a person, an organic unity of the spirit in the psychosomatic. But he has not yet expressed himself in the various dimensions of personality. Though he may give early indications of future development, it is largely through education that a child's personality is formed.

The second principle is that in teaching one must deal with the whole child, not merely one of his functions. The intellect, e.g., is not a separate entity which can be trained in isolation. Intellectual training involves emotional attitudes, physiological functions, and social relationships. Sometimes attempting to train only the intellect will develop feelings in the child which militate against the very goal sought by the teacher. We must always teach the whole-child-in-life. We must address ourselves to the person who self-consciously begins to order his functions in the dimensions of his personality according to the goals he accepts in his heart, that is, in his very being as image of God.

In our study we shall concern ourselves almost exclusively with the forming of personality as it takes place in the school as educational agency. The family too is a major agency in education. So is the church. They all seek the same objective, integration of personality as image of God. The school has a medium all its own in which this major task must be accomplished. Because of the distinctive task of the school, the classroom provides data for study peculiar to its situation. These data will concern us particularly as we proceed. The concepts we have developed thus far lay the foundation for our study.

We turn our attention first of all to a major problem on which all right understanding of learning and teaching in the classroom is based, namely, what constitutes a mature personality and how does its development take place?

QUESTIONS FOR FURTHER STUDY

1. A noted educator of the nineteenth century made the following statement: "The fundamental reason why children do not act right is because they do not have the conditions for right action." Appraise this statement.

2. Did the fall of man change the structure of the person?

3. Does one become a different person by regeneration?

4. How does our belief that we are by nature dead in trespasses and sins, according to Ephesians 2:1, affect our view of a child's educability?

5. Does a person become more intelligent when he is made alive in Christ Jesus?

6. How is one's personality affected by conversion?

SELECTIONS FOR FURTHER REFERENCE*

Overstreet. Chapter III of this volume will give you something to think about and appraise in connection with our study of sin and human personality. Appraise the concept of immaturity, especially in connection with our study of it in the following chapter.

*Reference here is cited by author's name. See Bibliography for title and complete publication data.

Part Two:

The Development of Personality

4

Theories and Principles of Development

DEFINITIONS OF GROWTH, LEARNING, AND DEVELOPMENT

(1) Growth.

We speak of a child's body growing, and of growth in his various bones, muscles, and organs. But we also speak of intellectual and emotional growth. In general, then, we shall speak of growth as *increase of capability* to undertake more functions in a richer way. Physically, growth proceeds from within the body structure to enlarge the several members and the whole. Psychically, growth comes about through increasing insights, which in turn make possible wider and deeper understanding.

(2) Learning.

We will reserve the term "learning" to refer to *specific achievements* such as learning to read, learning history, etc. Concepts are acquired by learning.

(3) Development.

Development refers to the *overall maturation process* which is accomplished when learning occurs in a growing organism. New capabilities arise with growth, and continued learning takes effect to further the development process. The total effect of learning is the progress of the whole person toward maturation or self-fulfillment.

We must recognize that God has ordained a *pattern* of development for all organisms, including human beings. This pattern can be modified only within certain limits; if these limits are transgressed, e.g., in the rearing or teaching of a child, only harm can result.

Development can be viewed as the unfolding of a pattern already implicit in the organism. The psychosomatic functions become increasingly organized and structured; activities become more precise and controlled. Babbling becomes imitative speech, which in turn becomes deliberately formed words and sentences. Handwriting moves from disordered scrawl to normal script. Abstract concepts come more and more to dominate thought and action. Wider interests arise, and a wider range of response. All this is development.

Though development does not take place uniformly in the whole personality, every specific bit of development affects the whole. Further, the potential for development at any given time depends on the whole personality. And finally, development never ceases; adults can learn, as well as children.

RELIGION AND CHILD DEVELOPMENT

MODERN SECULAR VIEWS

A. T. Jersild, a contemporary psychologist, has remarked that particular scientific studies of child development must be fit into "a larger view of life as a whole."[1] He adds that "in the interest of probing into the meaning of what we are studying and in the purpose of our study it is better to examine underlying viewpoints, and to disagree about them if need be, than to take them for granted."[2] One must see the child "in the light of a conception of humanity."[3]

In the context of this principle (which is certainly correct), Jersild develops two contrasting secular viewpoints regarding human development and explains the role of religion in each.

The first states that living is the activity prompted by a need to overcome obstacles. Conditions internal or external to the organism continually upset its static balance, so that the organism acts to relieve the tension caused by these irritants. According to this view, says Jersild, a child is like the dog Miltiades "who was never active except when he itched, and then the compelling passion of his life was to scratch the itch so that he might return to a state of inactivity. However, he never had a yen to go places and do things on his own accord."[4]

What place has religion in child life on the basis of this view? It is nothing more than an instrument for overcoming an obstacle to inactivity. The highest attainment of man is tension reduction. Some people need religion, belief in what we mean by God, to secure

1. A. T. Jersild, *Child Psychology* (New York: Prentice Hall, 1954), p. 22.
2. *Ibid.*
3. Ibid.
4. *Ibid.*, p. 23.

balance. Some kind of spiritual values, the less tangible things of life, are needed to scratch the itch. In some education theories religion and religious experience are treated precisely this way. In today's schools this view of religion is even more common.

There is a second answer among secular psychologists to the question of religion. Those holding this view reason something like this. "Living involves positive striving,"[5] says Jersild who is an advocate of this view. We shall let him speak for himself as he briefly summarizes it:

> The organism is endowed with an impetus to mobilize its resources and put them to use. It has what has been referred to as a self-actualizing principle. It does not seek simply to achieve equilibrium. The most significant developments do not consist solely in struggles to overcome a disturbed state, or to be rid of something, but also in strivings to gain something — to put potential abilities to use, to enter into experiences that utilize capacities for doing, thinking, and feeling and for sharing with others. According to this view, it is natural to seek, to strive, to struggle toward a kind of self-fulfillment. Included in this view is the implication that life does not consist solely in getting away from something bad but that the highest good in life is the living of it.[6]

According to this view religion represents the highest form of striving for self-fulfillment. In religious experience man lives on his highest possible level. It represents living at its best. Religion is not a body of unchanging truth to which man is obligated by higher authority to conform, but an experience that lifts men to the highest possible good in life. Whatever form of religious experience helps one be more and more what he can be, that religion is true for him.

This view too has found its way into educational thinking. It is this view which advocates strongly that religion must be reinstated in education. Advocates of this view frown on education without religion. They may even go so far as to advocate that the Bible be returned to public education as a source book in religion. For isn't the Bible one of our greatest treasures of religious heritage? To let a generation grow up without the Bible is to cut them loose from one of the greatest sources of power for self-fulfillment.

From what we have already learned of the Christian view of man it is evident that living is not exhausted in the surmounting of obstacles, even though such obstacles have come into life because of sin. Neither is living to be described in terms of mobilizing re-

5. *Ibid.*
6. *Ibid.*

sources for self-fulfillment. Human resources must be mobilized for positive action if the potential of man is to be realized. But self-fulfillment is the idolatry that man the sinner has substituted for fulfillment of the image of God in man.

Living is the activity of a person as he mobilizes his resources toward the fulfillment of what he really is, a son of God. Though his functions are out of harmony, man does not cease to be a son of God. His religious nature he cannot disown. He struggles endlessly for the fulfillment of his sonship. The sinner estranged from God does this unconsciously in terms of all manner of substitutes. The sinner saved by grace does this consciously and militantly as he fights for integration of his functions against forces within and without.

THE BIBLICAL VIEW: MAN AS RELIGIOUS BEING

Religion is central to the concept of development because, according to Scripture, man is essentially a religious being. We will now expand upon this thought by explaining six human qualities which characterize man as religious and can be attributed to no other organism.

Rationality. First of all, the human person is rational. By this we mean that a person has the capacity to know his experience as his own and relate it to foreseen, contemplated ends. He can reflect on his experience self-consciously, relate it to the past, and in a measure anticipate the future. There is a degree of transcendence of time and space in a person's self-conscious life. He can penetrate a situation in thought. The object of his knowledge he can judge true or false according to his comprehension of reality. In brief, a person can think. Thinking is a self-conscious process by which a person organizes concepts with a purpose or end in view. This is the self-expression of God in his eternality as it comes to expression in a creature.

Morality. The person is also moral. The morality of man is his capacity to place a value upon the object of knowledge as good or evil, as higher or lower, as greater or less, with reference to norms or standards. The person can recognize norms as obligatory upon him, can accept them or reject them, act upon them, and experience a feeling of justification or guilt in their execution. Because a person is moral he has a conscience. Conscience is a person's moral capacity informed by certain norms for living. A Christian's conscience is enlightened by truth according to the Word of God. This is the self-expression of God in his righteousness on the creaturely level.

Sociality. In the third place, the person is social. This quality refers to man's capacity for fellowship. Fellowship is possible only among self-conscious beings, for only they can communicate rationally and with a mutual feeling of value. Animals herd. Man fellowships. Animals are gregarious. Only man is social. Animals cannot fellowship for they know neither what they are doing or why. They only do. In animal life communication does not reach beyond a psychic affinity. In man communication is affinity of the spirit. Man's sociality is the self-expression of God as triune, as we understand communication within the deity among the three persons. A person's sociality is grounded in the organic unity of the race as image of God. Fellowship is an expression of this unity.

Aesthetic Sensibility. Fourth, a person is aware of the aesthetic. Man is capable of recognizing, valuing, and appreciating unity and harmony of expression, which is beauty. The Bible speaks of the "beauty of holiness"[7] and of the beauty of the Lord.[8] Man as image of God is created to give expression to the beauty of God's holiness, holy array, evident within himself and evident in the world. "The heavens declare the glory of God, and the firmament shows His handiwork," but only when recognized by the psalmist.

Freedom. Fifth, a person is free. To be free is to be self-determining, wholly directed from within. It is obvious that only God is free in this sense. He is the self-contained, the all-sufficient One. Man is a creature. As a creature man is limited to the nature God gave him, but also endowed with the capacities of that nature. Man is free when he accepts himself in his created endowments and limitations and rejects an order foreign to his nature. When he seeks to be God, he loses his freedom. This was man's original sin and the natural man persists in this error. It is also true that when man seeks a way of life beneath his created order he loses his freedom. This characterizes the man of sin as he caters to the lust of the flesh instead of bringing the flesh in subordination to the spirit. Man is a self-determining being when he is submissive voluntarily to the will of God for his life. In the fellowship of God's love man can order his way of life freely, for then he is subject to the law of God. Outside of the fellowship of God's love man does not subject himself to the law of God, and his freedom is turned to lawlessness and license.

Responsibility. Finally, a person is responsible because he is self-determining. He can be called to account for what he is and what he does. He must give answer for he makes voluntary choices. He can be judged as to his motives, for as self-conscious being he chooses

7. I Cor. 16:29b; Ps. 29:2; Ps. 96:9. The last passage the ASV has rendered "in holy array."
8. Ps. 27:4.

voluntarily. His choices transcend causation. He cannot escape the effects of antecedent circumstances, but he can judge them. His choices have the quality of purpose. He can foresee ends, judge them, and act according to them. Hence man can be approached with the question, "What doest thou?" God, being self-contained, is accountable only to Himself in the righteousness and holiness of His being. Man as creature is accountable to God and to God-ordained authority.

In the light of these qualities, what can we say about the goal of development, that is, maturity? The answer, evidently, is that a mature person is one who expresses the aforementioned qualities as richly as possible. And this is the goal of education in all its phases.

THE BIBLICAL VIEW: MAN'S THREEFOLD OFFICE

We gain another perspective upon the biblical view of man as a religious being by considering that as an image-bearer of God he has the offices of prophet, priest, and king.

Prophet. The person is a prophet. This means that he is a knower and can communicate his knowledge understandingly to others. He can know God, himself, others, and the world about him. Adam knew God as God, and communicated with him before and even after the fall. Enoch is said to have walked (walked about) with God. Even the unregenerate knows God, according to Romans 1:18-25, but holds his knowledge down in unrighteousness. Adam knew himself as a son of God. He knew the world about him so he could name the animals and dress the garden. Self-knowledge and knowledge of the world are seriously distorted in the disharmony of human functions. David cries out for greater self-knowledge in the face of God's all-searching providence (Ps. 139). Indeed, man is a knower and communicator of knowledge.

Priest. But the person is also a priest. Man is created to serve. He is not the original owner but the steward of all he possesses. Man is to serve God and his fellow man. He is to dress the garden and work on the animals, but to God and his fellow man he is one who serves. And his is to be a service of love. Even the authority vested in man is one aimed at service. His service is to be sacrificial in character. He is to find himself in losing himself. His is to be a life not only of self-knowledge but of self-surrender.

King. In the third place, man is a king. We are told in the Word of God that he that rules himself is better than he that takes a city.[9] The Bible also reminds us frequently of the creation

9. Prov. 16:32.

ordinance that gave man dominion over all creation.[10] Man was created to be vicegerent, to be king under God. He is to rule first of all in the domain of his own person and personality. Self-rule and self-control are a prerequisite for all other control. As he orders his way of life in keeping with God's will, he is capable of ruling in the world about him.

As prophet a person exercises self-knowledge; as priest self-surrender; as king self-control. All three are necessary for maturity, for independence, for a well-formed personality. The mature person in Christ orders every function of his person and every dimension of his life in keeping with his self-conscious commitment to the Word of truth as he has it in Jesus Christ.

PERSONALITY DEVELOPMENT IN THE CHRISTIAN SCHOOL

After having stated these ideals for education, especially education in a Christian school, we might well remind ourselves that their accomplishment does not rest wholly with the school or with the teacher. Other factors such as hereditary endowments, prenatal influences, and preschool training have already established a partial pattern for personality development of the child. Furthermore, the regrettable fact that all children come into the world suffering the effects of sin will immensely complicate the educational task.

Most important for the Christian school teacher, however, is the realization that God deals with youth in different ways. God's help is indispensable to the success of education; but God chooses to work in his own way according to his own wisdom, which we do not always understand.

The Bible is replete with examples of God's dealing with youth. We see in the lives of Samuel and Timothy, for instance, how the Lord early in their youth laid his hand upon them. Already as children they gave evidence of transformed lives, of restored righteousness. By God's grace they gave a full and rich life of service to the Lord. What a blessing upon parents and children whom the Lord favors in this way! But we also have the example of Paul, apparently a covenant youth, who persecuted the people of God and honestly thought he was rendering God a service. He was rescued from the darkness of sin only when God seized him in the midst of a misdirected religious mission. We also have the tragic examples of Esau and King Saul. Covenant youth they were too. But their developing lives betrayed the lack of righteousness. Temporary external conformance to truth and righteous living gave way

10. Ps. 8:6.

to inner hostility of spirit that sent them both headlong to destruction. They betrayed a motivation that characterized them as covenant-breakers. All sons of Adam are covenant-breakers. But these became covenant-breakers a second time when they failed to assume the responsibilities of the covenant of grace.

On the other hand we see Pilate, a pagan. Confronted with the Christ, he declared him innocent but crucified him just the same. He used his natural light to crucify our Lord so that he might save himself from the wrath of the multitude. How like the unregenerate man. He uses his knowledge of God to deny God or the right of God to control his life.

In the Christian school we can expect that most of the pupils come from Christian homes, that is, homes in which Christ is honored as Lord and Savior. Some from their early youth will give evidence of God's hand in their lives, as did Samuel and Timothy. Teachers in these schools will have Samuels and Timothys in all their classes and on all levels of schooling. But they will have Pauls too. Their Pauls seem to resist the work of the Holy Spirit and turn their energies into destructive activities. God, however, will use their present Christian instruction in his own time to discipline their lives in truth. In spite of the resistance he encounters, the Christian teacher works and prays, but he will not be discouraged. He is more intent on God's ways than on his own apparent success. But there will be deliberate covenant-breakers too. There will be Esaus and Sauls. They conform to the practices in the Christian community. They master the instruction in school. They go to church, attend catechetical classes in church, and perhaps even go through the form of confessing their faith before the church of God. But their hearts are not touched by the Spirit of God. Sooner or later they turn away and choose a life of more or less polite disobedience.

There may also be some Pilates attending Christian schools. The unregenerate world is pagan, be it in a more refined sense as a result of centuries of Christian influence. Should non-Christian children be in attendance at the Christian school, the teacher will see his task as bringing the gospel to one estranged from God. God is still calling his own from among sinners everywhere. Though Christian schools in our Christian communities are not established for evangelistic purposes, the Christian teacher will look upon the presence of a child from a non-Christian home as a providential act. God has his purpose. Such a child may turn out to be a Pilate who crucifies the Christ anew, but he may also be a chosen vessel for the Lord and his service.

THREE ASPECTS OF HUMAN DEVELOPMENT

Why does a child grow up at all? And why does he grow up in the particular way that he does? As we find so often, popular maxims suggest contradictory answers to these questions. "As the twig is bent, so grows the tree" seems to say that the growing up process is largely engineered from without, whereas "Mighty oaks from little acorns grow" indicates that the cause and direction of development lies wholly within.

Both maxims are partially true but oversimple. Growth and development *are* inherent in the organism; God has ordained that from a single fertilized cell a child should be born, and that the child should not remain so but become a man or woman. But development cannot be accomplished in isolation from an environment, so we must recognize that *nurture* as well as nature will contribute to the formation of the adult. In the following paragraphs we will discuss three distinguishable aspects of the complex human developmental process.

THE DEVELOPMENTAL URGE: DRIVE TO MATURITY

Studies of human development clearly indicate that there is some force of growth and development potential within the child which asserts itself from very conception according to a pattern. In general this is true of all organisms. Each develops according to its kind. Jersild speaks of this urge as a "positive forward impetus."[11] The Creator created all life according to its kind and each kind follows its ordained pattern. In man it is the pattern of a living being created in the image of God. The positive forward impetus in a child is that of a person as he is impelled to mature. It is the drive of the organic whole toward independent functioning.

The positive forward impetus is purposeful, teleological. It is not merely a force that somehow must be harnessed for development of the organism. The physiological structure, for example, does not merely grow bigger but matures. It integrates and coordinates structure so that it is capable of initiating function. When the structure for creeping is complete, all things being equal, a child will begin to travel even if he has no obvious external incentive. The same is true of neural and mental structure. There is a self-starter to action that impels growth and development. This impelling, purposeful drive is sometimes called the principle of indigenous motivation. This is a good name for it, for it stresses two important facts. First,

11. Jersild, *op. cit.*, p. 23.

that it proceeds from within a child. And second, that it is purposive.

When we view man as the living being created in the image of God we readily see the significance of indigenous motivation. The spirit as life principle impels the organic whole to maturity. The positive forward impetus is the expression of the spirit in organic union with the psychosomatic structure. The entire person is involved, therefore, in the indigenous motivation. Let us give this impetus the name "developmental urge." It is that urge which impels development of the person to self-fullfillment.

THE DEVELOPMENTAL GOALS: MATURITY AND FORMED PERSONALITY

Self-fulfillment is itself the most general goal of the developmental urge. More specifically, the goal of a human *child* is to become a human *adult*. More specifically still, his goal is to become precisely that *individual* implicit in his developmental pattern. A child is to develop every resource of his being as image of God in the threefold office which is his by divine appointment. Furthermore, God has endowed him as a person, and racial and ancestral relationships have equipped him with a given in his being which the developmental urge presses forward to self-fulfillment. The developmental urge impels a person to form himself in the dimensions of life into a mature personality. He forms himself and is formed by the truth. This forming of personality according to the pattern of truth is the developmental goal. The person is to become an independent personality, that is, able to make right judgments and order his life accordingly.

The Christian can speak of forming personality according to the truth. He knows the truth for he knows Christ. And Christ is the truth, the personal revelation of the Father, the author of all truth. He has received the Word of truth, the Bible, as the only infallible guide for thought and action. He can walk in the light of this truth.[12] This does not mean that the Christian can attain full knowledge of all facts and relationships. Though restored in spirit in the fellowship of God's love and therefore alive to the truth, the Christian still struggles in this life with broken functions of his psychic and physiological structure. He can err and the passions of a life estranged from God are still plaguing him. The old man has not been completely overcome, as we read in Romans 7.

The developmental goal is understood differently by the non-Christian. The most common concept today in our democracy is

12. See I John 2:20.

that of adjustment, especially social adjustment. Self-fulfillment, self-realization in the interchange of individual and social life is another way of stating it. Then there are those who view life more from the intellectual aspect and make training of the intellect or mental discipline the goal of development. It is recognized that not all can attain to the same level of intellectual achievement, but the goal is the same for all on different levels. Throughout history the developmental goal has been stated variously.

Even in Christian circles the goal has not always been clear with reference to the whole person. Some Christians have a dual developmental goal one for the spirit, namely, the Word of truth, and one for the psyche, mental discipline. They find it difficult to integrate these in terms of a total personality.

THE DEVELOPMENTAL TASK: EDUCATION

A third aspect of human development is the developmental task. The developmental urge is inherent, native, indigenous. It is not given by the environment. By virtue of being a person, the indigenous motivation of a human being is to become a formed personality. To attain the developmental goal of a formed personality according to the truth requires the process we call education. Education is the process by which a person is formed and forms himself according to the truth. In relation to the developmental urge *inherent in* the person, and the developmental goal *prescribed for* the person, the developmental task is set up *in behalf of* the person. Education works on the basis of the developmental urge and in line with it to achieve the developmental goal.

5

Theories and Principles of Development (II)

THEORIES OF DEVELOPMENT

THE FORCED MOVEMENT THEORY

We have seen that there is a positive forward impetus in a child, just as there is in all multicellular living organisms, that impels him to maturity. How are we to explain this indigenous motivation? A force that patterns a child according to propensities inherent in the physical structure? Such it is, according to some. Cell division, cell differentiation, maturation of the structure, and the dynamics of functions all go to make up the process which under given environmental conditions produce a human being. The whole process has its source in the impelling force of the positive forward impetus of development potential of the organism. This explanation is known as the forced movement theory.

THE HOMEOSTASIS OR EQUILIBRIUM THEORY

This explanation of human development carries the preceding idea a little further. The biological organism in its positive forward impetus produces within itself the tension of unfilled needs. The needs can be met by an environmental given such as food. But the organism must appropriate the food. When a problem situation confronts the organism the need for a solution arises. The necessary materials and processes for a solution must be appropriated. In the appropriated and assimilated object the tension is relieved and equilibrium is re-established. Development takes place as present equilibrium or homeostasis paves the way for further tensions and further balancing outcomes. Increase in achieved equilibrium is attained.

THE SELF-FULFILLMENT THEORY

A third theory carries the process still further. It recognizes a distinctive human potential called the self. What is the self? "The self," says Jersild, "is a composite of thoughts and feelings which constitute a person's awareness of his individual existence, his conception of who and what he is."[1] According to Jersild and others this self or "custodian of awareness," "that to which we refer when we say I," is built around a nucleus. Out of the nucleus comes forth the indigenous motivation. In the positive forward impetus the developing organism attains selfhood. The self is fulfilled in the process of development. A self patterned according to inherent growth and development potential and environmental opportunity is the indigenous motivation of the organism. This is the self-fulfillment theory.

The theories described thus far have in common that they view man as a biological organism whose basic structure is biochemical. All function, physical and mental, has its origin here. Even the nucleus of which Jersild speaks has its basis in the biochemical structure. The self is no more than a composite of functions.

THE THEORY OF HUMAN DYNAMICS: THE EGO THEORY

A fourth theory is beginning to influence thinking in education. This theory is difficult to label, for it is very recent and combines several concepts of man. It comes largely from psychiatry and psychotherapy, and these are influenced greatly by recent developments in what is known as psychoanalysis.

Exponents of this theory reason about as follows. The individual is forced into existence by the inherent impulse of the human race. The biological structure of each organism is the external manifestation of this impulse. Having come into existence as a discrete organism, the impulse moves forward along the lines of its growth and development potential. When the forward impetus can proceed in the organism without external interference the organism is at rest, secure. This is largely the case in the uterus, to a lesser degree in childhood than in the uterus, but more so in childhood than in later life. In infancy this security is afforded by the warm embrace of a nursing mother.

As the forward impetus impels the organism to growth and development, interaction with the environment sets up hurdles which require modifications called adaptations and adjustments. In the

1. A. T. Jersild, *In Search of Self* (New York: Teachers College, Columbia Univ., 1952), p. 9.

interaction the organism develops functions of thought, feeling, and purposing or willing which as a composite make up an awareness called consciousness. A self-awareness is achieved in which the organism identifies itself in the interplay of forces from within and without. This self is known as the ego. In the course of development the ego accepts certain demands made upon it by the culture in which it moves. This complex of demands is the superego. When desires from within and demands from without are in conflict he may suppress the former, thus adding to the unconscious impulses always present from earlier stages of development.

The explanation of development, according to this view, is to be found in a positive forward impetus which brings with it the confused memory of a racial and ancestral past (call this the id or it, if you will), the developing ego, the accepted superego, and an unconscious stirring of desire and drive which constitutes a mixture of the id and repressed desires and conflicts.

We see at once that we are dealing with a more mysterious explanation here. Its mystical element has caused many scientifically-minded psychologists to discredit it. This is not the place to appraise it, however. At this point what should interest us is its emphasis upon the desire for security. As Christians we recognize this for what it is, namely, the search for divine fellowship which every man needs. Man as religious being has his basic security in the fellowship of God's love. The forward impulse is not a blind urge of racial dynamics, but the dynamics of the spirit longing for the full consciousness of God's love. Reversions to infancy are abnormal expressions of this longing. Building "more stately mansions" for one's soul in this life is a more normal expression of this longing, for it develops the person to greater maturity. But refuge in Christ as the truth is the true fulfillment of the longing heart. "I count all things but loss for the excellency of the knowledge of Christ Jesus, my Lord," says Paul, the inspired writer of the epistle to the Philippians.

PRINCIPLES OF DEVELOPMENT AS RELATED TO LEARNING

Whereas the preceding section was concerned with competing *theories* of development, we now turn to six important *principles* of human development which are especially relevant to the understanding of learning.

THREE INTERACTING FACTORS IN DEVELOPMENT

The student may be aware of the venerable "nature-nurture" controversy, in which the two factors of heredity and environment have each been cited as the dominant influence on human development. Many studies have been made and conflicting conclusions have been drawn. For some time it was the consensus that the argument was meaningless, for both heredity and environment are equal contributing factors except in certain special cases. Of late the problem has come to the fore again. We cannot settle the issue here, but our discussion of development must take account of it.

One contemporary author makes bold to say that the weight should be cast on the side of nature or heredity. Says he,

> As we move into the second half of the twentieth century, it becomes abundantly clear that individual differences in children are lawful expressions of design for growing and that there is present no known possibility of obliterating these designs. In fact, there is a real probability that there are dangers in radical attempts to do so.[2]

Is there a "design for growing" inherent in every child which is interfered with at great cost to the development of a child?

We have seen above that studies clearly indicate a growth and development potential within a child that asserts itself according to a pattern. How well defined that pattern becomes in the early stages of development is open to controversy. Some hold that the early development pattern is much more flexible than is indicated by Olsen. Part of the difficulty originates in the fact that psychologists generally recognize only two factors in human development, heredity and environment. Because Christian psychology recognizes three factors, the controversy takes another turn.

H. H. Horne, late Professor of Education at New York University, frequently referred to three factors in human development by saying, "In part we are born, in part we are made, and in part we make ourselves." The first refers to our biological heredity, the second to our environmental relationships, and the last to the active principle within us called the self, which he as philosophical idealist viewed as the ultimate principle in man and in the universe as a whole.

Let us follow this thought of Horne a little more closely. In biological structure the child is a product of an ancestral line which has its roots in the first family as recorded in the Scriptures (cf. Acts 17:26). In the language of biological science, every human being is an offshoot of a branch of the racial tree. Both genetics and analytical studies in psychology and psychotherapy call attention to ancestral traces in child development. Development patterns come into evidence in childhood, both physiologically and in mental structure and function. Sometimes a distinction is made between human nature

---

2. W. C. Olson, "Redefining the Task of Education," *Educational Leadership*, IX (1952), 219-224.

and heredity. The former points to our characteristics as human beings, as a genus; the latter to specific characteristics that seem linked to immediate ancestors. For example, that one has a nose is human nature; that one has a sharp, long nose is heredity. So, in the language of Horne, in part we are born.

But how much of us is born? Are we largely the product of a maturing structure in which a growth potential asserts itself according to a pattern, so that development is an indigenous process of self-realization? Or are we being formed, shaped in our development according to an external pattern?

Horne said that we are also made. We are made by our environment. Environmental relationships lead to interaction of the organism with his environment immediately upon conception. Biologically a person springs from one fertilized cell. In the course of cell division and cell differentiation the environment provides the setting. As the human form takes shape by differentiation and integration, the environment increases its part in man-making. The environment provides the possibilities for growth and maturation, but also sets a degree of limitation.

Development before birth is thought to be almost entirely one of maturation. By maturation is meant the spontaneous process of growth in an organism in response to interaction with the environment. It is a ripening of structure. We distinguish it from learning in that learning involves the patterning or forming of the organism according to an external demand made upon it. For example, the sucking mechanism matures before birth. With the maturing mechanism comes the impulse to use it when the opportunity presents itself. This is part of the positive forward impetus we have called the developmental urge. The sucking instinct functions immediately at birth when an object is pressed to the infant's lips. But the infant learns to respond to the bottle with the urge to suck. Likewise with the growth of muscles, skeleton, and sense of balance, the infant begins to use his legs in a walking movement. When maturation of the walking mechanism is complete, the infant can learn to walk. To carry this a little further, the infant's vocalization becomes articulated sounds which by learning take the form of the English language. Thus the environment provides opportunity and form for development.

We may say, then, with Horne, that in part we are made. We do not choose our parents, our early associations, nor the cultural influences brought to bear upon us. To be born in a Samoan civilization, subject to a Samoan life style, or in industrial, democratic United States is not of our choosing. To be born in a Christian home where the Christian faith sets the basic pattern of life, or in a worldly, indulgent, pleasure-seeking milieu is not ours to determine. It is in the providence of the sovereign God that we are born of a certain parentage and in a certain community. We have nothing to do with these.

The pattern in which the growth and development potential asserts itself is flexible enough to permit forming according to an external pattern. The environment can form the person into a certain personality, not apart from the developmental urge, but in cooperation with it. So we are made, we are patterned, we are formed, we are shaped.

Horne continues, ". . . in part we make ourselves." And in a real sense this is also true, insofar as we are spirits or subjects made in the image of God. Our spirits are not in any sense identical with God, as Horne believed; but the six qualities of man as religious being (cf. Chapter IV) testify to his unique creation and cannot be derived from either ancestry or acculturation. The law of the spirit is not the law of the psyche or of the soma. Secretion of the salivary glands in response to food is a law of the soma. A feeling-tone of distress or pleasantness in the taste of food is a law of the psyche. Both cease at death when psychosomatic processes disintegrate. But the law of the spirit continues. Moses communicated with Christ on the Mount of Transfiguration. The spirit as subject manifests himself to us in self-consciousness. The spirit is the very life principle of the psychic or mental functions and of the physical functions.

Secular psychologies recognize only two factors in human development. Some speak seriously of self as a third factor, but when we examine their discussion critically we find that self or self-consciousness is a qualitative product of some irrational force or process. Self is only a name for a process. So is ego. Person and personality are descriptive terms of forms of behavior, not of being. One is his life-style. Hence person and personality are in the final analysis impersonal and irrational. In such an impersonal philosophy the basic truths of Christianity, namely, creation, sin, and redemption are irrelevant.

There are three factors in man-making, in the process of development and learning. Psychology and education must take this basic fact into account. The person is a subject who in a real sense makes himself. Heredity and environment are factors in and through which the subject is formed and forms himself.

A TWOFOLD UNITY

The three factors in man-making constitute a twofold unity in life. We have had occasion to note several times the fact of man's organic unity, and that this unity has two important facets. On the one hand there is the unity of the person, which is the I or ego in the psychosomatic. There is also a unity of the person in relation to his environment. We have called this the unity of a person's community. The three factors in their twofold unity constitute the basis for the understanding of child development. God endows the I, or spirit, with a potential for self-development according to the call he places upon a person in life. In his inscrutable wisdom he equips the spirit with a psychosomatic structure of corresponding potential. The same all-wise God in his providence places a person in a given environment. With a divinely-ordained place in life and qualified potentially to fill this place, the person enters life and living to assume his God-appointed place responsibly. The whole-child-in-life relationship is fundamental in child development if he as a subject is to attain to the understanding that enables him to assume his God-appointed place. The wholeness of the person and the wholeness of life are important principles of development, learning, and teaching. We shall have occasion to explore this principle of wholeness further.

While sin has not destroyed the reality of the three factors in their twofold unity, the absence of righteousness in the person and the resulting disintegration of structure and function have greatly impaired their effectiveness. The broken person, as illustrated earlier in our discussion, is able normally to maintain a semblance of unity, but the forces of disintegration from within and without are ever at work. The new life of faith restores the essence of unity by restoring righteousness, but in this life succeeds only in part to restore a unity of structure and function characterizing man before the fall. But if any degree of the forming of personality as a man of God is to be achieved, the principle of wholeness inherent in child development must be obeyed.

Felt needs a source of action

A third important principle of human development has to do with human needs. Man is a creature, and therefore is not self-sufficient. He has needs. He needs food to replenish his energy. To accomplish this he tills the soil and breeds animals. He needs protection against the forces of nature; he builds houses and hospitals. He needs tools to accomplish the tilling of the soil and to build houses; he builds factories. Man's industries are the product of his cultural activity to meet his needs as a creature.

A child is a person who is developing a personality. His needs are those of a developing person. His needs spell out his impetus to action. His need for food is the urge that impels the art of sucking. His need for expression gives rise to manipulation and articulation. His need for fellowship gives rise to seeking his peers. His need for reflection as a rational being gives rise to analysis and investigation. The environment must furnish the media and the goals in which needs of child life can find their fulfillment. He must have food to grow. He must articulate in meaningful sounds to communicate. He must meet situations calling for decisions to learn to think clearly. Needs of the person must have their fulfillment in the child's environment if his development is to move forward toward maturity, toward independent and responsible personality.

At the basis of development lies the need theory. It is a convenient concept for analyzing behavior and personality. "Whenever a person acts he is presumably trying to satisfy a need. If we can recognize his need we can help him find ways to satisfy it."[3] Cronbach gives a good illustration in the following words:

> If John insists on his way when serving on a committee, the remedy does not lie in scolding him, moralizing or removing him from the committee. His underlying need may be a desire to show that he is a grownup, and, especially intelligent. The teacher can help him by acknowledging the merit of his ideas, and by giving him ample opportunity to win approval for independent contributions. After he relieves this inner pressure for recognition of his intelligence, he is ready to be taught that a good leader helps others develop their ideas too.[4]

Needs may be defined in a broad, inclusive sense as tensional states in the person brought about by the absence of what is required for a person's fulfillment as a being created in the image of God. So defined, human needs are many and varied. Broadly they may be classified as somatic or physiological as, for example, the need for food: psychic or mental, the need, e.g., for a feeling of success; and spiritual, e.g., the need for truth and goodness. Though needs are predominantly of one of these classes or another, they are always needs of the total person. We speak of a good meal, for example. We mean that the meal was nourishing, palatable, well prepared, eaten in good fellowship, the fruit of honest labor, and satisfying to the person. We pray, Give us this day our daily bread, and we thank the Lord.

With reference to human development and learning, particularly as they take place in school, we can speak of a more functional

3. Cronbach, *Educational Psychology*, p. 100.
4. *Ibid.*, p. 101.

classification of needs. We shall classify needs as primary or original, and secondary or acquired. The former we have in common by virtue of being members of the human race and being persons. They are part of us as living beings made in the image of God. The latter are acquired as a phase of our life style. They are the fruit of our cultural activity. For example, that we need food is primary; that we need potatoes is secondary.

We speak first of primary needs. Almost all problems of development and learning of school children relate to the following primary needs: affection, adult approval, peer approval, independence, self-respect, and commitment. Each one of these will be discussed in later chapters in connection with stages of development. Here we give a brief explanation of each: (1) *Affection.* To love and to be loved is a requirement for all of life. Many difficulties in later life can be traced to a failure to meet this need in childhood. The need must be met according to the level of a child's development. An early adolescent cannot accept the affection bestowed upon an infant. He will revolt and reject it. (2) *Adult approval.* This is especially a need in the childhood stage. Parental approval and teacher approval are sought daily. (3) *Peer approval,* approval by one's equals or associates. This need becomes especially pronounced in early adolescence and continues to assert itself in varied forms throughout life. (4) *Independence,* or demand to act on one's own. "Let me do it" is heard early of children. When repressed it gives rise to many hostile feelings and actions. (5) *Self-respect.* This is closely related to the demand for independence. Every person needs to maintain his feeling of adequacy, of competence, and of individuality. (6) *Commitment.* This need is overlooked in current psychologies, but it is very evident in man as a religious being. Early in life he wants something or someone to trust in and to receive his loyalty. He wants an authority figure. This becomes especially pronounced in adolescence. Things, persons, and ideals become objects of reverence and expectation. This need comes to its highest and truest consummation when, in the words of the Heidelberg Catechism, one can say sincerely with all his heart, "That I, with body and soul, both in life and death, am not my own, but belong unto my Savior Jesus Christ . . . ."

Secondary needs follow from our life style. So, for instance, the primary need for communication gives rise among us to the felt need of English as a language. The primary need for food asserts itself in the desire (e.g.) for candy, since the taste for it has been developed. Secondary needs are cultivated. A felt need for good reading, a felt need for balanced living, a felt need for clear thinking, a felt need for right companionship; these are illustrations of secondary needs. The teacher is activating a felt need for reading when he reads a story to children up to a point of great suspense and then suggests that they complete the story. He activates a felt need by raising a problem in history as he points out that the treaty of Paris brought political independence to the colonies, but that then economically they were still very much under England's control. So teaching is largely a recognition of meeting primary needs and of activating secondary needs and meeting those.

Sometimes we find needs classified as need for recognition, for satisfaction, and for security. These are indeed basic needs of all, especially learners who are called upon to apply themselves to a formal program more or less detached from the everyday ways of life. We all need recognition. It is expressed especially in the primary needs for adult approval and peer approval, and in general in all primary needs listed above. We all need satisfaction, that is, a feeling of contentment and restfulness. Momentary annoyance may be a stimulus for deepening satisfaction. But constant annoyance throws us into confusion and frustration. And of security it may be said that it sums up all primary needs. It is a feeling of total well-being. Securities of all kinds can be had all through life, but the only ultimate security is expressed in the words of St. Augustine, "Thou hast formed us for thyself, and our hearts are restless till they rest in thee."[5]

FELT NEEDS BRING ABOUT A SEARCH FOR DIRECTION

The needs of a person are fulfilled only by environmental interaction. He can function as organic unity within only to the degree that he can bring external relationships into organic unity with himself. The developmental urge sends a person into his environment to establish a communal relationship. In other words, the developmental urge sets a child to work at a developmental task. Learning, therefore, is spontaneous, need not be forced. One cannot keep a child from learning. Therefore a school does not provide learning but the *medium* in which learning toward right goals may take place.

Needs, then, give rise to a person's search for direction. Felt needs, both primary and secondary, give rise to a positive forward impetus in the person that seeks direction. The developmental urge can be given direction toward ends in keeping with who a child really is, a living being in the image of God.

5. *Confessions* I, 1.

FELT NEEDS ARE MET BY SATISFYING GOALS

Felt needs, as we saw, are a source of action and give direction to action. The tension involved in felt needs calls for an object of satisfaction, an object that can resolve tension. The satisfying situation becomes a goal of the person. A goal is a thing we seek. What we seek promises to involve the satisfaction of some basic need or needs.

Goals play a dynamic part in the forming of personality because they are discerned by the person as meeting his felt needs. Learning has been described as goal seeking. Life itself may be so characterized. Psychologically considered, one of the chief purposes of education must be the selection and adoption of right goals capable of meeting the true needs of the person.

Many goals are capable, when attained, of satisfying the child's need's to some degree. Furthermore, any one goal may satisfy more than one need. Learning to read, for example, meets the needs of adult approval, group acceptance as a literate person, feeling of independence, the felt need for knowledge that right commitments may be made, etc. Also the same goal can satisfy different needs when it is adopted by different people. One student, for example, selects mathematics because he is looking forward to the field of engineering. Another takes mathematics because it is a minimum requirement to get into medical school. Again, one may commit himself to goals which to some extent satisfy present needs, but which ultimately lead to conflict and frustration. Acceptance by his peer group, for example, is satisfying to a youth and essential to the fulfillment of his needs as a social being. But suppose his peer group has doubtful moral standards. Acceptance in such a group can never prove wholly satisfying. His needs as a moral being call for satisfaction too. Conflict and frustration will result. Only those goals can prove satisfying which meet a person's true needs as a religious being.

Developmental goals are not final goals. The former are only transitional. We find this thought in the Bible, too, in the words of Paul, "When I was a child, I spake as a child, I felt as a child, I thought as a child; now that I have become a man, I have put away childish things."[6] The concepts of *channeling* and *canalization* make clear the relationship between felt needs, developmental goals, and final goals. "The transmutation of needs into operating goals, i.e., the actual shaping of motives, is brought about by the opening of certain channels of action through which the constant pressure of needs can

6. I Cor. 13:11.

discharge itself."[7] As these needs "discharge themselves" into goals, new needs arise and new goals are found. They are developmental goals that constitute links in a great chain leading to final goals of the person as religious being, the forming of personality in the image of God. Developmental goals are directional process goals that direct the process of development to its consummation.

Let us illustrate this concept of channeling and canalization. To play a game of ball with mutual satisfaction and contentment is a developmental goal. A child learns to give and take in a ball game. He learns to serve. But the ball game is a transitional goal to broader and richer goals of love, co-operation, service, consecration, loyalty, and devotion. These are more ultimate goals into which needs, transitional goals, and further needs and goals are channeled.

READINESS DETERMINES EFFECTIVENESS OF GOALS

Readiness, in general, can be defined as the level of development at which new learning can profitably be undertaken. A newborn infant, for instance, is not ready to eat solid foods because his digestive organs have not developed sufficiently — or so it had been thought until recently. And analogously, the third grader is not ready to study geography because he lacks the requisite background of experience.

Readiness is related to goals in this way. If a child has not developed sufficiently to *appreciate* a given goal, that goal cannot possibly motivate him effectively. Even worse, trying to force upon him an activity for which he is not ready can undermine his sense of security. But of course one can also make the opposite mistake of failing to provide opportunity for achievement when the child *is* ready. In this case he may divert his energy toward attaining available but undesirable goals. So we see that the enlightened parent and teacher must be sensitive to the readiness level of the child.

SUMMARY OF BASIC DEVELOPMENTAL PRINCIPLES

(1) There are three factors involved in the forming of personality. They are the spirit (I or ego), the ancestral line in heredity, and the challenging and patterning environment.

(2) The three factors in the forming of personality function as a two-facet unity, the unity of the person and the unity of life. This twofold or two-facet unity is expressed as the whole-child-in-life relationship.

7. J. L. Mursell, *Psychology for Modern Education* (New York: W. W. Norton Co., 1952), p. 67.

(3) Felt needs of the person are the source of action which leads to the forming of personality.

(4) Action prompted by felt needs gives rise to a person's search for direction.

(5) A person's search for direction is consummated in satisfying goals. Motivation is the arousal of the will to act in pursuit of a goal.

(6) The effectiveness of desirable goals as a source of satisfaction depends upon the readiness of the learner.

THE DEVELOPMENT OF CHRISTIAN YOUTH

The role of education in child development should now be apparent. Education is a process in which the educators (parents and teachers) provide *guidance* for that inherent forward impetus which is resident in the educand (the child).

The Christian educator, therefore, finds great significance in the biblical mandate "Train up a child according to his way" (Proverbs 22:6).[8] There is a God-ordained way for a child to develop, which we may describe both according to the *principles* and the *goal* of that development.

With respect to the principles of development we refer to the previous section of this chapter. These principles constitute a God-ordained way which the educator must understand and observe in the conduct of his work. The goal of child development is also prescribed by God. A child is to be formed into an adult who voluntarily serves the Lord in all dimensions of his personality according to the measure of grace bestowed upon him in this life.

In this connection it is well to note how secular educational theory views the relationship between development and education. For modern education the relationship is one of providing the right conditions. An infant is a biological organism with human potentials among his functions. Given the right conditions, the human potentials can reach their maximum development. Education is the process by which appropriate environmental conditions are set up or provided for the positive forward impetus of a biological organism. Mursell points out two conditions necessary for personality development.[9] First, a challenge must be presented to a person relevant to his interests. He must strive to deal with the challenge that has for him what is sometimes called "ego-relevance." In the second place, in striving to meet the challenge he should achieve a newly organized

---

8. According to most Hebrew scholars, this is the preferred rendering of the text. It is given in the latest Dutch translation, and marginally in the ARV.

9. J. L. Mursell, *op. cit.,* p. 15.

mode of dealing with his environment. The person must be aroused in his will and find his way to a satisfying solution.

But Mursell's conditions do not exhaust the prescription for personality development. We know that we are dealing with a person, a living being created in the image of his Creator. He must be understood as such and educated as a rational, moral, social, esthetic, free, and responsible being. We know the norm according to which a person is to be formed into a personality. Not a dead uniformity, but a dynamic diversity in one organic unity according to gifts of God's grace to each person is the goal. We must look to psychology, sociology, and to studies in learning and teaching to help us get a better understanding of how we can guide the forming of personality.

THE HOME

To whom must we look to assume the developmental task? The Bible does not leave the answer in doubt. Marriage is a divine institution and one of the purposes of marriage, according to the Scriptures, is the bringing forth and rearing of children. God himself has instructed parents concerning their parental responsibility. God made the family the unit of society. It is the cradle of child life and education. Man's attempt to tamper with the integrity and rightful functions of family and home life brings devastating results for the individual and society. Sin has impaired this divine institution, but in the covenant of grace the parental responsibility is re-emphasized (cf. Genesis 17:7). To the parents and their children is the promise of the covenant. But the covenant of grace, like every covenant, has a second part. Christian parents take their vow before the Lord and his church to assume the second part of the covenant, namely, the responsibility to educate their children in the way of the covenant. The family is the God-ordained institution to provide the fellowship of love in which a child can be brought up in the security that love alone can afford.

THE CHURCH

But parents cannot assume this responsibility alone, especially in the complex modern age. They must look to auxiliary agencies.

The first among these is the church. It must first be observed that the church has an original as well as an auxiliary function in the education of covenant youth. The church, being a divine institution, has a claim upon parents and children alike. Children are born into the church from parents who are saints, believers in the Lord Jesus Christ. As mother of all saints, young as well as old, the church fulfills her teaching function by direct mandate of God. The church of Christ authoritatively exercises maternal care over parents and children.

But the church also has an auxiliary function in bringing up the covenant youth. Parents need the teaching ministry of the offices of the church to help them lead their children to conscious, voluntary acceptance of the second part of the covenant. The Reformed churches have consistently sought to carry out this task through catechesis. In this capacity the church functions as auxiliary educational agency. It assists parents by instruction and pastoral care to bring up their children in the holy faith.

THE SCHOOL

The school is another auxiliary educational agency. It is not a divine institution with an original function, but an extension of the home made necessary by the complexity of modern society. Not only has the scope of knowledge gone far beyond most parents' competence to teach it, but the teaching process itself has become sophisticated to a degree that it requires specially trained personnel.

In summary, we see that the teaching of Christian youth is a single task with a single goal, namely, the rearing of covenant youth in the fear of the Lord. The responsibility for this task falls primarily upon the parents, who in turn seek assistance from the church and the school. Thus we find that there are three agencies of education, each using its peculiar medium to effect its part of the unitary task. The parents use the informal milieu of family life. The church uses the Word of God and the doctrines of the Christian church. The school uses the culture and civilization as organized body of knowledge. But the media do not change either task or goal.

A CASE OF WHOLESOME CHRISTIAN DEVELOPMENT

Before we turn our attention to further details in the dimensions of personality, it is profitable to look at a realistic picture of a youth whose development we may characterize as wholesome and Christian.

Mildred Kort is fourteen years of age and in the ninth grade. She enjoys good health, is attractive, of normal height and weight, and is maturing normally. She is well thought of by her teachers and accepted by her fellow pupils, even to the extent of being popular in a wholesome sense. Her school work is always above average, even superior at times, though she is not the topmost scholar. Her record shows an I.Q. of 120, which is better than average, and an achievement in her school subjects of a B or better. She applies herself diligently to her studies but takes time for fun too. She loves to read, but reading is very evidently a hobby, not an escape. Recently she has taken up sewing because this is the only way she can get some of the clothes she likes to have.

Her basic needs are met but her wishes and desires are kept in balance by a well-ordered home life. Her home is generous with affection so that all members of the family feel secure. Mildred is the oldest of three children in a family that enjoys a moderate standard of living. Mrs. Kort has always devoted herself to making home for her husband and children a place of affectionate fellowship and devotion. While giving the children plenty of affection she holds them responsible for certain chores according to their maturity. Mr. Kort spends much time with his family. They enjoy doing things together. There is authority in the home, but it is exercised in love and toward increased self-discipline and responsibility of the younger members.[10] The children participate in making decisions according to their maturity and involvement. Consequently the children respect their parents, rather than fearing the consequences of wrong acts. Mildred, being the oldest, shares with parents the care of the younger ones, but not to the point of lording it over them.

Mildred attends church services regularly with the family, is beginning to participate in church activities, and has for some time attended the class in church for special instruction in Bible history, Bible doctrine, and personal spiritual guidance. She assumes responsibility for family devotions when her turn comes. She is talking about a desire to teach a Sunday School class as soon as her age permits.

Among her friends Mildred is known as a charming girl who can be depended upon to do her share of the work. She is not found in the front lines. A teacher was heard to say, "How can you call Mildred such a charming person, so well-adjusted? You'll rarely see her volunteering any work. She should be the first with her ability and attractiveness. Instead she waits until others call upon her." Another teacher, hearing this, replied, "This is precisely what I think so wholesome about Mildred. She is not driven by a desire to shine or stand out. She is perfectly willing that another should take the honors when she does the work." One's judgment of others often depends upon one's own disposition.

Mildred has her problems. There is a reserve about her that some of her peers are inclined to interpret as snobbishness. She has her friends, selects them rather carefully, does not shun others, but acts

10. On the importance of authority and obedience in child development, see C. Jaarsma, *Fundamentals in Christian Education* (Grand Rapids: Wm. B. Eerdmans Publishing Co., 1953), pp. 91-117, 356-366.

rather cool to some. This is primarily because of her standard of values. Her home life, while flexible in several ways, has set for her a high tone of spiritual and moral values. She cannot tolerate the interpretation some girls give to "fun and frolic." She has yet to learn how to deal with these problems without irritating others.

Adolescence has thrust upon her a new feeling of independence which Mrs. Kort sometimes fails to understand. Consequently a bit of anxiety is developing which sets up friction between mother and daughter not known until recently. Mildred very evidently is exploring this new feeling that has come over her and neither mother nor daughter fully understand. Mildred has her quiet moments at home, is sluggish about doing things, and is somewhat resentful of criticism.

All in all, however, Mildred is developing normally. She must work through her problems and she needs to be understood while she does so. It is not likely that Mildred will lose balance. She has enjoyed a security and a positive direction in her life that, all things equal, can bring her to maturity without debilitating conflicts.

STAGES OF DEVELOPMENT

Dr. H. R. Wyngaarden, a psychologist at the Free University of Amsterdam, has observed that the overall life span of a person can be divided into three stages.[11] The first stage, which lasts until about the eighteenth or nineteenth year, is a period during which the person comes to an initial understanding of the world and his place in it. When he begins to assume a more responsible role in life, during the latter part of adolescence, he enters the second stage. This is a period during which the person actively gains stability, discretion, and acceptance of life. It is difficult to determine when this stage ends and the third begins because individuals vary so much, but in most people it occurs at about forty-five or fifty years of age. During the third period the person has achieved a mature perspective which gives him a settled basis of judgment and often enables him to be very productive.

Our interest, of course, is in the first of these stages. This is the period in which personality is formed, and therefore it is most relevant to education. And now we may subdivide this first stage into three parts: the *preschool period,* the elementary school period of *childhood,* and the high school period of *adolescence.* For reasons that will become evident later, we will also divide the pre-school

11. Wyngaarden, *Hoofdproblemen der Volwassenheid* ("Major Problems of Adulthood") , ch. 3.

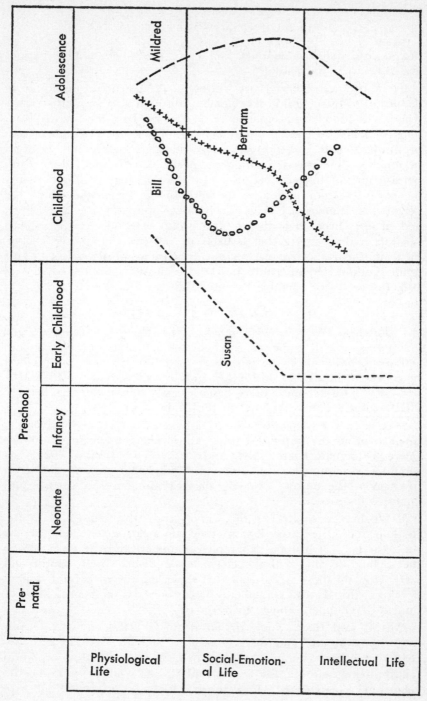

Table I

STAGES OF DEVELOPMENT

period into *neonate, infancy,* and *early childhood.* These periods are summarized in Table I.

In the balance of Part II we will employ the structure indicated in Table I to trace child development through the periods of pre-school, childhood, and adolescence. This may be done in two ways: *longitudinally,* by tracing one dimension of personality through from beginning to end, and *transversely,* by viewing the development of *all* personality dimensions during *one* period. Both methods are important for our purpose because child development does not usually move neatly from period to period. In one particular child the personality dimensions may not be developing at the same rate, and in any chronologically uniform group of children (e.g., a class of sixth graders) the teacher is likely to find many stages of development in the respective personality dimensions of his pupils. This point is illustrated in Table I by the indicated "profiles" of Susan, Bill, Bertram (see Chapter I), and Mildred (this Chapter).

QUESTIONS FOR FURTHER STUDY

1. Teachers are at times amazed at the drive that young people manifest at a ball game, in a school band, or in some social club activity. They express the wish that such forceful motivation could be generated in algebra, history, geography classes, and the like. Is it because the former meet more basic needs? Or is it perhaps because vital goals are not formulated in the study of the latter?

2. A teacher was heard to say, "If I were to take account of the interests of all my pupils I'd never know where I am, for children's interests fluctuate by the day. And furthermore, I think youngsters should be disciplined early to do some things that are not of interest to them at the outset." Analyze the reasoning of this teacher and appraise his views.

3. We hear it said, "Let the schools train the youngsters in the fundamentals, the three R's, so they can read, write, figure, know the basic facts of history, geography, grammar, and the like." When the schools do this will they have accomplished their educational task? How do those who speak this way view the process of human development? Is this judgment based on facts and principles of human development known to us today?

4. It is said that schools in our democracy fail to teach pupils to think, evaluate, and discern because they incorporate such activities as home economics, typing, printing, metal and wood work, family living, etc. in the second curriculum and projects in the elementary curriculum. How do you analyze this reasoning? Appraise it.

5. How would you appraise the oft-repeated statement that man is a product of heredity and environment?

6. To what extent should a teacher interest himself in a pupil's past?

7. Why is close cooperation of home, church, and school essential?

8. A teacher who had just completed some courses at a university summer school was heard to say, "All this talk about motivation sounds good in books, but when I get back to my classroom I've got to cover the course of study and the textbooks. How will I get time for determining the needs of my pupils, help them formulate goals, and the like, that books in education speak of?" What had this teacher failed to learn in his summer course?

SELECTIONS FOR FURTHER REFERENCE*

Blair *et al.*, Chapter II, "Biological and Social Bases for Behavior."

Coladarci, Chapter II, "Developmental Aspects of Behavior."

Cronbach, Chapter IV, "The Stream of Development."

Crow & Crow, Chapter II, "The Fundamentals of Human Development."

Gates *et al.*, Chapter II, "The Development of Behavior."

Havighurst, Chapters I-XIV, "A Study of Developmental Tasks and Adolescence."

Jersild (1)

Jersild (2), Chapter II, "Nature and Course of Human Growth."

Jordan, Chapter II, "Heredity, Maturation, and Environment."

Morse & Wingo, Chapter IV, "How Children Grow and Develop."

Mursell, Chapter II, "The Sources of Motives."

Sorenson, Chapter V, "Our Needs, Wants, Urges, Drives, and Motives."

*References are cited here by author's name. See Bibliography for title and complete publication data.

6

Physiological Development

To understand how development of the total personality takes place according to the principles discussed in the preceding chapter, we shall find it necessary to view development in one dimension at a time. We must emphasize again that it is not given us to view the whole at one time. We must analyze for understanding, but likewise remind ourselves that we cannot see one dimension of the whole-person-in-life independently of other dimensions. When we look at the physiological activity of a person we are also looking at the other dimensions, for they are all involved in one another. For example, we may be observing skeletal and muscular growth. But these are associated with movement by the person, his sense of balance, a focusing of the movements in attention, a feeling of success, thwarting, or frustration, goal of movement, and the like. A child is an organic unity from the outset, and he grows, develops, and learns as a unity.

We shall, therefore, try to view the development of the whole by taking a look at each dimension of the personality separately and observing each as a facet of a functional whole. But we shall find ourselves constantly crossing over from one dimension to another.

GENERAL PHENOMENA OF PHYSIOLOGICAL DEVELOPMENT

GROWTH, DEVELOPMENT, AND LEARNING

Because the concepts growth, development, and learning are likely to be confused, it is well that we distinguish their meaning once again at this point. When speaking of the physiological, the distinction can be more clearly pointed out than in the other dimensions of the personality.

We say that a child is growing when his bones, muscles, and bodily organs take on larger proportions. In other words, growth refers to enlargement of structure. Development, on the other hand, refers to the co-ordinated *use* of the growing structure. When an infant begins to grasp the toy that he sees, we say that he has reached a new level of development. Finally, learning refers to some specific achievement such as holding a spoon between the thumb and first two fingers. Thus development depends upon growth, and learning depends upon both growth and development.

How, for example, does a child become a well-mannered table guest? Growing skeleton and muscles in arms, hands, and fingers adapt their use to integrated action. Focusing the eyes and movement of the mouth are co-ordinated with action of large and small muscles of arms and hands. The child learns how to hold a spoon, when to use the knife and fork, how to sit, what to pass, etc. In the learning he develops good eating habits and acceptable social intercourse. He gains insight into being at ease himself and how to put others at ease in eating. He is formed in his personality.

The growing insight referred to indicates that we can use the words growth, development, and learning with the same distinction in other dimensions of the personality. We speak of a child learning the fundamental processes in arithmetic, that is, specific, defineable achievements are attained in number relations. However, we speak of a growing insight in arithmetic, which means that the mental structure in arithmetic is being enlarged. He is developing greater facility in arithmetic as growing insight and specific attainments are co-ordinated and integrated.

It is well that we keep these terms distinct, lest we be found to confuse issues in more involved discussions about learning and teaching.

PERSISTENCY OF THE DEVELOPMENTAL URGE

A phenomenon that strikes us as we view the physiological development of a child is the dogged persistency of what we have called the developmental urge. God has laid down an inner drive to maturity. A child must grow up, though some parents and other elders seem at times to think they can prolong childhood. This positive forward impetus lies behind the superabundant activity of the normal child; he is on the way; he *must* be on the way. The developmental urge will express itself in various ways, but in all cases it is a primary factor in the explanation of child behavior.

INDIVIDUAL VARIATIONS IN DEVELOPMENT

We also observe that the developmental urge is not equally strong in every child, nor is it uniformly potent throughout each child's development. Every child develops at his own rate depending upon internal or external circumstances. A well-nourished child who is given ample opportunity for rest and physical activity will grow normally according to his developmental urge. But a youngster who is inadequately nourished and who is denied sufficient sleep and activity will be thwarted in his development.

The important thing to remember about differing patterns of physical development is that they must be accepted by parents and teachers and by the child himself. If they are not — if the tall child is made to feel that he is too tall, or the short child that he is too short, for instance — there will be repercussions in the total personality of the child. He will feel inadequate and lose self-respect; and because there is little he can *do* about the growth of his body, his frustration may well be expressed in the failure of other functions. In an intelligent school program every effort will be made to avoid such frustrations; for instance, physical activities can be selected in which every child has a reasonable chance to succeed.

UNITY, DIFFERENTIATION, AND INTEGRATION

The three words above indicate a general *sequence* of physical development. Consider, e.g., prenatal development. The single fertilized ovum is a unity. Cell division begins, and soon clusters of cells differentiate themselves to perform specific functions. These functions, in turn, are integrated to serve the organism as a whole. Again, the simple function of following a bright-colored object in early infancy becomes differentiated in being attracted by many objects. The many stimuli become integrated in the interpretation of a colored picture when a child recognizes a boy running after a ball.

The process of development from a unity through differentiation to a greater unity underlies a child's learning and development in general. It lies at the basis of what is called whole-part-whole learning. A child does not begin by learning parts and then arriving at the whole. He responds first to whole situations in an undifferentiated way. Differentiations follow, and they are directed to new integrations. A child enjoys an entire scene in a picture before he singles out the boy and the ball separately. The story of the boy running into the water to get the ball follows. Likewise in reading, house and door of a house precede the word, and the word precedes the letters. Out of the words sentences emerge, and out of sentences the reading of a story. We shall see that this process of wholeness constitutes an important phase of the learning process. Look for further discussion of it under the heading of perceptual field.

STAGES OF PHYSIOLOGICAL DEVELOPMENT

PRENATAL

Psychologically the prenatal period is largely shrouded in mystery. The three factors involved in development (the self, heredity, and environment) function in a unitary way from the very beginning. There is a self at work as basis for the total organism from the start. Not only is it said of Jesus or of Jeremiah, that he was called from his mother's womb,[1] but of all human beings we may say that God calls them into being for a purpose. The prenatal position of Jacob and Esau is held significant in Scripture. Samuel was conceived in answer to prayer. Illustrations of the significance of the prenatal life could be multiplied from the Bible.

Our scientific knowledge of prenatal development is limited entirely to the physiological. We know that cells multiply, differentiate, and subsequently integrate to form a physiological structure, but that is about all. Nearly all prenatal growth may be subsumed under the concept of *maturation*.

Maturation means the growth of structure to the functional stage. For example, the sucking and swallowing mechanisms of an infant are complete at birth. When a nipple is presented he automatically sucks, and when liquid enters his mouth, he swallows. These mechanisms are developed and further perfected by learning.

We also know that the so-called endocrine glands play a large part in maturation, even prenatally. They are formed in the fetus before the nervous system is complete and are believed to affect its growth directly. Thyroid deficiency, e.g., retards development of the fetus as early as the sixth month, though mild cases can be remedied by early treatment of the infant. The teacher should be aware that endocrine glands have an important causal influence on child behavior, and should become familiar with their functions in development.[2]

The effect of the birth experience on child development is largely conjectural. Birth is obviously a violent change of physical circumstance, but prenatal maturation has largely prepared the way. Some psychologists say that birth is always a traumatic experience, but under normal circumstances this does not appear to be necessarily true. Indeed, considering all the hazards attending prenatal development and birth, we may marvel with the Psalmist, "I am fearfully and wonderfully made; marvelous are thy works" (Psalm 139:13-16).

1. Isa. 49:1,5. Jer. 1:5.
2. See Figure V and references at the end of this chapter.

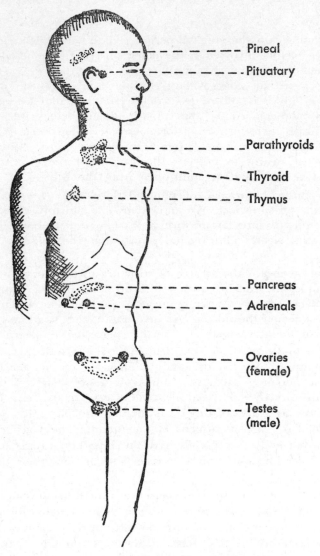

Pineal

Pituatary

Parathyroids

Thyroid

Thymus

Pancreas

Adrenals

Ovaries
(female)

Testes
(male)

Figure V
LOCATION OF ENDOCRINE GLANDS

Neonate

The first two weeks of infancy are known as the neonate period. It is a critical period of orientation for the infant as he adjusts to new functions and new environment. Mass action and random movements of startling speed and variety are characteristic of this stage. They are spontaneous, impulsive, unorganized, and ceaseless. All these movements enter into the maturation of body structure on which important functions such as walking, grasping, talking, will soon be built. During this orientation period it is important to continue the comforts of prenatal life. Maternal nursing is the closest approximation. Pediatricians and child psychologists recognize this and advocate what is known as "lying in" after birth, that is, the infant with the mother as much as possible. Maternal attitudes and practices in handling the baby afford him an inner feeling of security basic to later development. This feeling facilitates normal physiological processes of digestion, circulation, and glandular action. It constitutes an infant's first feeling of acceptance, a basic need of life and development. Some psychiatrists are of the opinion that during this period of orientation an infant should experience no discomforts. He should be picked up whenever he cries. And these psychiatrists are not necessarily advocates of permissiveness. They would have parents be firm with children, make demands upon them, but not until a child has experienced love and is able to return a degree of affection.

Infancy — First Year

During the first year the processes of differentiation and integration are much in evidence. Random movements develop into bodily skills. The infant holds his bottle, picks up a block, get up on his knees, pulls himself up by a chair, etc. These constitute an integration of differentiated movements. Movements are coming under his control for purposeful activity. Mental discriminations follow a like pattern. The infant stretches out his arms to mother, signaling for mother to take him. Language skills are acquired in associating spontaneous vocalizations with mother ("ma-ma-ma"). When asked, "Where is your ball?", he looks about him. Social distinctions are being made as when he responds with great jubilance to the presence of children. Some individuality in life style is coming into evidence too. We recognize, for example, one baby to be much friendlier than another. An important fact to note is that physiological, social, emotional, and intellectual development go on at the same time, and that every one of them involves the other.

INFANCY — SECOND YEAR

The second year of a child's life is marked by three climactic events which are of great significance in total development and illustrate many phases of learning and development that appear later. We generally speak of these events as the three "musts" in the life of the infant, namely *walking, talking,* and *control of elimination.* We see maturation and learning working together in these processes toward total development of a child's personality. A child can learn to walk when his skeleton, muscles, sensation of balance in the inner ear, and focusing of eyes have matured. The developmental urge functioning as a positive forward impetus impels action leading to walking. Encouragement and assistance from elders strengthens this action. A child learns to talk when the physiological mechanisms of vocal chords and mouth are matured to function in articulation. Again encouragement from his environment promotes it and furnishes the forms for articulation, namely language. The same can be said of elimination.

Why do we speak of walking, talking, and control of elimination as musts? Because achievement in these activities is necessary for normal communication among associates. Normal development in these areas meets a child's primary needs, especially adult and peer approval. When anyone of these accomplishments is delayed, a child fails to get this approval and he loses normal contact with others. A child's normal intercourse in play, for example, depends upon the development of all three processes. Failure to attain normal relations socially and emotionally may have a retarding or distorting effect upon his physiological and intellectual development. His entire personality is affected adversely.

In these areas of development the normal range of individual differences also obtains. Should a child be slightly slower than the average, not coercion but understanding and sympathetic helpfulness are needed to help him catch up. Coercion will press a child to the frustration point, so that he feels threatened and becomes inhibited or violent through fear. Some children entering school are suffering the effects of abnormal development in these areas. Their problems in pupil-pupil relations and teacher-pupil relations may have originated in a parent's faulty dealing with one or more of these "musts." Teachers should bear these facts in mind.

READINESS, THWARTING, AND FRUSTRATION POINT

When is a child ready for walking, talking, toileting, tricycling, reading, number exercises, etc.? Must we wait for a "favored moment" to appear before which nothing can be done? And when that moment is past, is a golden opportunity lost? Not in the sense of "now or never." Development is a continuous and cumulative process. We can "ready" a child by providing for the use of structure and function. A mother does this when she encourages baby to use his little legs in pushing himself up, or when she helps him reach for a toy. Telling stories to a preschool child, showing him pictures in connection with stories, conversation with children on subjects meaningful to him, visiting points of interest to children, etc. provide "readiness" for reading upon entering school. But to force a child to read when the readying is absent puts him into a situation where he is not able to handle himself and consequently his primary needs are not met, but violated. The result is a deep feeling of insecurity. He is driven to a point of frustration.

Readiness. Whether a child can successfully undertake a new experience involves at least three things. First, his equipment, such as physique, sense organs, and mental attainments. Second, needs and goal. If the new experience constitutes a satisfying consummation of a felt need, it can be successfully undertaken by a child. Third, ideas and skills. If in the new experience meanings emerge, he can relate the experience to himself and actively identify himself with it.

Cronbach calls our attention to four general principles regarding the development of readiness:[3]

(1) All aspects of development interact. A change in one facet of a child's development affects the whole person and thereby his readiness for this or that.

(2) Physiological maturing is a large factor in preparing one to profit from experience. Changes in the nervous system and glandular structure involved in growing up are important conditioning factors.

(3) Experiences have a cumulative effect. No experience remains an achievement by itself. All experiences add up to a snowballing effect upon total development.

(4) Certain times in one's life are formation periods when basic readiness for an activity is established. The three musts we referred to illustrate this clearly. School work also illustrates this principle. A child's intellectual ability in reading and number work come into play in the first years of schooling. His own attitude toward intellectual activities will be conditioned by his feeling of success or failure at this time. Readiness for further intellectual advance is being formed thereby.

3. Cronbach, *Educational Psychology,* pp. 75, 76.

Concerning these principles Cronbach adds the following:

> These principles imply that teachers must be acquainted with all aspects of development and with all periods of life. What went on before the person came into the classroom predetermines what he will do there. And what happens to him in the classroom must be judged in terms of what it contributes to his later readiness. Despite the fact that each individual has a unique history and a different pattern of readiness from his neighbor, the teacher who understands the process by which all children in our culture develop can make a sounder interpretation of each one.[4]

Cronbach's statement is too deterministic, but it contains an important truth. The teacher should recognize that every pupil is a child-with-a-history and should not be treated in isolation from that history. But Cronbach errs if he believes that the past totally determines the present and the future. It is the very essence of man, as God has created him, to be able to transcend his own past, at least in part.

Thwarting. Thwarting refers to a momentary obstruction in development. It results from a failure to attain a goal a person sets out to achieve. The result may be a reinterpretation of one's goals, felt needs, or choice. If a person seriously doubts he can attain a goal that brings approval, he is likely to be frustrated.

Frustration Point. The frustration point is reached when a child's initiative has been taxed beyond maximum endurance. It is the point at which, in spite of all encouragement and help, he gives up effort to attain. This point varies in children according to their personalities. Degree of readiness for the new experience is an important factor, as is also the extent to which felt needs in a child's life are being met. In an emotionally stable child the frustration point will, all things equal, be higher than in a child beset by phobias. Again, all things equal, a child who has experienced success after persistent effort has a higher frustration point than one who generally gets things easily, with little effort. A child's frustration point can be raised. For example, a child who has experienced frustration in learning to read suddenly begins to pick up reading skills when he changes teachers. The new teacher provides him a feeling of security based on acceptance that he failed to experience in the former class. Or again, a child's health may improve because of recent medical care. With it the force of his whole personality goes up. The frustration point is, therefore, not a stationary kind of thing. The raising of it is a constant objective in the lives of some children.

4. *Ibid.*

EARLY CHILDHOOD

We usually call the three years following infancy "early childhood." They constitute more specifically the pre-school period because certain things must happen in the development of the child before school begins. The beginning school age of five or six is not arbitrary, but the recognition of a readiness level.

Physiologically, this period is known for two important characteristics: the first growth spurt, and the "runabout" feature. (1) From about the beginning of the third year to the end of the fifth year there is a rapid increase in body structure and weight. Internal organs and neural structure grow more rapidly during this period than either immediately before or after. (2) All this growth is accompanied by abundant energy, which is also expressed in other dimensions of the personality. During this same period the child is constantly on the move, stopping only when overtaken by sound sleep. The "runabout" feature of this period provides a child opportunity to explore the world about him. His walking carries him from the protective custody of the mother and makes him rely on his own resources. The needs of a growing feeling of independence and self-respect are being met. His play among peers tests his growing feeling of security in the group and begins to pattern his social behavior.

Nursery School and Kindergarten. Actually the nursery school is not a school in the strict sense, since there is no formal program for learning with specific goals. But the nursery school can take account of the two development characteristics noted above by providing selected materials for the spontaneous channeling of individual and group activity.

The kindergarten can be viewed as a transitional stage. Play activities can be channeled into a more purposeful and formal program for all. It is a "readying" place for orienting children to more formal schooling. Not all children need an equal amount of this "readying." Hence, the kindergarten program must be very flexible.

Schools should avoid two extremes at this point. On the one hand a child may be regimented into formal schooling by the setting up of a planned program of activity before he is ready for it. A preschool youngster in his "runabout" stage is not ready. To coërce him into a formal program of learning lowers his frustration point, defeating the very end we seek. In the transitional period of the kindergarten, about the age of five, a child still learns largely by spontaneous play with alternating rest periods following energetic activity. But when a school operates a first grade as a kindergarten or nursery school, it does the very opposite. We then prolong the preschool stage and encourage immaturity. This too proves frustrating to a child who is ready to take on firmer, disciplined tasks. As schools of yesterday often tried to rush a child into maturity, so schools today are apt to prolong infancy and preschool characteristics into the childhood or the elementary school period. Both set the stages for problems in the personality development of children.

Does a child need nursery school or kindergarten? Of the former it may be said that home life and a community with children that can constitute a peer group provide everything and more than a nursery can provide. Nursery school is a good place to compensate for deficiencies in a child's development. In the case of the kindergarten we have another situation. The kindergarten as a "readying" of a child for formal learning is essential. Kindergarten activities must be provided even though no kindergarten is included in the graded program of the school.

Let it be said that the significance of the preschool period for personality development is not easily overstated. Many later problems in living can be traced to this age when a child's life style is being formed. Teachers who seek a better understanding of their pupils with reference to school work should include information about this period of a child's life among the data for analysis. It is the great importance of this period that has led some psychologists and educators to say that a child's basic life style is fixed by the time he enters school. This is an exaggeration of the truth, but to discount the significance of this period is to ignore the facts of life.

CHILDHOOD

In general, the most important fact about physiological development during the childhood period is that it slows down to a uniform rate. This uniformity holds with respect to the various parts of an individual child's body, and also with respect to age groups as a whole. Should you enter an elementary school, you will notice that in spite of variations most children in a given grade will approximate the same height and weight.

There is a danger, however, that teachers will confuse physical uniformity with uniformity in other dimensions of personality. Children in elementary school exhibit much greater variation in social and emotional development than they do in physical. And if this fact is ignored by requiring rigid subject matter mastery in a given grade as a condition for promotion, we invite frustration. Of course it is impossible to grade children on a social-emotional basis, but it is imperative that this dimension be taken into account in the teaching and learning process. Our ultimate aim, after all, is development of the *total* personality.

Physical Education. Though subject matter is the principal medium for development in the school, physical education also falls within its legitimate scope. This is true because, as we have urged many times, the total personality of the child is involved in the learning process. Physical education can serve several functions: for one thing, supervised play which is organized in terms of child readiness can provide opportunities for social-emotional development much more readily than subjects such as arithmetic. Furthermore, some children who cannot excel in academic work will be able to achieve the necessary ego-status in physical activities.

In selecting a physical education program the teacher must remember not to over-emphasize competitive games. Some children who are undersized or unskilled may be left out of activities needed for their total development, and others may become demoralized by repeated failure. Every child must experience some success if the program is to be educational, and not merely activity as an end in itself.

ADOLESCENCE

Second Growth Spurt. In early adolescence we observe a second growth spurt with all the complications involved for the total personality. Rapid physiological growth rushes a youth toward bodily maturity long before he experiences like development in the other areas of his total personality. The lengthy skeleton of a boy of fifteen or sixteen may prove too much for him in the posture and poise expected of him. His changing voice is unstable in pitch, causing him frequent embarrassment. Sex organs ready to function are being stimulated, but the consummation of normal functions must wait for years. The maturing body demands adult activity but adult standards make this impossible. The physical size of a youth may encourage adults to expect adult performance of him, but these ideals simply do not fit the developing personality of the adolescent. David cannot move freely in Saul's armor. Youths must develop at their own pace and in their own way to feel secure. "Their own way" does not mean that they should do as they please, but according to the ways of God-ordained development.

Individual Differences. There are great variations in rate of growth among early adolescents. During these years of puberty some young people begin to take on manhood and womanhood, the girls being generally ahead of the boys in this matter. In the eighth, ninth, and tenth grades one is likely to see a great variation of size and degree of maturity and immaturity, physiologically speaking. Either extreme of growth may cause considerable embarrassment. A feeling of inferiority or inadequacy may temporarily overcome a youth of fifteen or sixteen with a boyish voice, of a girl with underdeveloped breasts. The physical education teacher who moves among pupils in locker rooms has a golden opportunity to help young people over this hurdle which can prove very frustrating to them. Teachers in junior and senior high schools in general should take account of personality complications that may result from differences in physiological development on this level.

Glandular Activity. Recent biochemical research has contributed much to our better understanding of the chemical processes involved in adolescent growth. The functioning of the pituitary gland in physiological growth, especially in its relation to the gonads, or sex glands, and the latter in producing primary and secondary sex characteristics tell quite a story of physiological growth. The knowledge of the interrelation of both with the hypothalamus is of even more recent origin. Knowledge of the functioning of glands and nerve centers with reference to developing personality is "stock-in-trade" for one who would understand learning and teaching. Biology and physiology furnish important information to psychology in this matter.

We recognize that a large part of adolescent development is sex-linked. Many studies have indicated a positive correlation between developing sexual maturity and a change of interests. For example, early adolescents maturing sexually showed greater interest in personal adornment, strenuous activities, realistic (in contrast with earlier imaginative) activities, and heterosexual activities than did the less mature. In his desire for peer approval and self-respect the youth begins to notice the opposite sex. His need for affection may lead to early "crushes" which are apt to fluctuate with changing moods.

Physical Education. Physical education has an important place in the secondary school. Indeed, it is so necessary for total personality development that some form of it should be required of every adolescent. A well-directed program of physical education will provide a variety of activities that help to form worthy ideals and habits of body care that produces self-esteem and responsibility. Interscholastic athletics is sometimes a real hazard for such a program. Though it may benefit the participants directly and others indirectly, it constantly threatens to usurp the center of the stage.

CONCLUSIONS

We may conclude our study of physiological development with the following general observations:

(1) Growth and development are fairly consistent and continuous. Slow development in the first years usually means somewhat slower development in later years as well. Likewise a precocious child will show superiority all the way through life, other things being equal.

(2) Development is dimensional in the total personality, that is, it follows dimensional lines. Dimensions do not necessarily keep pace with one another. While the rate of development in the dimensions of a single person normally does not differ greatly, there are many children who deviate from this general rule. The child with a high IQ may be a shy or even antisocial youngster. The very average child academically may prove to be a leader among his peers. These deviants we call "split growers." They can constitute serious problems in school if not understood.

(3) While growth and development have a tendency to level off after early rapid increase, the opposite is not uncommon. Frequently we see children somewhat retarded for several years, especially in their physiological growth, and then suddenly shoot up. This accounts for some individual differences in learning in the classroom.

(4) Individual differences extend to every dimension. In the final analysis growth and development are individual, though fairly consistent with themselves in a given person. Individual differences preclude any formula in dealing with children in directing their development.

(5) As teachers we are placed on our guard by the many exceptions to the usual trend of growth and development to avoid predicting a child's progress for the future from any measure we have of his present development or of the past. Teachers must consider all the aspects of development in understanding the significance of any particular difficulty.

QUESTIONS FOR FURTHER STUDY

1. Do you think that body structure or body type can tell us something about personality as a whole? Explain.

2. No one doubts the importance of physiological development to physical health. Why is its importance for mental health and personality as a whole often overlooked?

3. Going back to Susan in Chapter I, what developmental problem do you envisage for her?

4. A teacher was heard to say, "I find it extremely hard to help a left-handed pupil with his writing. I insist that my pupils use

their right hand. After all, it's merely a matter of habit." Do you agree?

5. Mary is five feet six inches tall at fourteen years of age. Do you expect her to become a tall person?

6. How do you account for the fact that junior and senior high school girls generally prefer the company of boys a year or two older?

7. How would you organize physical education in the elementary school? In the junior high school? In the senior high school?

8. In the preceding chapter we saw that felt needs prompt a person to action. What bodily needs are a source of drives and urges? Can they be ignored with impunity in the classroom?

SELECTIONS FOR FURTHER REFERENCE*

Beaumont & Macomber, Chapter II, "Organic Bases of Activity."

Cole & Bruce, Chapters III, IV, "The Physical Growth of the Individual."

Gates, Chapter III, "Physical and Motor Development."

Jordan (2), Chapter III, "Growth, Physical and Motor."

Mursell, Chapter XII, "The Growth Plan."

Sorenson, Chapter IV, "Human Physical Growth and Development."

Stephens, Chapter IV, "Physical Growth and the Problems of Health."

Witherington, Chapter V, "The General Nature of Growth."

*References are cited here by author's name. See Bibliography for title and complete publication data.

7

Emotional Development

EMOTIONAL AND SOCIAL: A CLOSE ALLIANCE

There are reasons for believing that emotions in a human being derive basically from physical needs, and perhaps should be explained wholly in terms of the body. An infant, for instance, may be crying and throwing his limbs about in a wildly random way as he lies in his crib. We would say, properly, that all of this behavior is an expression of infantile emotion. But how is this expression changed? How is his tension relieved? By closing his open diaper pin, by giving him appropriate medication, or (most likely) by presenting him with a bottle. All of these are physical acts which presumably affect emotions deriving from physical needs.

But surely this is a one-sided conclusion derived from hasty observation. As we have pointed out many times, the whole person is present even in the infant, and no single aspect of that unity can be reduced to another. When we extend our observations a bit we notice that baby's discomfort is often relieved not by food but simply by his mother's presence and loving attention. In fact, as a child develops we find that his emotional life is tied more closely to *social* than to *physical* considerations.

This point is especially important for the teacher, because the primary felt needs of child life as related to schooling, namely affection, adult approval, peer approval, independence, and self-respect, are social-emotional in character. The child cannot learn adequately unless these needs are being met satisfactorily at his level.

Because the social and emotional dimensions of personality develop together so markedly, we will often speak of them as one, the social-emotional. But for the purpose of clarity we will proceed first to discuss them separately in this and the following chapters.

109

DIFFICULTIES IN UNDERSTANDING EMOTIONAL DEVELOPMENT

All behavior is permeated to varying degrees with feelings and emotions, and at no time before the twentieth century has this fact been recognized and emphasized as much as it is today. But along with this intense interest in emotional development there has been great controversy and confusion — much of it stemming from a failure to recognize that man is a religious being created in the image of God. So, for instance, the conflicting theories of Freud and Jung about the unconscious both point out facts which are suggested in the Bible and should be recognized by the Christian, but at the same time they both fail to set these observations into the biblical perspective.

But there are other, more general reasons why it is difficult to gain insight into the emotions:

(1) Our culture seems to frown on emotional expression. We tend to shy away from our feelings. We hesitate to reveal how we feel about a situation, nor are we encouraged to reveal it. Our feelings are suspect. They seem to say more about our true selves than any other phase of human behavior. There is within us the desire to appear to be what we are expected to be, not to reveal who we really are. As Christians we readily recognize this phenomenon as an unconscious recognition by the religious being that he is not what he ought to be. Original sin and a feeling of guilt constitute a potent force in the cover-up of our true selves. The tendency is to think that a well-trained, cultural person acts unemotionally or nearly so. But God created us with an emotional dimension in our personality and it calls for expression as a perfect man in a perfect creation.

(2) Norms for emotional expression are difficult to determine. That we must express ourselves emotionally is clear. Repression without substituting channels for expression in our emotional life is contrary to our created nature and often lies at the basis of our bodily troubles, such as ulcers, gall bladder, and the like. But when is emotional expression legitimate? The Bible instructs us, "Be ye angry, and sin not; let not the sun go down on your wrath" (Eph. 4:26). How not to sin when becoming angry is our problem. We are enjoined to love, for love is the fulfillment of the law. But how are we to love in given circumstances? How much we need norms for emotional expression! Surely, the seeking of legitimate emotional expression according to true norms is a major goal in learning and teaching.

(3) Scientific study of emotional expression is difficult. "Objectivity" of the sort found in chemistry, e.g., simply fails to grasp the sort of thing emotions are. It appears that only empathy, based on person-to-person communication, will provide the needed insights. From a strictly scientific point of view this situation is far from ideal.

TOWARD AN UNDERSTANDING OF EMOTIONAL DEVELOPMENT

In spite of the difficulties outlined above, study of emotional behavior has made important contributions to the theory of learning, showing how the child develops in his personality. Here we take note of some of these contributions.

INITIAL OBSERVATIONS

(1) *Emotion as feeling-tone.* When one person asks another with reference to a situation, "How do you feel about it?," he is not merely asking for an individual judgment based upon some observed facts. He is really saying the following. "Place yourself in this situation. What tensions do you experience. How would you react if you found yourself involved in it? Would you be disturbed? Could you rest in it as is? What is your present mood with reference to it? Can you accept what is involved?" In other words, one is asked to identify himself with a situation and describe his feeling in so doing. Our emotional life seems to register how we are doing in our total person in a given situation.

What do we mean by feeling or feeling-tone? Feeling is the state of one's person that gives an awareness of an external event its peculiar personal reference or quality. That feeling or feeling-tone is intensely personal is evident from the fact that the same objective qualities may produce quite different subjective meanings when feelings come into play. A situation with which one is not called upon to identify himself or become involved in readily may have the same or similar meaning for one as for another. But when asked to relate oneself personally to it, the meaning changes. Hence what feelings a situation provokes is often more important in learning than the information it provides.

That the emotional life represents the feeling-tone of the total person is illustrated in several ways. A feeling of guilt will disturb the whole person to the extent of abnormal functioning of the whole personality. The depressed feeling which it engenders may throw off one's digestive processes and involve other physiological complications. It distorts one's anticipations and blurs one's whole purpose in life. If not founded on fact, the disclosure of this to the understanding of the person may relieve the entire situation. If based on fact, a genuine feeling of having been forgiven engenders new hope and idealism. Or again, desires which the individual regarded as illegitimate may have been repressed. But they only disappeared from the surface of consciousness and were not consciously invoked as motivations of thinking, willing, and doing. They turn up in the unconscious as hostilities toward certain persons or certain kinds of people, thus making certain situations intolerable. A certain personality irks one, or a certain environment "drives you mad." As a consequence everything goes wrong. This may be back of a pupil's getting along better with one teacher than with another, though both teachers get along well with most children. When one comes to understand the sources of these drives, he can actively pursue a remedial program of readjustment and redirection.

So we see that the emotional life expresses how-we-are-doing in our total personality. The day is past, or should be, when we thought of the emotional life as a faculty or compartment of the mind, or as an entity or power in the mind. Feeling is not, no more than thinking and willing, a faculty or power that calls for concentrated training as does a group of muscles. It is an activity of the whole person. Development of the feeling-tone of the person is an integral phase of the development of a child. We sometimes use the word *attitudes* to express a person's feelings. This is not wrong, as long as we remember that what we recognize as an attitude, say of helpfulness or assertiveness, may have a deeper motivation than the feeling-tone of a person.

Several passages of Scripture refer to the feeling-tone of the total person. One of these is Romans 12:11, where Christians are admonished to be "fervent in spirit," as the American Standard Version has it. The Revised Standard Version translates this phrase as "aglow with the Spirit." And Weymouth makes this passage read, "Have your spirits aglow . . . ."[1] To be on fire in the spirit as servants of God, as Paul urges upon Christians, means, psychologically speaking, that the feeling-tone of the whole person is charged with the service of God. In this sense the emotional life is *the energy of the total personality*. There are other forces at work that energize, such as passions, impulses, drives, and the like. But these are, whether they operate unconsciously or consciously in the person, an integral part of the emotional dimension of the personality.

(2) *The psyche and the soma are closely related.* As we pointed out at the beginning of this chapter, there are reasons for associating

1. It is interesting to note that the recent Dutch Revised Version also translates this phrase as aglow or on fire: "vurig van geest."

the emotional very closely with the physical. In fact, there is no clear-cut experimental method for discerning precisely where the physiological leaves off and the emotional begins. If we did not have a scriptural understanding of what human nature truly is, we would be in constant danger of identifying the psyche with the soma.

The following example illustrates this point. Some psychologists, reasoning from the premise that man is essentially a biological being, see in the hypothalamus an approximation to a link between certain centers of bodily control and personal subjective feelings. But when we substitute for this bias the clear teaching of Scripture that the spirit is the life principle of the organic whole we know as a person, we see soul life and body life in other relationships. In the functioning of the hypothalamus as nerve center and in the subjective feeling related to it, the same life principle is operative. We are glad to see in the development of recent psychological studies a greater recognition of the organic unity of man. The organismic and dynamic emphases in psychology are in a position to make a greater contribution to Christian thinking than were earlier mechanistic psychologies. But only a naturalistic bias will confuse these emphases with organic unity and motivation centered in the spirit, as taught in the Scriptures.

The issue whether we can ascribe motivational or causal functions to emotion is easily answered by the layman. Doesn't a child run because he is afraid? And don't we all adopt a fighting attitude because we are angry? Doesn't anxiety have typical drive characteristics; as do love, hate, jealousy, etc.? The layman was shocked when the James-Lange theory (1890) stated that "we are afraid because we run." Cannon's counterview, called the emergence theory of emotions, was a homeostatic view. This theory holds that emotional experience arises as a balancing influence between conflicting forces. Others have advanced the thought that emotion energizes behavior.

What is the answer? True, we have no experimental evidence. The difficulty secular psychology encounters is that it seeks the explanation of the person in his functions. Dynamic schools of psychology recognize that love, hate, anxiety, and the like are functions that generate behavior. Physiologically oriented schools of psychology call this view of dynamic schools a conscious or unconscious predilection for a metaphysical assumption. A good example of how a physiologically oriented psychologist treats emotional experience is this quotation from Bugelski: "How the subject feels about having given a correct answer or having made a correct response is unimportant in itself. The important feature is that the stimulus pattern involved in the learning situation has been accommodated by the brain activity and is no longer enforcing a change in the pattern of that activity."[2]

The Christian does not find the explanation of the person in his functions, but in the organic unity of his being. Emotions issue forth into behavior because the spirit is the life principle of both soul-life and body-life, and they constitute an organic whole. This is not based on a conscious or unconscious predilection for metaphysics, but upon a plain acceptance of what God says about man.

(3) *Emotional life is deeply imbedded in the total personality.* The roots of emotional experience reach deep below the level of consciousness. It takes a psychoanalyst much prying into the inner life of a person, and the overcoming of much unconscious resistance, to bring the sources of disturbance to the surface of a patient's consciousness. There is an emotional past in the life of every person. This emotional past has become very much a part of the total personality structure, and it often determines a person's anticipations and qualifies the meaning he derives from a given situation.

As the child comes to school, his personality has a history. The teacher should be aware of this. The aggressive boy in the fifth grade may be working out a long-standing inner conflict, or again, he may have a problem of more recent origin. Some understanding of this boy will help the teacher direct his work more realistically toward the child's needs. But the teacher should remain within his province; he is a professional in the art of teaching, not psychology or psychiatry, and hence if his most carefully-conceived pedagogy fails to reach a child he should consult a professional in the relevant field.

In spite of the truth in the above very necessary warning, it is well to note with Percival Symonds that there are many similarities between psychotherapy and teaching. He points up the following:[3]

(i) "Both teachers and therapists should treat children as individuals with potentialities for progressively taking over direction of themselves.

(ii) "Both teachers and counselors should be warm, friendly, outgoing, pleasant, and kindly.

(iii) "Both teachers and therapists are counseled to accept the child as he is — no matter how stupid, lazy, resistive, or disorderly."

We may add:

2. B. R. Bugelski, *The Psychology of Learning*, p. 463n.
3. Percival Symonds, "Education and Therapy," *Journal of Educational Psychology*, XL (Jan., 1945), 5-20.

(iv) Teachers and therapists may also be expected to be permissive, but to a degree only.

(v) Both teachers and therapists have a responsibility to understand a child.

(vi) Both teachers and therapists should be sensitive to feelings expressed by the child and should help the child to be aware of them.

(4) *Emotions cannot be identified simply with certain forms of expression.* Joy, happiness, hope, fear, anger, anxiety, and the like constitute emotional experiences that can find varying channels of expression. One may cry for joy, for example. Or a person may pose as being very happy because he would like others to think so and to encourage himself in this feeling. But both the crying and the apparent happiness are parts of a larger whole, a larger context of experience in which crying may involve joy, and apparent happiness may be related to anger or fear. Education in the emotional life is more than cultivating some favorable or acceptable emotional expressions. The total feeling-tone of the person is involved.

(5) *The frustration point is largely determined by emotion.* Frustration is a feeling of helplessness or uselessness that comes over one as he engages in some kind of activity. A child may be driven or drive himself to a point beyond his endurance. A "give-up" feeling comes over him. Individuals differ in their ability to take defeat and failure, but in the life of every person there is a point at which, if pressed beyond it, he gives up in despair. One pupil can be pressed considerably beyond his present level of attainment and accept it as a challenge. There is emotional stability of confidence and assurance that enables him to carry on. Another will collapse under the pressure. He feels threatened by it in his inner life. In the process of child development the frustration point can be raised by effective teaching. Teachers should recognize the frustration point of their pupils. They should likewise know how to raise it so that the child may reach out confidently toward new goals. Gradual raising of a child's frustration point constitutes an important phase of guiding him to maturity.

CUES TOWARD BETTER INSIGHT INTO THE EMOTIONS

(1) *The emotional life is an integral part of the total personality.* Every experience produces a feeling-tone in the total personality. Emotional expression, therefore, is a tell-tale of the tone of the total personality. A teacher does well to take careful note of the feelings of a pupil. They are strong indicators of what a child is learning and how a learning situation is affecting him in his total personality.

Guided by the observation made above, that no simple list of emotional expressions is sufficient to determine a child's emotional experience, the teacher will view an emotional expression in the context of a child's personality. The teacher must know Mary as a person to understand why she cries so quickly, why Jack breaks out into such hilarious laughter.

(2) *The feeling of security is a basic emotional need.* We distinguished earlier between human primary and secondary needs, and said that for our purposes there can be distinguished six primary needs (affection, peer approval, etc.). But these and all other primary needs are really manifestations of an all-inclusive basic need for *security*. Man has been so created that he cannot be at rest without it. When the infant cuddles to his mother; when the kindergartner holds up his paper for teacher's approval; when the senior high school girl plays up to the boys; these are all manifestations of the child's constant search for security. The teacher must understand this fact, must attempt to assist his pupils in their quest for security, and must above all manifest security in his own person.

(3) *Emotional development does not proceed uniformly in the individual.* There are many spurts, plateaus, and even regressions. This is to be expected, since everything that happens to a person affects his emotional life. If the teacher is aware of this, he will not draw hasty conclusions from the observed behavior of a child but will study these fluctuations within the total personality context of the pupil.

(4) *There is a marked variation among pupils in emotional maturity.* It is a commonly observed fact that children of the same chronological age vary greatly in their readiness to assume responsibility, for example. One will depend upon the teacher or upon other pupils, while another will launch out for himself and confidently assume group leadership. Generally this ability to function independently and responsibly finds its ground in a feeling of self-respect and assurance. Teachers know of children who are intellectually far ahead of their age group, but who fail utterly in assuming leadership in group activities. A child's emotional maturity is often a more important consideration than intellectual attainment when considering his promotion or retardation in the grades. In every case it is an important fact to consider how well prepared a child is emotionally to handle himself in the advanced group.

STAGES IN EMOTIONAL DEVELOPMENT

Though the "longitudinal" stages of emotional development possess less clearly-marked boundaries than the stages of physiological development, we now proceed to characterize them in a general way. It is important that the teacher knows something about these stages, because emotional security in the pupil is absolutely necessary for learning in the school situation. And here an important principle of teaching should be enunciated: *if the child is to progress, he must first feel accepted for what he is.* If he does not accept and respect himself, he is not ready to improve himself. And ultimately, learning and developing are processes that must come about from *within* the child.

INFANCY

In infancy emotional development can hardly be distinguished from the associated physiological processes. The neonate gives one the impression of a behaving organism more helpless than other species. Even the first smile which parents wait for so eagerly and recognize at about six weeks is no more than a reflex, a response of the muscles of the face to certain stimuli from the faces of others when the infant's eyes begin to focus. The self and soul-life we spoke of earlier are surely not in evidence. But as months pass the subjective feeling of a conscious subject becomes clear. That smile becomes a conscious expression of a feeling-tone of satisfaction and joy. He seeks out his favorite toy for effective manipulation. He creeps away from daddy in play to give him a merry chase. What actually constitutes a life-long search for personal security, for inner contentment, finds expression in such simple activities as running to mother and trusting in father's strong arms after a daring leap. As we know from the Bible, these simple manifestations of the basic human need for security can ultimately be satisfied only by deep and abiding love. Christian parents and teachers will provide this love, imperfectly; and will lead the child to the God who is Love.

EARLY CHILDHOOD

In early childhood emotional development appears to be closely associated with certain organs of the body, and then with the body as a whole. The order seems to be clear. In the neonate emotional satisfaction seems to center around the mouth. This continues during infancy while other centers develop. Elimination appears to be a source of great satisfaction. When the time comes for regulating this process, there is inevitably a period of tension. For infants to fumble the genitals is a natural development of bodily satisfaction. Parents and other adults create a problem when by their expressions they associate ugliness with this activity. A youngster in early childhood who discovers the difference in anatomy between the sexes is merely making a factual discovery. (It does seem to create in little girls what is known as penis envy. They seem to feel that they lack something.) But on the whole, normal satisfactions can be had by youngsters from these experiences if parents and adults will refrain from attaching adult values to them. When adults interfere, these experiences often acquire a neurotic setting that plagues a child early with a feeling of guilt, followed by shame and anxiety. As he approaches the childhood period he can learn in a natural setting to observe proper decorum in personal appearance, just as he learns to control elimination. When a child is ready for standards pertaining to proper appearance among others and proper attention to be given to others, he generally has little difficulty learning to observe them.

The positive forward impetus, or developmental urge, is clearly evident from early childhood. From the very beginning we observe the whole person striving for maturity. The ego begins to express itself in the psychosomatic life — first in body-centered activity, then gradually more and more in the psychical. Experience continues throughout life as psychosomatic.

In the drive for emotional expression a child can be given support toward integrating his experience so that inner unity rather than tension results. We have already referred to parents accepting as factual a child's discovery of sexual differences. A child's natural fear reaction to loud noises may become accentuated when during an electrical storm parents show fear. But when parents point a child to the beautiful light in the sky and refer to thunder as a sound to be enjoyed like the blowing of a trumpet, they give him support toward integrating his emotional experience so that no inhibiting fear results that periodically breaks out into hysteria and anxiety. Helping a child develop courage, sympathy, and responsibility has the same effects. We call these *sthenic* emotions, i.e., supporting, sustaining emotions.

In this connection it is helpful to observe that early training in obedience is a positive support for emotional development. The child who must make decisions for which he is unprepared feels insecure. Compare, e.g., the behavior of preschoolers who have learned good manners at home with those who have not. When the former go visiting with their parents in the tidy home of a friend, everyone can relax while the children play normally with the toys at hand. The undisciplined children, however, incite general anxiety by their unrestrained behavior. As long as parents and teachers do not frustrate the child by demanding impossible standards of behavior, the emotional experience of obedience is a sthenic emotion to be cultivated early.

CHILDHOOD

Though in a sense the childhood stage exhibits less rapid development than the preceding stages, and hence may be called a period of latency, there are two characteristics of this period that have pronounced emotional significance especially for schooling. They have intellectual and social aspects as well, but here we will emphasize the emotional aspect.

Freedom. The first of these is the demand for freedom. When a child arrives at school at the age of five, he has already been weaned to a degree from mother's and father's protective care. Approval of father and mother and other adults still means much to him, still gives him a feeling of satisfaction, but the approval of his peers has also come to be significant. Adult approval now begins to include his teacher, who embodies for him the whole school and all of adult society. The circle of peers increases. Class approval and approval by peers on the playgrounds take on significance. Home loyalties are gradually being replaced by boy gangs and girl cliques. A child begins to launch out for himself. This weaning process has a painful side for parents, but their better knowledge tells them their children must grow up. When the author's children were two or three years of age, he often remarked to his wife, "I'd like to keep them this way for a while." But his better sense told him otherwise. Parents may at times be shocked by a child's blunt rejection of earlier parental concern over them. Bob may need the admonition "Be careful" when he goes swimming, but he doesn't appreciate the warning, especially when it is said in the hearing of his peers. Youngsters may even seem cruel and brutal at times. "My teacher said wind is air set in motion by air pressures. And, believe me, he knows." The implication is that mother or dad, to whom he is speaking, do not know as well.

Actually what is happening in a child's life is that his peer group and respected adults in the wider social sphere are becoming a stronger educational influence than parental direction. A child who at this stage fails to find a secure foothold in his group should become a parent's and a teacher's special concern. This transition is necessary in the developmental urge, which calls for a growing feeling of independence. The tight hold upon child life by adults and superiors should gradually be relinquished and exchanged for more indirect ways of guidance and direction.

A teacher who understands this is gradually working toward greater individual and group responsibility in his classroom. Always according to a child's readiness, of course, recognizing too that readiness can be cultivated. We need not sit and wait for it to arrive. Group activities of many kinds providing for group communication and group presentation are becoming of increasing significance. So is individual activity which is group oriented.

Educational psychology is experiencing a new thrust from social psychology. In the past it has very much concerned itself, almost exclusively, with the individual's reaction to situations. Now sociologists are pointing out how intra-group relationships contribute to learning and development. We are hearing much about group dynamics. With the development of the field theory of experience and the personality field concept new avenues of learning and teaching open up to the classroom teacher.

Some years ago the author visited a fifth grade where the teacher was alerted to the psychology we have developed here. From this experience the following illustration is derived:

As I knocked on the door of a classroom I was advised to visit, a smiling fifth-grade girl came to the door, opened it and said, "How do you do, sir. My name is Nancy Hall. Yours, please, sir?"

"My name is Mr. Jaarsma," I replied, somewhat taken aback by such courtesy.

"What can I do for you, Mr. Jaarsma?" the young lady (for such she was) continued.

"I would like to visit your classroom, please," was my reply.

As I entered I looked toward the teacher. She had turned her face toward me, smiled, nodded a friendly hello, and continued to work with the group at the window.

"Would you like to see our transportation project?" I was asked by my friendly hostess.

"I certainly would," was my answer.

With this she proceeded to lead me to the rear of the room. Here was an exhibit of booklets, maps, drawings, bulletin board clippings, a mural, models, etc. They were labeled and organized according to the historical development of transportation to the modern day. The "young lady" proceeded to explain the study of transportation and the results. I asked a few questions which appeared very welcome and were ably answered.

While we were discussing this project, a fifth grade boy had walked up quietly. I had not noticed him until my attention was called to him.

"Mr. Jaarsma, may I present David Martin?" asked Nancy as she introduced me.

"How do you do, David," I said, not knowing where he came in.

"David will show some of our art and music work," continued Nancy. With this she quietly retired.

David, in a very intelligent and courteous way, explained to me the work in these areas. Subsequently I was introduced to two other pupils who explained the botanical studies and some arithmetic work. The class library was also explained to me.

When this was done, the last pupil, John Stewart, asked "Would you like to meet our teacher, Mr. Jaarsma?"

"Gladly," I replied.

John took me to the center of the room where the teacher was helping a few pupils with geography study.

Said John, "Miss Thompson, may I present Mr. Jaarsma? He has visited our room and has seen some of our work." With this he retired.

Was this teacher teaching attitudes? Can attitudes be taught? Pupils were learning attitudes, to be sure. We shall try to answer these questions later.

What would you say to a teacher who was developing a spirit of independence and responsibility in her pupils? All the while I was given this conducted tour by four young ladies and young gentlemen, the rest of the class together with the teacher kept busily at work. And this was in a common, ordinary school in a common, ordinary district. I was so impressed with the natural, home-like atmosphere of this class that I breathed a prayer spontaneously, "Lord, give us more teachers and classrooms like this."

And when these children left the classroom for recess, they showed no urge to race or push, for they had given expression to the urge for communication and group relations in legitimate ways in the classroom.

I shall not proceed to analyze this situation in all details. It is merely given here to point out how children's growing demand for freedom can be met with effectiveness educationally.

A situation like this, however, is achieved by a teacher who not only recognizes a child's primary needs, but also his secondary needs. For in satisfying a child's primary needs, we must help him recognize and accept that they can be met with satisfaction only under certain conditions and in certain situations. Miss Thompson certainly had made demands upon her pupils. But she had done so in the consciousness of their ability to assume the required task. The principle of readiness was ever being observed.

In a Christian classroom there need be no absence of obedience, but it should be an obedience which includes the opportunity for activity that furthers a child's growing feeling of independence. Obedience thus becomes gradually internalized as a voluntary acceptance of responsibility. Control by others must become self-control. Emotional security demands it. A child gradually begins to accept norms for his way of living, though they are still crudely realized. Not all children in Miss Thompson's room were ready to serve on the reception committee, but she was leading them all up to it. Thus in school group work is essential. Today we call it group dynamics. Especially from the third grade on it should take a large place in classroom work. The quiet classroom of individual study and recitation still has its place, but the dynamics of group activity and free communication is as essential for a full education.

Creative Activity. A second characteristic of the childhood stage of development that has emotional significance with reference to schooling is the desire for what is often called creative activity, making and doing things independently and spontaneously. In the kindergarten and primary grades it is important that teachers select things to do in connection with the fundamentals in reading, writing, and number work. Activities of many kinds can be worked out, individually and cooperatively, which require the use of fundamentals in knowledges and skills. Activities are also provided merely for the sake of expression, because the urge for constructing is so great. Providing an outlet with certain tools, such as brush and easel, affords opportunities to learn many things: holding a brush, position from which to work, selecting colors, and developing perspectives.

As a child proceeds through the grades, the urge for construction can be directed from things to ideas and appreciation. Handicrafts, sculpture, and printing may still be continued, but in several cases it can be directed into literary arts such as short story and poetry, or into music, drawing, and sketching. Throughout the elementary school, however, the need for creative activity associated with things remains an important medium of learning. Many children derive much emotional satisfaction from these activities.

In this connection it should be said there is a difference between an *activity school* and learning through well-selected and guided activities. The former often seems to stress activity for activity's sake. There is a place for this in undirected childhood play. But the school is no playground or backyard activity for fun. The school is an institution that has a program according to which a child must learn certain things. When a teacher selects activities appropriate to this program designed to develop a child according to the ways of childhood, these activities become significant learning media. They give a child deep emotional satisfaction as well as providing content for knowledge and understanding.

A word of caution should be given in the use of the word "creative." More will be said later in connection with learning by thinking. But let it be said here that the word "creative" applied to childhood learning means a directed or guided spontaneity of expression. There is originality and spontaneity in it, but also direction according to standards.

Indeed, the period of childhood is one of positive progress toward maturity. The school makes a vital contribution, emotionally as well as intellectually. And all of learning takes place in the setting of the feeling-tone of the whole person. Hence we should be reminded again of this important principle in learning, namely, that the feelings which a situation evokes are often more important than the information it provides.

ADOLESCENCE

With the onset of adolescence, the beginning of which is often referred to as pubescence, marked and swift changes begin to take place in the development of a youth. The young person goes through a second growth spurt, to which we already referred in connection with physiological development.

That rapid physiological development should have potent emotional complications in the lives of the early adolescent is natural. The physiological changes themselves generate a feeling-tone of striving and unrest. Things are on the move on the inside and the youth feels it intensely, but cannot define it.

In his social relationships there is also a new striving and unrest. The early grower finds himself in a short time outgrowing his peers. Or retarded development gives another a feeling of inferiority. Uneven development within the adolescent or among adolescents creates problems for the school as well as the home. Teachers must be very patient and understanding. The early adolescent who is both child and youth is trying to find himself in his new role. He needs much guidance by one who understands.

The move for greater independence gains new impetus in the adolescent. As his body takes on the appearance of an adult, he wishes to achieve the personal integrity of an adult. But he is in an ambiguous situation which requires much wisdom and love on the part of adults. He wishes to be recognized overtly as an adult, but at the same time he needs to know that his very real continuing dependence on his elders is not being jeopardized. To deflate the adolescent's ego by sarcasm or otherwise, when his need for self-respect is so great, creates barriers that make future guidance ineffective.

The spontaneity and openness of childhood is no longer present in the adolescent. It is often difficult to discern just what he really feels, as he attempts to adjust to the prevailing patterns of the community around him. He responds most readily to the adult who commands his respect but at the same time makes himself approachable and is a willing listener. Such a person or persons may very readily become the basis for what is technically called an *ego-ideal* — the pattern of personality which the youth identifies as the goal of his own development. Very often the ego-ideal is personified by the pastor, a teacher, a youth leader, and the like; frequently the approval of this person by the youth's own parents will weigh heavily in his choice; but curiously, the ego-ideal may not resemble very closely the character of the person from whom, supposedly, the ideal has been derived.

The important point to notice here is that the adolescent wishes, and ought, to choose his *own* ego-ideal. This is the point at which he properly begins to internalize, to adopt as his own, those standards of conduct which were required of him earlier in terms of external conformance by way of *obedience*. At this point the *example* rather than the *precept* of his superiors is absolutely crucial — a fact which ought to make them extremely careful of their own behavior.

Adolescence is also a period in which major life commitments are prepared for, if not actually made. These commitments involve the whole person, to be sure; but emotional satisfaction is an indispensable criterion of a genuine commitment.

One of these commitments involves the person's *vocation*. Here the junior and senior high school may serve by providing an exploratory curriculum, a curriculum in which the student may gain the knowledge of alternatives which is required for a satisfying choice later on. Another commitment for which the student is preparing himself, especially in middle adolescence (15-18), is the *marital*. At this age romances begin to bloom which frequently mature into life-long marital companionship. The church and school must assist the home in providing associations which will encourage the selection of suitable mates. Finally, and most important, adolescence is often the age at which *spiritual* commitment is made. The church urges its youth to stand publicly before her, to confess hatred of sin and love for Jesus Christ. Although for most covenant youth this commitment is the culmination of a gradual process, it is nevertheless a deeply emotional experience.

Of all these major choices it may be said that they involve the feeling of security of youth. Undue delay in any one of these choices is a source of major problems in later life. Floundering in one's vocational interests makes for economic insecurity. Postponement of marital ties may become a source of sexual deviations and personality patterns which give one considerable difficulty. Procrastination of young people from Christian homes in their religious profession can lead to hardening of one's life in the way of sin. Emotional unrest in the wake of postponement can easily be rationalized by alibis which later become pet projections of one's feeling of guilt. The youth who makes emotionally satisfying choices based on truth and right sets the stage for a fruitful and productive life in the service of God.

THE THREE CONSTELLATIONS OF EMOTION

Can emotions be identified with forms of emotional expression? We have given reasons for believing that they cannot. Can an exhaustive list of emotions be drawn up? We have seen that this is also an oversimple idea, and substituted for it the concept of feeling-tone. The popular idea that emotions are merely forms of behavior, each connected as a response to a particular stimulus (the so-called "connectionistic" theory), has been shown by later organismic and dynamic approaches to be unduly naive and atomistic.

But is it impossible, then, to classify emotions in any way? Cole and Bruce have suggested that it is not: that by speaking of "clusters" or "constellations" of emotions we may avoid the extreme of atomism and at the same time subject the range of human emotions to fruitful analysis. They list three such constellations, as follows:

> Love and its concomitants: responsiveness, friendliness, sympathy, admiration, generosity, respect. These functioning in a myriad of integrations lead to happiness, joy, hope, quiet calm, relaxation. All are summed up in a sense of security and gratifying growth.
>
> Rage and its accompaniments: a sense of frustration, of being thwarted, of being rejected by a world that is cold, unfriendly, indifferent, hateful. To challenges of this type the person responds with an admixture of anxiety, hate, and a view of the world that is distorted by his own unhappy anticipations.
>
> Fear and its satellites: fused in manifold ways, these express themselves in anxiety, withdrawal, grief, and despair, and are gathered together in insecurity and frustration.[4]

For our purposes this list of emotional constellations is helpful, and we will proceed to discuss each of them in greater detail.

4. Cole and Bruce, *Educational Psychology*, p. 216.

LOVE

When we consult the biblical use of the term "love," we discover that its significance lies very deep, at the roots of human nature. Dr. Wyngaarden has expressed this superbly in the following words: "Love is not merely a matter of the emotions, impulse, or attitude, nor merely an emotional cluster or constellation; but it is one's acceptance of being bound; in other words, it is that state of being of man in which he without reserve and in all freedom directs himself to another and opens himself to him. He does not overpower the other, but draws the other to himself by impelling, magnetic interrelationship."[5]

Notice the words "state of being of man." Here we see an indication that love is not simply an emotion and not even a "virtue" in the ordinary sense, but rather a summary description of what every person ideally ought to *be*. Love is the fulfillment of the divine creation ordinance; as Jesus said, is it the fulfillment of the law. When love is perfect, the man is perfect; in this sense love casts out fear and overcomes rage. The ability to love is the measure of maturity.

We read about God that he hates sin, that he is a consuming fire against all wickedness, that his wrath rests on the wicked. But this anger or hate in God is not the result of thwarting and frustration, for God is sovereign and his will is supreme. God's anger is rather to be understood as his judgment upon sin because of the holiness of his love. Likewise in man as the being created after God's image, perfect love includes judgment upon all that militates against it. But the man without God and impaired in his functions experiences fear and rage in the absence of love. The disintegrating forces of fear and rage are ever at work to destroy love.

The love Scripture speaks of is man's response to the love of God in Christ. It is in the supreme act of love that a person can order all dimensions of his personality in the service of God in Christ, and thereby in the service of others. Only the Christian, the person whose life is Christ, can love in the scriptural sense. The non-Christian is able to order the dimensions of his life in the love constellation to a degree because God's goodness is still manifest in persons who are estranged from him. But he lacks the life-giving fellowship of God, and therefore fails to attain genuine harmony of spirit. In the sanctified Christian life fear and anger are being overcome by perfect love.

5. Freely translated from Dr. H. R. Wyngaarden, *Hoofdproblemen der Volwassenheid* ("Major Problems of Adulthood"), (Utrecht, the Netherlands: Erven J. Byleveld, 1950), p. 140.

It should be clear from our discussion why love is primary in education. As we can speak of the primacy of love in the psychic life, so we can speak of the primacy of love in education. For a classroom to be genuinely Christian, the atmosphere must be one where love is supreme. Among the qualities that make for distinctively Christian education, the love of the teacher for his pupils and the developing love response in the lives of youngsters are of elemental significance. A biblical interpretation of the facts and principles of life will be Christian in the context of love. Where love is lacking, these principles lack the motives for effective personality development. Children learn best in a situation aglow with loving hearts.

RAGE AND ITS SATELLITES

This constellation is the very opposite of love. Love seeks its object for the sake of fellowship and preservation, whereas rage rejects, despises, and seeks to destroy.

Ever since Adam sinned, the forces of hate have been deeply rooted in human nature. We see the rage constellation operating at the dawn of human history when Cain slew Abel. In that first fratricide the disintegrating effects of both fear and rage are well illustrated. For, "wherefore slew he him? Because his works were evil, and his brother's righteous."[6] Abel constituted a real threat to Cain's security, for Abel reminded him of his own wickedness. Instead of confessing his guilt he removed, not the source of his feeling of guilt, but the object that reminded him of it. He slew his brother.

It has sometimes been pointed out that love and hate are polar opposites which, in a sense, require each other. When we love something we hate its opposite. Thus we are enjoined to love truth, but hate error; to love righteousness, but hate unrighteousness. Even of God, who is love, it is said that he is a consuming fire and his wrath is upon all unrighteousness. Therefore, in this sense, we may say that hatred is sometimes a moral *duty;* it is the *object* of our loves and hates that makes all the difference.

For our purpose it is important to note that deep-seated hostility expresses itself in essentially one of two ways. On the one hand, open rebellion gives evidence of hostility. A child may openly rebel against a teacher's reasonable direction, against the administration, or against the school as a whole. There will be contributing factors which a teacher should seek to understand, but these should not be permitted to camouflage the basic source of a child's trouble. Christian teachers will not be misled by a "good-boy" theory. They will recognize the

6. I John 3:12b.

"prone to hate" while they seek to take care of secondary contributing factors that can be resolved.

On the other hand, complete submissiveness may likewise be an expression of hostility. A child may appear "very good" in the classroom. He generally gets his assigned work done. He is quiet and submissive throughout the class period. He is no problem to the teacher, except that he generally fails to take any initiative and occasionally fails to assume responsibility for an assigned task. He never manifests any open hostility to the teacher. Actually he may be smarting under self-hate. He suppresses all feeling of aggression and hates himself for his display of weakness. Inside he is constantly accusing himself of being a coward, a fool. He is a problem to himself more than to the teacher. Only a discerning teacher who gets beneath the surface of children's lives would view him as a problem. Yet he may be a potential psychopath. In fact, he is much more likely to experience maladjustment and disintegration of his personality than the former.

Both the aggressive and the submissive child must be brought to recognize their own problems and view them for what they really are, a hostility that needs straightening out if they are to live happily. The teacher should consider it a major factor in a child's education to help him recognize his hostilities and learn how to deal with them. Helpful self-understanding is a major goal of education. A child can be brought to better understanding of himself by a teacher who understands himself and his relation to his pupils.

FEAR AND ITS SATELLITES

This negative constellation of emotions includes the anxiety, insecurity, and frustration that tears a personality into shreds. A child controlled by fears is kept busy trying to circumvent them, or to fight them, or to find alibis for avoiding the source. A child in whose life fear is the controlling force can have no constructive, unifying goal. Fear of reprisals at home for misdeeds at school causes him to resort to lies. Fear of discovery of having told lies keeps him busy concocting others. Fear of the consequence of a low mark in a test encourages him to cheat. Fear of detection leads him to undercover, secretive activity. Fear of rejection by his peers encourages slovenly work to avoid being known as the bright boy of the class. And so we might continue to show how fears dissipate a child's energy into divisive channels.

But in a world badly distorted by the effects of sin, and among persons whose functions are broken, fear is a necessary source of control. Radar control on the roads keeps motorists from speeding, for they may be caught. Fear of failing tests may keep students from skipping classes. Fear of church discipline may cause some members to attend church with at least some regularity. Fear of consequences keeps some citizens within the requirements of law. Because we live in a world in which not love of the truth but love of self is the primary motivating factor, fear is a necessary form of control.

Neither can we remove fears from life. In a world filled with insecurities, physical, economic, moral and spiritual, fear is bound to exist. Constant threats to our physical well-being by disease or other natural forces, constant danger to our income which furnishes our daily bread, constant temptations to moral digression, and the ever-present issues of the meaning and purpose of life give us no peace. They are replete with one fear or another. Likewise fears are ever present in children's lives. Fear of not being able to compete with his peers, fear of adult disapproval, fear of loss of status, and the like constantly beset a child. We, and a child too, must learn to live with our fears. Fears cannot be removed from life. They are learned as integral phases of living. Only to a degree can they be overcome.

Conflict is of the essence of our emotional life. The theory of conflict is a foundation of most psychogenic interpretations of abnormal behavior. Psychogenic means that the psyche or soul life is an indigenous source of motivation. The theory of conflict is a basic principle of Freudian psychoanalysis. Impulses of the id which are unacceptable are in conflict with noble and acceptable principles of the superego. Neurotics are people who cannot make up their mind in a conflict. Psychopaths are complete victims of their tensions. Freud held that most difficulties of personal adjustment are due to repression of anxiety, though he also thought of anxiety as a major cause for repression. Animal experimentation has shown neurotic effects of strapping animals down for experimental purposes.

With reference to the education of children it is important to recognize that they can learn to know fear-producing agencies for what they really are. So fear of the dark acquired through some unfortunate experience can be cleared up when a child learns to recognize that not darkness itself but certain threats under cover of darkness should be feared. It is dangerous to walk on the road in the dark, for example, for the motorist cannot see a pedestrian distinctly. Fear of storms is in the same category. Likewise, the fear of water. Fear of coming home with a poor report card can be analyzed to the point that a youngster begins to understand how he can approach his problem constructively through better work at school.

In the Christian classroom, as in the Christian life, discipline exercised in love overcomes inhibiting, paralyzing fear. So the Lord deals with us, his children. He does not permit us to suffer beyond what we can bear, and in the midst of our suffering he speaks to us of his mercy and lovingkindness. Likewise a Christian child in his struggle with inevitable fears in his life is undergirded in his struggle by discipline administered with a warm heart. In such discipline all paralyzing, inhibiting fear is banished, and the love response of the person is called forth. Only the Christian knows of the perfect love that overcomes all fear.

QUESTIONS FOR FURTHER STUDY

1. A teacher who is capable of discerning emotional patterns in children will soon discover several kinds. He must be able to deal with them in a positive way if he is to promote child development. Conditions in the classroom which upset Mary may not upset John and even prove to his liking. How should a teacher approach these differences? By avoiding conditions that upset a pupil? By catering to immediate emotional needs? By setting up situations that help a pupil surmount his emotional limitations to meet deeper and more permanent emotional needs? Explain and illustrate in terms of a specific case.

2. It is not what a teacher says and does in the classroom as much as how he is interpreted by pupils that counts in their development. Why? A teacher's own life style, for example, is bound to affect pupils. How does an aggressive teacher affect learners? A fearful, reserved teacher? Why?

3. We hear much about security today; economic security, personal security, national security. We learned that man is a chronic security seeker. Some one has said that man may seek security, but it is idle dream. He cannot have it. What he can learn to do is accept insecurity with equanimity. Do you agree? Explain. How much security must we give children? How can Christian education develop genuine security in child life?

4. Schools sometimes face the problem of damage to school property, such as desks badly marked, lavatory walls defaced, broken windows or lights, and theft. May there be school policies that contribute to such action? How can school authorities meet such behavior in a constructive way?

5. We have noted several times that how a child feels about what he is required to learn is as or even more important than what is required. Should we interpret this to mean that the feeling of pupils is the criterion for what they are to learn? Explain.

6. How would you as teacher approach an angry pupil?

7. How would you help a timid child to enter into class discussion?

8. How can an aggressive pupil learn to be cooperative in a group situation?

9. In terms of emotional development of children explain why a fraternizing teacher loses control of his class. What constitutes fraternizing? Is it the same for all teachers? Explain.

SELECTIONS FOR FURTHER REFERENCE*

Beaumont and Macomber, Chapter V, "The Effects of Success and Failure."

Blair *et. al,* Chapter XIII, "Basic Processes of Adjustment"; and Chapter XV, "Promoting the Personal and Social Adjustment of Pupils."

Coladarci, Chapter III, "Assessment of Social-Emotional Climates..."; and Chapter V, "Learning: Motivational Aspects."

Cole and Bruce, Chapter VI, "The Emotions: Energies of Man"; and Chapter VII, "Motives: From Drives to Purposes."

Cronbach, Chapter XVII, "Reaction to Thwarting"; and Chapter XVIII, "Personal Integration."

Fullagar *et. al,* Chapter IIC, "Emotional and Social Development"; and Chapter IIIB, "The Classroom Atmosphere."

Gates *et. al,* Chapter IV, "Emotional Development."

Morse and Wingo, Section 5, "Emotions and Reactions to Stress"; and Section 6, "Mental Health and Therapy."

Mursell, Chapter IX, "Emotional Learning."

Skinner, Section 3, "Emotional Development."

Sorenson, Chapter VI, "Mental and Emotional Development."

Stephens, Chapter XVII, "Adjustment in Major Aspects of Personality"; and Chapter XXI, "Improvements in Adjustment and Attitudes."

*References are cited here by author's name. See Bibliography for title and complete publication data.

8

Social Development

Sociality is an essential feature of human nature. This fact is already indicated in the divine pronouncement, "It is not good that the man should be alone" (Gen. 2:18), whose meaning is not exhausted in the need of a man for a wife. God is himself a social being, as the doctrine of the Holy Trinity shows; and man, created in the image of God, needs the fellowship both of God and others of his own kind.

It is important to make clear that human sociality cannot be reduced to animal herding instincts. The human community has dimensions (in particular, the *religious* dimension in its richest sense) that are not found, e.g., in a herd of cattle congregated under a shade tree on a hot summer's day. But only the Christian, having received a revelation of man's creation as a religious being, truly appreciates this distinction between human and subhuman groups.

STAGES IN SOCIAL DEVELOPMENT

INFANCY

The infant is first aware of his mother. But soon he begins to respond to other adults, and other children, of whom he becomes aware. He delights in being the center of attention, and begins to assert himself to gain that attention. These social assertions are necessary to call forth the love of others and to experience the first rudiments of loving. It is in this early social relationship that a child feels the security of love which must help him later to surmount momentary hostilities due to frustration when controls are applied.

Parents are in danger of making one of two serious mistakes in this early development. On the one hand, parents may be tempted to prolong the period when a child aggressively asserts himself for adult attention by failing to apply restraints. This is known as permissiveness. On the other hand, they may apply controls only for their own convenience, totally disregarding the effect they have upon the feeling-tone of a child. This is arbitrary repression. In general it may be said that frustration by external control should be at a minimum, for at least the first six months and even the first year. A child is learning to accept love and to love. These are both very necessary when parents begin to apply reasonable controls in keeping with the child's nature. The firm hand of discipline must be applied, even during the latter part of the infancy period. And when it is, mutual love may not break down, though hostilities may momentarily prevail.

Neither permissiveness nor arbitrary repression gives a child the security he needs to function acceptably among his fellows. Permissiveness fails to provide the support of a disciplined life. To do what we want to do when we want to do it lays the foundation of maladjustment, delinquency, and crime. Arbitrary repression drives a wedge between parent and child that bears the fruit of personal hostility. A child must assert himself and express himself to grow up, but only assertion and expression with a feeling of legitimacy generates security. Effective discipline consists of guiding self-assertion and self-expression so that it carries adult and group approval. This will give the child a feeling of legitimacy and of being accepted.

EARLY CHILDHOOD

In connection with social adjustment in early childhood it is well that we center our attention on play. For, indeed, play occupies a central role in child development.

It is in play that a child seeks the association of his peers, that he makes his forays into a broader social scene. At first play consists of individual activity in a group. There is little or no sharing or participation. Gradually play becomes a group enterprise in which participation is the much-desired end. What is played is not as important as the feeling of acceptance that is brought about in play. To be permitted to join in, to be recognized as a participant, and to get a hearing in the participation are new experiences that enhance the ego-status of a child. He needs this. The weaning process from mother and from parental dependence is taking on larger proportions. The necessary feeling of belonging must be extended beyond the parental bosom.

It is readily seen how unfortunate a child is who fails to enter into group play. His weaning process cannot take a normal course. Arriving at school he is still mother's baby. As a result he may have difficulty with adjustments in the larger group at school. He may get off to a poor start in the learning process.

CHILDHOOD

When a child arrives at school well oriented to his play group, the weaning process gains new momentum. His expanding peer group and new facilities and opportunities call for new challenges. New interests develop and former interests are being modified. The school takes advantage of expanding motives and interests by providing appropriate activities. But the effort of a child in school work should not be gauged by passing childhood interests. New interests within the range of a child's understanding must be developed. New interests are cultivated effectively through group activity. The dynamics of group life in the classroom in which everyone is a participant have not been sufficiently explored for effective learning. Much is being done today to gain a better understanding of learning in group relationship.

In connection with seeking to cultivate new interest in a child, a teacher should guard against two fallacies. The first is to coerce a child to his frustration point. Some coercion is essential. Activity in the group cannot be left to the caprice of the individual. A firmness of control is essential for a child's own feeling of security. But this does not mean that a teacher can ignore a child's frustration point with impunity. When the child gives up, constructive learning ceases. The second fallacy is that a teacher may accept too low a conception of a child's frustration point. What appears to be real frustration may be only a momentary hurdle that can be surmounted. Understanding of a child in his life style is essential to know how far a child can be pushed along a certain course with some hope of securing acceptance and participation.

A close relationship has been found to exist between the social stratum of a child's home life and his readiness for school.[1] We shall not go into a discussion of social strata here, except to point out certain values and attitudes characteristic of these groups that have a decided effect upon childhood ideals, purposes, and interests as children come to school. And these ideals, purposes, and interests affect the readiness to learn. Because the great majority of the children in Christian schools come from homes of the upper division of the lower class (called the upper-lower) and from the middle class, we confine ourselves largely to them.

Table II shows the way in which sociologists generally indicate social strata. The percentage of population in each group will, of course, vary with the community.

The fact that most children in Christian schools come from the upper-lower and middle classes gives these schools a definite atmosphere characteristic of these classes. Families in these classes are not

1. Cronbach, *Educational Psychology*, pp. 130-139.

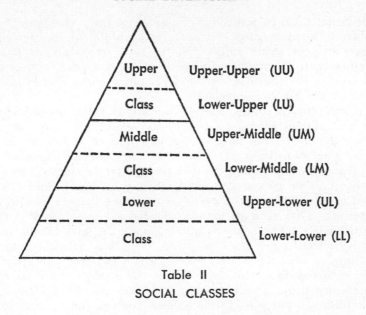

Table II
SOCIAL CLASSES

economically underprivileged and they enjoy some social prestige; but at the same time they often are greatly interested in *increasing* their fortunes and their reputations. They wish their children to be "better off" than they are, and often this advancement is stated in worldly terms rather than spiritual or even cultural ones. Industry, conformity, and competition are the keynotes of these classes; and while there are some who exercise conscientious Christian steward-ship, by and large economic pressures tend to dull these sensibilities. The children are under great pressure to achieve, to attain, to excel.

In this situation teachers and school administrators face a genuine moral challenge. Will the Christian school increase the pressure upon children by a competition for high marks or other competitive attainments? Will the Christian school further accentuate personal achievement, or can the curriculum and organization of the school develop a keener sense of stewardship? Will the school place major emphasis upon intellectual mastery, or should the school go all-out for the development of personality qualities inherent in a deep per-sonal commitment? The social-economic tide is against sacrifice and stewardship and service. Can the school help stem the tide and give place to the leadership of the spirit?

ADOLESCENCE

One of the primary facts about social development of the child is his increasing need for peer approval. This need is stronger in adolescence than in any other period. In early childhood father, mother, brother, or sister can provide the buffer of security against failures in peer relationships, but no such recourse is available to the adolescent. His need for independence and self-direction demands that he gain the esteem of persons in his own group. Self-esteem and group esteem are closely related.

For this purpose youths in early adolescence will form gangs among boys and cliques among girls. Not to belong to a gang, or to be outside the clique, can have disastrous effects of withdrawal upon a youth. The youth must feel that he belongs, and only group feeling can give him the feeling of belonging that he needs. So group activity must be encouraged. But when gangs and cliques become closed groups that practice exclusiveness, they become educationally dangerous. They tend to develop self-righteousness, hyper-criticism, and hypocrisy. The school can transcend the loyalties of smaller groups by challenging them as groups as well as individuals to work for a larger cause, the school as a whole, for example. Interscholastic athletics accomplishes this, but often at the expense of greater values. Community projects such as the Red Cross or Civil Defense can accomplish the purpose. Intrascholastic competition of wide partici-pation often helps transcend close-knit group loyalties.

A word of caution should be given here with reference to the Christian day school. The Christian school is a necessity. But this very necessary grouping of children from Christian homes for edu-cational purposes may have evil effects, especially upon early adoles-cents. Children from Christian schools have been known to reject other children from other Christian homes with the words, "She doesn't attend the Christian school." The Christian school should by word and deed cultivate a feeling of stewardship toward others. By working not merely for the school but also for the community, the barriers otherwise created may be leveled in the emotional life of children and young people.

Another significant feature of the adolescent period is the youth's forming of moral standards for his own life. In addition to the discussion of this point in the previous chapter, we now add some further remarks on the subject of moral training.

There are two related mistakes which parents and other advisors of the adolescent may make in the area of moral instruction. One of these is simply *neglecting* to tell the youth what is right and what is wrong, and *why*. A warden of a reformatory for boys relates this incident, which serves as a good example. In talking to one of the boys in his institution he asked the lad these questions, "Do you know what a law is? What are laws for? What authority has law? Who makes laws? Why must you obey law?," etc. Then the warden proceeded to develop the authority of law and the authority of the lawgiver for him. "You know, warden", said the lad, "no one has ever talked to me that way before." Early in life a child must learn what is right and why, and what is wrong and why. Morals and morality are essential in the security of youth.

But a second mistake is not uncommon. In the adult's desire to have a young person respect law and order, obey truth, and accept moral law, he may confuse morals with mores and custom. When this happens non-moral customs acquire in the mind of the subject moral significance. When the youth is called upon to break with a custom, he cannot do it without a feeling of guilt, for his conscience speaks. As a result of this conflict a youth may revolt against all morals as crippling restrictions upon attaining his "new-found" freedom. We have experienced this in connection with unreasonable demands upon youth in observing the Lord's Day.

In developing moral standards for young people it is essential that mores and customs be distinguished from morals. The former two carry group approval or disapproval. But they should not have moral implications for youth. A well-mannered family invited a guest to dinner who apparently had not learned the finesse of good table manners. When the guest failed to put his napkin on his lap, mother left hers on the table too. When he reached across the table, dad said nothing and permitted him to reach. When pie was served for dessert, the guest ate it with a spoon. And, of all things, mother did the same. Billy and Joan were both much bewildered by this time. But they said nothing. After dinner, when the guest had departed, mother began to explain to Billy and Joan why father and she broke some of the well-mannered practices at the table. They did not want to embarrass the guest. Should the guest come again, they would gradually practice all good manners, hoping that the guest would follow. Mother and dad had an opportunity to distinguish between the binding of morals and mores or customs. Right is right and wrong is wrong, but customs are in themselves non-moral. It is important for young people that they learn to abide by the moral relentlessly, but apply flexibility with customs and mores.

The thing to be remembered in all basic commitments in adolescence is that they require peer approval. "Dare to be a Daniel, Dare to stand alone" is a good challenge. But we know that a youth is still too peer-conscious to make it fully applicable when needed. Group approval, even among his peers, must come from somewhere. If it isn't from his immediate buddies, as in the military, at least it must come from a group in church, at home, at school.

THE ROLE OF THE SCHOOL IN SOCIAL DEVELOPMENT

Going to school is a socializing experience, and thus the school cannot help contributing, for better or worse, to the child's social development. Let us first take note of two interesting features of the child's social relationships which are of practical value in the managing of a classroom.

First, to be *ignored* is a painful experience which the teacher may sometimes use effectively as a disciplinary measure. All of us want to be recognized, even if we are not liked; and for some children this social need may provide the means for effective reprimand. But the teacher should use this method intelligently: if a given child already has feelings of inadequacy, this will aggravate them. A child's need for group acceptance is so deep-seated that it should constitute a major consideration in the management of a classroom situation.

Second, the teacher should know how to recognize and deal with both the submissive, withdrawing child and the child who is dominating and outgoing.

The submissive and withdrawing child is quiet and unassuming. He rarely raises his hand in class. He may be quietly at his work or toying with some object behind a book or underneath the desk. He generally does what he is called upon to do to avoid any kind of resistance. If he is in the group at all on the playground, he stands back and follows where he must. Often he will withdraw and engage in some individual activity in which he can experience success, even if only on the imaginary level. This child must come to experience success in the group. Often a teacher can find some latent talent, such as drawing or constructing, in a submissive child that catches the attention of others and secures the approval of the group. If so, this is often the initial step to group acceptance. The child may also be harboring some repressed hostility for which he is unconsciously accusing himself. In this case the teacher may need advice on how to get at the child's problem and how to follow it through.

A child who is of the dominant, outgoing kind makes himself felt in the classroom as well as on the playground. He must be seen, heard, and obeyed, or there is trouble. Everything goes well, as far as he is concerned, until by force of circumstances he is pushed to the background. Then he does something about it, and generally in some noisy and boisterous manner. When a teacher understands that often a child's self-assertion and domineering ways are a compensation for a felt inadequacy, he can direct his attention to the source of a child's difficulty rather than merely dealing with symptoms. Punishing a child for his boisterous conversation in class or for his dropping and throwing things will not correct the situation. This may be necessary for momentary control of a classroom situation, but continued punishment will only increase hostility and create further problems.

A feeling of insecurity in the group motivates both types. Each type does something positive about it, generally according to the life style he has developed to that time. One child is more disposed to submission or dominance than another. The desirable social development of a child demands that both submission or withdrawing and dominance or outgoing be integrated to a greater purpose. This greater purpose is co-operative effort. Many people will in most things be followers. Others will develop into leaders. But even followers are at times called upon to lead, and leaders to follow. A child matures socially when in the group he begins to recognize and accept his rightful place as follower and as leader.

In general, the school can no longer be considered merely a place where children go for a few hours per day to learn skills and information that are not available at home. The process of socialization, the learning of community tasks and activities, has now been removed by our complex modern life from its earlier place in the home to the school.

It is an established fact, psychologically, that we learn best from the process of living. It gives us that first-hand contact with things that gives concreteness to ideas. But most ideas must be had vicariously, without reference to the thing itself. Most of our knowledge is verbalization of the experiences of others in earlier days. We shall see this more adequately when we study the learning process in the next section. But even knowledge as verbalization has a social context, for it must be shared to be of value to us. We must be able to communicate it. The modern classroom provides a social setting in which ideas as verbalizations acquire concreteness in communication. We help each other to understand what we are talking about. Hence the community aspect of the classroom is a vital phase of learning.

But there is more. For true knowledge to become effective in the forming of personality, group participation and peer approval are essential. One cannot learn and live unto himself. A child as a person is a social being. Right and true knowledge cannot secure its effective rootage in the total personality without the feeling of sharing and mutual acceptance. As we live and learn together our common knowledge and understanding develops goals and motivations for living.

The group dynamics of a classroom needs further study, and is presently being explored. But even now we know enough about group life and peer approval to guide the classroom teacher to make this community life in the classroom a major factor for the forming and integration of personality.

QUESTIONS FOR FURTHER STUDY

1. How may we describe the social status of a Christian teacher in a normally Christian community? How does this affect his attitude to pupil motivation?

2. Are Christian teachers generally trying to move upward in the social scale? How does this affect their sense of mission in the classroom?

3. Try to chart your school community with reference to social classification. How do beliefs, goals, and citizenship in general compare?

4. Following the longitudinal levels of child development, indicate at what points beliefs and moral and social practices begin to divide children from their peers. What problems of development do these pose?

5. How can Christian schools as a comparatively segregated community cultivate a general social responsibility and universal sense of mission?

6. How can we help children distinguish between morals and customs, and still uphold the validity of custom in community practice? Are youths apt to feel that custom may be broken at will?

7. To what extent should a Christian youth develop self-confidence? How can we relate self-confidence and genuine trust in the Lord in the life of youth?

8. When may we speak of a person as comparatively socially mature?

9. How can classroom organization and school organization in general contribute to personal maturity?

10. How can group activity be organized to facilitate individual learning?

11. How can a teacher deal constructively with undesirable gangs and cliques?

SELECTIONS FOR FURTHER REFERENCE*

Blair *et al.*, Chapter XI, "The Social Psychology of Teaching and Learning"; and Chapter XV, "Promoting the Personal and Social Adjustment of Pupils."

Coladarci, Chapter II, Selection 8, "Methods of Child Rearing in Two Social Classes"; Chapter III, Selection 13, "Assessment of the Social-Emotionnal Climates . . .", Selection 14, "Relationship between Sociometric Status . . ."; Chapter IV, "The Class as a Group."

Cole & Bruce, Chapter VIII, "Growth and Development in the American Culture."

Crow & Crow, Chapter IV, "Personal and Social Development During Childhood"; Chapter V, "Personal and Social Development During Adolescence"; Chapter VII, "Personal and Social Bases of Adjustment."

Fullagar *et al.*, Chapter II, "Emotional and Social Development," Section C.

Gates *et al.*, Chapter V, "Development of Social Behavior."

Morse & Wingo, Chapter IX, "Learning in Groups."

Peterson *et al.*, Chapter II, "The Social Environment of Youth."

Remmers *et al.*, Chapter VI, "How May the Community Contribute to Child Adjustment "; Chapter VII, "A Sociological Perspective in Education."

Sorenson, Chapter IX, "Social Growth and Development."

Stephens, Chapter XVIII, "Social Patterns."

Stroud, Chapter IV, "Race and Culture."

*References here are cited by author's name. See Bibliography for title and complete publication data.

9

Intellectual Development

As we have stressed many times, man should be viewed as a two-fold unity: the unity of the person in the psychophysical structure, and the unity of the personality in the structure of personality dimensions.

Knowing involves both aspects of this unity. It involves the person in the sense that it is primarily a psychic function, though it requires physiological concomitants such as the nervous system and particularly the brain. The brain does not think, nor do thoughts; but the person does think, using the psychophysical structure. Again, knowing involves every dimension of the personality; it depends on the sensory function, and it is conditioned by social and emotional experiences. Especially do our unconscious impulses and drives play a large part in the knowing process.

Moreover, knowing is the act of a moral and religious being. To be aware of an object of knowledge is at the same time to place it in a value-system, and all value-systems are at bottom religious. Hence knowing, like every other kind of human act, cannot be divorced from the religious center of man.

THE INGREDIENTS OF KNOWLEDGE

Let us look upon knowledge as a kind of *product,* the end result of a process. Then it will be possible to speak of three conditions or ingredients of that product: the knower's capabilities, called *intelligence;* the thing known, called the *object;* and the process itself, which we may call simply *coming-to-know.* We will now discuss each of these in greater detail.

INTELLIGENCE

(1) *The Definition of Intelligence.* We have said that intelligence is a name for the capabilities of the knower. But this is

still very vague. So that we may move toward a more precise definition, let us make some distinctions.

The first distinction is between *intelligence* as an abstract noun and *intelligent* as an adjective (or *intelligently* as an adverb). Of course the grammatical terms are not our interest here, but rather what they signify, namely, that we can think of intelligence either as a kind of *thing* or as a *mode* of a person or his acting. It is preferable, by and large, to avoid thinking of intelligence as a thing, an entity, and instead to regard it as a quality of a person's being or acting. This will help to keep our thinking concrete, and at the same time will help us avoid the temptation to carve up the human person into separate faculties.

The second distinction is between three *kinds* of intelligence.[1] (a) Abstract or verbal ("academic") intelligence is the capability to deal effectively with ideas. This is required especially in the study of language, mathematics, theoretical science, and philosophy. (b) Mechanical intelligence is the capability to comprehend and manipulate physical objects, as is demanded in the various branches of technology. (c) Social intelligence is the ability to understand persons and to have rewarding social relationships.

Now it often happens that a person is well endowed with one of these kinds of intelligence and less well endowed with the others. We are all familiar, e.g., with the student who excels in his school work but is disappointingly ineffective after he graduates. Others will be mediocre in school but become standouts in "real life." Because this is so, some have distinguished between "abstract intelligence" and "effective intelligence." But the main point of these distinctions is that there are different sorts of intelligence, and it is therefore misleading and unfair to reserve the term "intelligent" for those who possess only one particular kind of excellence.

We come now to the task of finding a common element in all these kinds of intelligence which will serve as the basis for a general definition. One such general definition, which is representative of many others currently offered, is that of Stoddard:

> Intelligence is the ability to undertake activities that are characterized by (1) difficulty, (2) complexity, (3) abstractness, (4) economy, (5) adaptiveness to a goal, (6) social value, (7) the emergence of originals, and to maintain such activities under conditions that demand a concentration of energy and a resistance of emotional forces.[2]

1. Cf. E. L. Thorndike, *Human Nature and the Social Order* (New York: Macmillan, 1940), p. 57.
2. George D. Stoddard, *The Meaning of Intelligence* (New York: Macmillan, 1943), p. 4.

This definition does, indeed, describe some of the main characteristics of intelligence, but like most modern psychologists Stoddard neglects to describe the subject of intelligence and the object of his knowing, but focuses exclusively on his activity. As Christians we cannot be content with these omissions; we must take account of the fact that the knower is created in the image of God and that he must be formed by things as they really are, i.e., the truth.

Resuming our quest for a definition, then, let us consider what is involved in any intelligent action. Whether the situation in question requires the solving of a mechanical problem, or of seeing an abstract relationship, or of fitting into a new social context, it would seem that the intelligence which is required has to do with "sizing up" the situation so that meaningful action can be taken. We propose, therefore, the following definition of an *intelligent act*: it is a self-conscious act in which the subject focuses his attention upon an object of knowledge for the purpose of penetrating it in thought and apprehending it in the knowing function. *Intelligence,* then, is the aptitude of a person in his soul life to see the coherence of a situation almost immediately as he focuses his attention upon an object of knowledge for apprehension.

(2) *The Sources of Intelligence.* There are four sources for the aptitude that we have called intelligence. (a) The first of these is *heredity*. Studies have shown that biological structure, as determined by genes and chromosomes, plays a large part in determining intelligence. Unfortunately little is known about the exact *how* of this determination, and what role is played by prenatal growth and development. The legacy of heredity is a predisposition, however, to some degree of intelligent action. (b) The second source is *divine endowment*. Here we mean to speak of the fact that the inner self, the spirit, is a special creation of God which is joined to the psychophysical organism according to his perfect will. Hence intelligence, along with all other human capabilities, derives ultimately from the disposition of God. (c) The third source is *environment*. Opportunities for wholesome development can greatly enhance intelligence, and poor schooling or other unfavorable environment can have correspondingly disastrous effects. These assertions run counter to the popular belief that intelligence is a fixed given from birth, but they have been amply demonstrated by careful studies. (d) The final sources of intelligence is *choice*. To some degree we determine our own intelligence through decisions taken deliberately or unconsciously. This may occur by virtue of the environment in which we place ourselves, the moral values which we choose, or the emotions with which we meet our tasks. Any of these can enhance or constrict our knowing life and hence our intelligence.

(3) *The Measurement of Intelligence.* Quantitative measurement is an ideal of all science, and it can be seen that *if* we could measure intelligence on some objective scale we would have in our possession a very useful instrument for educational purposes. We shall see that existing techniques of measurement fulfill this practical purpose remarkably well, though the theoretical rigor of measurement in (e.g.) physics has not yet been approached.

The typical intelligence tests used for educational purposes are the so-called general intelligence tests. These are not achievement tests; that is, they do not test knowledge or skills gained in specific subject matters. Rather, they seek reactions pertaining to the child's daily experience, out of school as well as in school. They are attempts to measure the child's capability for knowing-in-general.

Of course there really is no such thing as knowing-in-general. Therefore it must be added immediately that every so-called general intelligence test incorporates certain biases. Most tests, e.g., slant more heavily toward urban experience than toward rural experience, so that urban children frequently gain higher scores. Again, to incorporate a proper balance between abstract, mechanical, and social intelligence in a general test is well-nigh impossible. The best one can do is to construct a test as "culture fair" as possible; that is, to minimize the effects of variations *within* a culture, recognizing that no test can operate effectively *between* cultures. Then, having taken these precautions, ". . . most psychologists are [still] quite prone to attribute a heavy loading to experience in interpreting intelligence test scores . . . ."[3]

We now turn to some key concepts involved in the use of general intelligence tests. The first is *mental age,* generally written as MA. Suppose, e.g., that a certain child, age eight, reaches the raw score of 75 on a given test. From the key accompanying the test we find that this child has a MA of 10; that is, he performed as well as at least 50% of the ten-year-olds who had taken the test previously. This eight-year-old has the *capability* of the average ten-year-old.

The second concept is *intelligence quotient,* usually IQ. This is the ratio or quotient arrived at by dividing mental age by chronological age (CA) and multiplying by 100 to eliminate the decimal. Hence for the child mentioned above we find an IQ of 125: 10 divided by 8, and the quotient multiplied by 100.

The difference between mental age and IQ should be carefully noted. Mental age is a measure of *relative maturity;* it tells us the level of present achievement in terms of standard age groups; and we *expect* this number to change as the child grows older. Intelligence

3. Bugelski, *The Psychology of Learning,* p. 383.

quotient, however, tells us how *bright* the child is; it is an attempt to abstract from the child's actual age to get at his capability as such; and we would not expect this number to change much as the child becomes older. If our previous subject is compared to another child, age 10, MA 12, and IQ 120, we would say that the two are about equally bright but not equally mature. The two measures tell us different things, and we need them both.[4]

The third concept is *age of arrest*. Every intelligence test has a point at which performance on that test does not improve. On a certain test, for example, a group of people of forty years old would do no better than a group of twenty years old. The actual age at which performance on a test stops improving is the age of arrest. So if the age of arrest on a given test is sixteen (CA) and a person of forty years scores a mental age of eighteen, the ratio would not read 18/40 but 18/16. The age of arrest varies by tests. What does the age of arrest mean? That mentality or mental maturity does not reach beyond a certain age? Not at all. Mental maturity has been found to increase but means of measurement begin to fool us. Too much has been made of the age of arrest. But intelligence tests such as we have give us little of value beyond the age of eighteen.

(4) *The Use of Intelligence Tests in Education.* To the degree that intelligence test results are accurate, they furnish a valuable objective measure of a child's maturity and capability for learning at a certain level. But the teacher should remember that intelligence test results may be misleading, and they *never* give the whole picture of a particular child. The test measures only *some* things about that child, based on performance at *one* time in his life (i.e., while he is actually taking it). Actually, the teacher is in a position to know many more relevant facts about the child (e.g., his health, emotional problems) than any test can show. He should look upon intelligence test results, therefore, as one of his many available *tools* to evaluate patterns of development and to choose wisely a manner of instruction.

It also follows from these considerations that several IQ scores obtained at intervals in the child's development are more helpful than only one score. If an intelligence test has been given in the first grade, in the third, and again in the sixth, a junior high school teacher has some helpful information. All things being equal, the intelligence quotient has been found to remain relatively constant. If Betty has an IQ of 105, 110, and 108 consecutively on three in-

4. As the reader has no doubt inferred, the average IQ is 100. It is interesting in this connection that Binet, the originator of intelligence tests, did not develop the concept of "intelligence" in connection with his work. This awaited the work of Stern, who in 1914 devised the formula for IQ.

telligence tests given at reasonable intervals, a teacher may expect this to represent a fair estimate of brightness. If, however, Joan has an I.Q of 105 on a test given in the first grade, 95 two years later, and 115 on a subsequent test, a teacher should know what to look for and what to do from here on.

(5) *The Range of Intelligence*. Statistical studies of IQ distribution among the population are available, which are summarized in the following Table:

IQ		Percent of Population Below This Level
140		99
130		96
120	Likely to succeed in college	87
110	Level of median college entrant	69
100	Average of unselected population	50
90	Unlikely to complete traditional high-school program	23
80		8
70		3

Table III

GUIDE FOR INTERPRETING THE IQ[5]

Though no classroom contains a completely representative population, the teacher can expect that *in general* he will find about 30% of his students to be potentially superior (IQ of 110 of higher), about 45% to be average learners (IQ of 90 to 110), and about 20% to be slow learners (IQ of 70 to 90). Children below 70 should not usually be in a regular classroom, since they often need some sort of special instruction.

Even apart from IQ test results, the observant teacher can readily distinguish the "bright" child (sometimes: the "high deviate") from the "dull" child (the "low deviate"). The bright child is capable of making many and complex associations quickly; he detects errors readily; he can "stay with" a task for a comparatively long time; he can shift activities without confusion; he is versatile and imaginative. On the other hand, the dull child cannot concentrate well or for a long time; is easily distracted; reads mechanically and with minimum comprehension; and likes routine rather than variation. But once again, we must remind the reader that individual children may excel in *some* activities far more than in others, and that the blanket categories "bright" and "dull" are far too coarse to be applied uncritically (cf. our previous examples of Bill and Bertram in Chapter I).

What can be done for the bright, superior, or gifted children? In this country we have tried to find the answer in terms of the comprehensive school attended by all children except the mentally handicapped. If they are to be grouped according to ability, surely mental tests are no basis for classification. They cannot produce homogeneity when they give a statistical measure of a single phase of a child's personality, but no complete appraisal. A child does not learn better when he is in a group of similar ability. "Covering the material" rather than group co-operation then becomes the supreme motivation. Homogenous grouping implies the wrong conception of the function of a group in relation to learning. Homogenous grouping can only be an administrative device, but no answer to the real problem. Whatever means is employed to take care of individual aptitudes is better arranged in a comparative group relationship.

This is especially true in Christian education where the aim of stewardship is of supreme value. The gifted must learn to develop their blessings along group lines as well as individual lines. The child who has been given much is called upon to cultivate his abilities, but not for his own sake. He must learn to use them in the service of others. The Lord blesses us in order that we may be a blessing. In the Christian school the problem of the bright and dull learners takes on added significance. All children in Christ are precious in the sight of the Lord. All have not the same calling in life, but all are called to serve.

With regard to differences in sex, it may be said that variations of intelligence within each sex are far more significant that differences between the two sexes. Certain characteristic differences which do exist between the sexes, as, e.g., the fact that in junior high school girls are generally superior academically to boys, or that adult males generally dominate the professions and business, are to be explained rather by physiological and social causes than by innate superiority. In junior high, boys who excel academically are usually not well accepted by their peers; and in the adult world, the woman's tasks and interests generally focus her capabilities on other than theoretical problems. Similarly, the alleged inferiority of certain *races* has never been demonstrated. Here again, environmental causes undoubtedly play a very great role.

5. Cronbach, *Educational Psychology,* p. 192.

THE OBJECT OF KNOWLEDGE

The object of knowledge can be any idea or any thing. But this statement should receive two important qualifications:

(1) "Things" are created by God, and together they constitute an orderly *cosmos*. The "ideas" we have about this cosmos must therefore reflect the pattern of interpretation which God himself has established for his own creation. God has given us the capabilities of sense experience and intelligence by which to apprehend this pattern, but (especially because of sin) even the skillful use of these capabilities is wholly inadequate to give us the essential truth. Therefore, in order to apprehend this truth, we need the special word-revelation of God. Only thus can we in some way "think God's thoughts after him."

(2) To know something is not merely to know "the facts about it." Knowledge involves valuation; it requires acceptance or rejection by the person. To know about the squalor of life in India without being moved to sympathy and action is not really to know it. To know God, in the deepest sense, is to love him. To know the devil is to hate him. All of this follows from the principle enunciated many times heretofore, namely, that *any* activity of the person is an activity of the *whole* person and cannot ultimately be separated from his other functions.

COMING-TO-KNOW: STAGES OF DEVELOPMENT

In previous chapters we have alluded several times to the intellectual aspect of other phases of development. Moreover, Part III of this book will discuss the learning process in detail. Hence in this chapter we will limit ourselves to the preschool period and to the general significance of schooling in intellectual development.

Infancy and Early Childhood. We mark off four important developments in this period.

(1) The sensory organs rapidly assume their functions of making possible discrimination and identification of objects in the world. At first all is confusion: the eye, e.g., cannot focus upon an object clearly for several weeks after birth. But soon the rapid development of sight, touch, taste, smell, and hearing provide basic data for further development of the knowing function. When one or more senses are defective, this development is retarded and often permanently handicapped.

(2) Attention span lengthens. At five years of age, e.g., a child may be able to maintain concentration upon a particular object or task for as long as twenty-four minutes. At first such concentration is directed wholly from outside; the child is mainly a *responder*. But

gradually the child becomes capable of *choosing* objects of his attention, and by the time he enters school he should be responsive in some degree to the ministrations of the teacher. *What* will interest him depends greatly on his preschool environment.

(3) Language facility improves. Long before he uses conventional words and sentences, the infant communicates vocally. But because he is usually encouraged to do so, the child rapidly "picks up" the techniques of spoken language. Language is primarily a means of communication, and by using it the child attains the feeling of belonging to the human community — a need deeply rooted in man's religious nature.

The reader may be surprised to know that a normal child has a conversational vocabulary of 2500 to 5000 words when he enters school, and often can understand as many as 16,500 words. Nursery school and kindergarten teachers too frequently underestimate their pupils on this score, especially those who practice the unseemly technique of "baby-talk." It should be added, however, that *reading* vocabulary cannot be identified with the vocabularies of (auditory) understanding and conversation. Reading is a separate skill which requires the recognition and interpretation of *written* language, perceived *visually*. Although having a rich spoken vocabulary does assist the beginning reader, it does not guarantee success.

(4) There is a development of play activity. Play is spontaneous activity in which the child engages himself individually or socially with objects and games. Because it stimulates the imagination, creates challenges of communication, and encourages skill in manipulation, play makes definite contributions to the development of the knowing life. The teacher will observe that very young children are mostly individualistic in their play, rather than group-minded; he will respect this fact, while at the same time encouraging as much co-operation as possible.

The Role of Schooling. The difference between schooling and the more or less spontaneous activities of home and play life is determined by the peculiar *objectives* of the school. These objectives are understanding and wisdom, organized according to the patterns of God's creation and directed ultimately to the love of God in Jesus Christ.

The transition from preschool to school life is always a major one for the child, requiring that he adjust to new associates and begin to participate in assigned activities. Hence the kind of introduction he receives to school life is extremely important. Two extremes must be avoided: On the one hand, the sudden exposure to adult-level regimentation which was so common a generation ago is unjustly demanding on very young children. Such children are hardly ever ready, emotionally or physically, for long periods of enforced quiet, exacting lessons in writing, and the like. On the other hand, the school must not make of itself simply another place for unrestricted play in its eagerness to make the transition easy. Its task is to prepare the child for more mature living, and it must not delay unduly in beginning that task.

The objective of schooling has often and appropriately been stated as the achievement of a *liberal education*. That is to say, the truth can and should make one *free*. The school can implement this objective in three ways: (1) by helping the child to face the truth, to come to grips with it; (2) by teaching him to express the truth through effective communication; and (3) by conveying and making available to him bodies of factual information.

(1) Even in secular theories of education we find that the school is viewed not merely as a place where skills and information are acquired, but where the child should gain insights into the truth which are meaningful for his entire personality. Speaking of this deeper task of the school, Mursell, e.g., says, "What should be done is to reveal arithmetic or history to pupils as interpretations of reality, symbolizations of experience which have profound implications for thought, feeling, and action, and which can serve as foci for the integration of personality."[6] In the context from which this quotation is taken Mursell is pointing out that games and other devices for learning subject matter have their place. But, says he, the deeper significance for learning comes from the subject rightly understood.

For Mursell, interpretations and symbolizations are what form personality. And to a degree he is correct; for instance, it is not enough to teach the mere *fact* that Washington crossed the Delaware at a critical hour in the Revolutionary War. This fact must be interpreted: i.e., it must be set into a meaningful context where its relevance is shown to the whole struggle of American colonists for self-determination as a people. And further, these events symbolize man's perennial right and duty to secure and maintain his integrity by legitimate means against outside encroachments. In this way an historical event becomes the occasion for the student to face truths and to make personal capital of these truths. But Mursell falls short in failing to recognize that these are *God-given* truths; that coming-to-know should be coming-to-know God; and that only the knowledge of God can make one truly free.

(2) Man was created to express the excellencies of his Creator and the creation, but because of sin his capabilities have become blunted

6. Mursell, *Psychology for Modern Education*, p. 6.

and distorted. Hence he must learn *how* to communicate as well as *what* to communicate. Since language is our chief means of communication, the language arts have a large place in the school curriculum.

(3) Finally, it is impossible either to face the truth or to communicate it unless one is well-supplied with information and the skills for gaining more of it. Hence the school must not take lightly its task of inculcating conscientiously the materials and the love of learning about the nature of reality.

QUESTIONS FOR FURTHER STUDY

1. Examine several intelligence tests and try to answer questions like these:

    a. How do they increase in difficulty at various age levels?

    b. How wide a range of experiences are drawn upon?

    c. Suppose these tests were translated into Korean and given to children living in the mountains. How far would they get with them? What do you conclude as to the importance of life style in the appraisal of test results?

2. Can you defend the thesis that intelligence tests measure inborn capacity?

3. We should make a distinction between test intelligence and effective intelligence. Why? Of what importance is this distinction for the classroom?

4. From your study of human development, which of the following do you think should be a school's policy with reference to those who show up poorly in intelligence tests?

    a. Give them extra drill in verbal-symbolic learning and retard their promotion until standards are met.

    b. Eliminate these pupils from school as soon as possible.

    c. Arrange a program of non-verbal learning to meet their needs; shop, for example.

    d. Group them by themselves (homogeneously) and teach them less of the usual verbal-symbolic material and at a slower rate.

    e. Have you still another solution?

5. If genuine knowledge involves the acceptance of truth, and the love-constellation is the feeling-tone that opens one's life to the object of knowledge, then what do you conclude as to the importance of the feeling-tone with reference to genuine knowledge? Do you subscribe to the statement that how a learner feels about the object of knowledge is as important or more important than the information he accumulates?

SELECTIONS FOR FURTHER REFERENCE*

Cold & Bruce, Chapter V, "The Development of Effective Intelligence."

Fullagar *et al.*, Section IIB, "Mental Ability."

Gates *et al.*, Chapter VI, "Mental Development"; Chapter VII, "The Nature and Measurement of Intelligence"; Chapter VIII, "The Practical Use of Intelligence and Aptitude Tests."

Jordan, Chapter XII, "Intelligennce and Intelligence Testing."

Mursell, Chapter XI, "The Concept of Mental Growth"; Chapter XIII, "General Intelligence."

Peterson *et al.*, Chapter III, "Mental Development in Infancy and Childhood"; Chapter IV, "Mental Development in Adolescence"; Chapter XV, "The Measurement of Intelligence."

Sorenson, Chapter X, "Measuring the Capacity for Learning"; Chapter XI, "Mental Growth and Development"; Chapter XII, "Intelligence, Its Meaning, Organization and Relationships."

Stephens, Chapter V, "Growth in Intelligence and the General Use of Symbols"; Chapter VII, "Mental and Physical Growth: The Role of Non-Scholastic Factors."

Witherington, Chapter VI, "Intelligent Behavior."

*References here are cited by author's name. See Bibliography for title and complete publication data.

10

Some Related Concepts in Personality Development

We have now completed our discussion of development according to the distinction of personality *dimensions*. If our analysis of personality was correct, we should now be able to begin a study of our next major topic, how the child *learns*. But it is wise to pause for a bit at this point, to ask whether there may not be certain well-known concepts popularly associated with human development which are relevant to our inquiry. Three such concepts present themselves: *moral-spiritual* development, *character* education, and education of the *will*. We shall, therefore, pause to discuss each of these briefly.

MORAL-SPIRITUAL DEVELOPMENT

Current educational literature is replete with this term. Moral-spiritual values are said to be higher values, and as such they are distinguished from social and material values. Money, e.g., is a material value, and neighborliness a social value. But respect for the genius and dignity of man, as exemplified by appreciation of art and literature and acts of philanthropy, embodies values which represent the highest cultural achievements of man. The spirit of religion, it is commonly said, is the highest expression of human culture; because it encourages reverence for the divine and love for one's fellow man, it must be encouraged in the youth.

Though Christians certainly have no objection to the moral and spiritual development of youth, we must distinguish sharply between the view presented earlier in this book and the basically humanistic approach contained in most modern literature. The latter is guilty of at least two serious faults: (1) Because it takes no account of sinful depravity in human nature, it supposes that moral-spiritual development can be fostered simply by *adding* something to the usual secular curriculum (e.g., released-time religious instruction). (2) Because it views religion as a cultural product of *man,* it promotes the development of higher values for the sake of man, rather than recognizing that man is created to live in the service of *God*.

We have seen that man is indeed spirit, for God created him such. As spirit, he is religiously related to God, the Spirit. This relation defines him, constitutes his essence; and for this reason we may say that *all* values are spiritual values. Similarly with morality: man is moral because he is spirit, rational and able to choose good and evil.

What then is moral-spiritual development? It is nothing less than development of the whole person in all dimensions of personality such that consecration of the spirit to the service of God and moral righteousness find expression in the fullness of life. In the love and service of God the person directs his life in channels of righteous living. He knows God in the sense of loving him as God. He seeks to do God's will in every area of his life. Moral-spiritual values of the Christian flow from a restored relationship to God in faith and a humble obedience to his will as he makes it known in his Word.

CHARACTER EDUCATION

It is sometimes said that reputation is what men say you are, but character is what you really are. Though this will hardly define character for us, it does give us a clue: like reputation, character has to do with good and bad. So character education has something to do with education in *morality*.

We may see the nature of character more clearly by distinguishing it from personality. Personality, we said, is the integration of qualities manifested by a person as he extends himself in all dimensions of life. Now we may view this whole complex called personality from many points of view, depending on what aspect of it interests us at the time. When we speak of a person's character, we view his personality with reference to his *conscience*. As a material object has color, so a personality has character. To describe the color of something is to describe the whole thing from a particular point of view, not to say everything there is to be said about it; to describe character is to describe the *whole* personality, but *not* to describe it *wholly*.

What is conscience? Like intelligence, it is not a separate thing or faculty but a capability to function in a certain way. It is the capability of a person to make correct evaluations and to act according to them. Character has reference to conscience; therefore we speak of good and bad character, and also of strong or weak character. A person who is morally alert and "conscientiously" motivated has a good character; another person may have equally keen but distorted moral judgment and acts accordingly; he has a bad character. Thus bad and good characters are, in a sense, "strong"; but a third possibility exists, that a person is morally insensitive and volitionally indecisive; such people have weak character.

Now this all means that good character, bad character, and weak character describe the color of a personality with reference to conscience, a person's capacity for moral insight and effective action accordingly. Development of character, therefore, follows the lines of the development of personality. The principles of development of personality apply in the development of character. We develop character when in understanding we come to grips with truth pertaining to the moral relationships of life. As a child begins to embrace this truth with a feeling-tone of love he accepts it in his heart and begins to order his way of life accordingly. The learning process which we take up in the next section is as applicable to character forming as it is to all forming of personality.

Moreover, to separate the concepts of religious and character education from each other is misleading. Character is moral, and the moral cannot be separated from the religious.

EDUCATION OF THE WILL

How must we conceive of will in the forming of personality? Nowhere in our discussion have we spoken of the will as a faculty of the mind. Rather, we have emphasized that the functions of the soul life are not to be thought of as entities or independent faculties. There is no thing called the will which we may train or break, as there is a muscle that may be exercised.

What is will? We can say that personality has character. Does personality have will in the same sense? Hardly. We say a person wills. As a person in his developmental urge self-consciously begins to achieve purpose in his life he is developing will-function in his personality. In his knowing life he begins to recognize meaningful goals for himself, comes to accept them, and in embracing them directs his personality accordingly. It is in the will-function of the personality that accepted goals become the motivations of life. As the person purposes he wills. As he wills he develops. Will is the goal-related activity of the whole person.

What, then, is education of the will? It is the establishing of goals in a child's life which he, in understanding and in love, can embrace for purposeful action. Because man is rational, he can understand goals. Because man is moral, he can value and love goals. Because man is free, he can choose goals. Because man has these qualities, because he is religious in being, he can will. He can develop will-function in his soul life that forms his personality according to the pattern of the image of God.

QUESTIONS FOR FURTHER STUDY

1. We read of spiritual and moral values in current literature. What values are generally meant?

2. When we as Christians speak of cultivating our spiritual life, to what are we generally referring? Are we using the word "spiritual" in the same sense as the above question?

3. How are the moral and the aesthetic related to the spiritual?

4. How is the word "character" used in daily conversation? In literature?

5. Sometimes we speak of character education, or education for character. Is this sound terminology?

6. Can we break the will of a child? Explain.

7. The subject of free will has been warmly debated over the centuries in both theology and philosophy. When we think of will as a function of the person, what happens to this controversy?

8. Do we have a conscience, or is it more correct to speak of functioning conscientiously?

9. Why have most books on development, learning, and teaching little or nothing to say about character and will?

Part Three:

How the Child Learns

11

How to View Learning

TWO LEARNING SITUATIONS

We are visiting a first grade in an elementary school located in a large metropolis. The school is surrounded by business establishments, apartments, and tenement houses. Most children in this community never look beyond the large city buildings that surround them. Their playground is the hard-surfaced schoolgrounds and the busy streets. Their homes are the crowded tenement houses of the community.

"What did you have for breakfast this morning?" asks the teacher of the entire class.

All hands go up. "Jackie, will you tell us?"

"I had orange juice, milk, whole-wheat cereal, and toast."

"That was a good breakfast," continues the teacher.

Many other children report a similar breakfast. Nearly all had milk.

"I am glad you all had milk. Milk is good for boys and girls. For older people too, but especially for children. Why should all children drink milk, Mary?"

"It makes them grow," replies Mary.

"How many of you boys and girls think Mary is right?"

All hands go up.

"I think so too," agrees the teacher. "Do you know where the milk you had for breakfast comes from?"

Some hands go up. Some hesitate. Another group, then another, until nearly all hands are up. Some very vigorously seek the floor.

"Bennie, you tell us," says the teacher with a broad smile, for Bennie was on his feet by this time.

"From the milkman," replies Bennie with all the self-assurance he has. "He brings it in bottles, and my mom puts it in the refrigerator. It is cold . . . and good too."

"Where do you suppose the milkman gets the milk?" continues the teacher.

Several hands go up, but most of the children look perplexed. "Henry, you tell us."

"My daddy says it is brought in by big tank trucks."

"What is a tank truck?"

Few pupils seem to know.

"John, will you tell us?"

"That's a truck that has a big (he stretches his arms to full length in opposite directions) tank on it."

"Now I am going to ask a question that may be a little harder for us. You are right when you say that milk is brought to us by tank trucks, the kind of trucks John described to us. This is the question. You think about it. Where does the driver of the truck get the milk?"

One hand goes up; another; but few try to answer the question. The answers that are given do not even approximate the right one.

LEARNING AS VERBALIZING

"Well, that is a hard question, isn't it? Then I shall tell you, if you listen carefully. Ralph, are you listening? Will you remember where the trucker gets the milk, after I tell you, Joe? This is the answer. The truck driver goes to the country, outside of the city, and fills the tank truck from large cans on the farm. The farmer fills the cans after milking his cows. When the tank truck is full, the truck driver brings the milk to a large milkhouse. Here the milkman heats the milk to kill all germs. When the milk is cooled, the milkman puts it in bottles. Now the milkman brings as many bottles to each house as the people want."

The children look at the teacher with a feeling of strangeness.

"Do you think you can tell us now where milk comes from, Wallace?"

Wallace tries; Henry tries; but each seems to be repeating words without getting a connected story.

"Let us make a story about milk on the board."

The teacher writes and reads while she writes:

The farmer milks the ——.

"Cow," quickly responds Louise.

The teacher continues on the board.

The farmer sells the milk to ——.

He brings the milk to town by ——.

When the milk is brought in he heats it to ——.

Then he lets it cool and puts it in ——.

Jackie fills in the right words in all the spaces. He gets an A. He knows where milk comes from. Mary missed two spaces. She gets a C. But does Jackie know milk? He can tell us all *about* milk.

Later it happens that Jackie has the first opportunity in his life to visit a dairy farm at some distance from the city. As one filled with curiosity about the strange environment in which he suddenly finds himself, he walks around in utter bewilderment. As he walks into the barn he sees a farmer milking a cow, a strange sight for a city-bred boy who was *told about* milk.

"What are you doing to the cow?" asks Jackie of the farmer.

"Milking, my boy, milking," replies the farmer. "We have to do this every morning and evening."

"Milking?" asks Jackie in amazement at what he sees. "Milking?" he continues. The word seems to register with him, though he does not at once recall the connection with what he learned about milk. "Do you get milk by pulling on the cow like that?" and he goes through the motions.

"Yes, my boy," the farmer went on, "this is milk." When he says this he holds the bucket of milk with foam on it toward Jackie so he can see it. But Jackie backs away as he takes a good look at the milk. "Do you want some? It is good for you. All boys and girls should drink milk if they want to grow."

Where had Jackie heard that before? He reflected for a moment. "You mean . . . you mean . . . that there, that you pulled out of that cow? Is that milk?"

"Yes, it is. But perhaps you don't like it warm from the cow. Come with me to the milk cooler. You may have some cold milk if you like."

Jackie follows with a mixed feeling of misgiving and curiosity. But he goes. At the cooler the farmer offers Jackie cool milk in a dipper. Jackie looks, comparing it with the milk he saw the farmer draw from the cow.

"Is that the same as what you just pulled out of the cow?" asks Jackie looking up to the farmer.

"Yes, try it. You drink milk, don't you?" asks the farmer.

"Yes, but my mommy gets it from a big bottle," says Jackie.

"Well, this is the same," retorts the farmer.

But Jackie pulls back. "No," he says at last, "I don't think I'll like it."

Does Jackie know milk? We have defined knowledge as the apprehension by a person of the object presented. We distinguished knowledge by acquaintance and knowledge by acceptance. To know is to be informed of the truth pertaining to the object of knowledge. Genuine knowledge, however, is apprehending the object in its reality and integrating it in life for what it really is. Has Jackie accepted milk in his life for what it truly is?

Jackie accepted milk as it came from the cold bottle in the refrigerator. Everything else he had heard about milk left him unaffected. It did not change him inside. Milk fresh from the cow was repulsive to him. Jackie saw no connection between the milk coming out of a cow and the milk he learned about in school as coming from the farm. He had learned milk in the artificial context of a refrigerator. What he learned of milk beyond that consisted of words about milk.

Is this learning? Three centuries ago Comenius, the Moravian educator, spoke of the schooling of his day as words, words, words. A century later Pestalozzi, the Swiss educator, repeated this description of the schools of his day. Apparently very little change had taken place. And how much do we rely today upon mere words for effective learning? Jackie too had learned about milk in words. He had repeated the words of the teacher and received high approval for it. When he faced milk in its real context he was unable to accept it. He failed to recognize milk for what it truly is, and appraise and accept it accordingly.

Isaiah, the great prophet of God to Israel, complained of something similar in his day. The Lord says of His people, ". . . their fear of me is a commandment of men learned by rote" (Isa. 29:13). They excused themselves from knowing the law by saying that the book of the law was closed to them or that they could not read. But the Lord tells them that the law for them consists of a repetition of words.

We call this kind of learning (if it may be called learning) *verbalization*. The perceptual field that gives the words meaning is lacking. Hence, the words used do not represent understanding of the relationships involved. Words are merely sounds that are repeated. Farmer, feeding, milking, grazing, warm milk from the cow, and the like are words for Jackie that lack a perceptual field. They do not constitute a unity in experience. Likewise for the people of Israel the law consisted of ritual or forms to be memorized and repeated, but life remained unaffected by it.

Words, words, words. But words alone do not constitute language. Language is the articulation of human needs for communication. The needs grow out of understanding. One may have something to communicate to another, to make known. He does so when the occasion arises, that is, when the need is felt. He then communicates in articulations which signify certain perceptual experiences. The language will be understood by others when they have similar experiences for which the language is an articulation of felt needs. If I want to communicate the serious illness of another I may say,

"Henry is sick unto death." When the other person understands that sickness and death stand in cause and effect relationship to each other, I am communicating. Otherwise I am merely sounding forth words. Sounding forth words and repeating the words sounded forth are often mistaken for learning.

Verbalizing, therefore, cannot constitute learning, for it is not based on understanding. Without understanding there is no communication.

LEARNING AS EXPERIENCING TRUTH

Suppose that the first grade teacher is well aware of the fallacy of verbalization in learning. She knows that a child brought up in a metropolitan community who hardly sees a blade of grass lacks a perceptual field for meaningful communication about milk. She knows too that merely telling the boys and girls in her class about milk will not provide them the perceptual field needed.

But why should Jackie know that milk is a product of cows raised and milked for the purpose of feeding people? Because this great truth understood by Jackie will form his personality. He will come to accept the farm, the farmer, the cow, and dairying as a valuable phase of his life and that of others. He will be formed in the physiological dimension of his personality as he drinks milk with appreciation of its food value. In the social-emotional dimension he will be formed by his attitudes to farming and farmer. In his knowing dimensions he will be formed by the knowledge of milk in its broad context of farm products and food.

However, these outcomes follow from understanding and communication, not from repeating words. Words, words, words cannot form personality. Neither can mere facts, but only truths disclosed by these facts.

How, then, does the teacher who understands learning proceed? Rather than saying, "I shall tell you" when she reaches the point at which children begin to wonder where milk comes from, she continues with something like this:

"How many of you would like to follow the tank truck to the place where the driver picks up the milk?"

All hands go up.

"Where will the truck take us, Joan?"

"To the country," answers Joan.

"To the farm," remarks Howard.

"All right, we'll all go to the country and to the farm."

To accomplish her purpose the teacher takes her class on an imaginary journey by picture and story, the closest possible substitute for living on a farm. To know the farm one must live on the farm. But not all people can live on the farm. Instead of a concrete experience of living on the farm and engaging in farming chores, a city-bred youngster can experience the farm and farming vicariously. At any rate farming and farm life must have perceptual content for a child to know milk. The class visits Uncle Bill's farm where the tank truck picks up milk to bring it to the city. They see and hear the animals on the farm. They visit the barns. They observe the feeding of animals, milking, and other farm activities. In school the farm and farm life begin to live in their experience. In the course of their visit the children begin to feel dependent upon farming and the farmer. They begin to respect the farmer as a valuable worker that provides food for many people. Among the many indispensable contributions of the farm is the milk that they drink so lustily for breakfast, dinner, and supper. And the cow provides us the milk. How hard the farmer works to feed the cows! What a valuable animal the cow really is! These, and many like impressions, develop new understandings and attitudes in the children.

Following the study of the farm, Jackie returns to his breakfast and drinks his milk with a new understanding of and feeling for the farmer and farming, and a feeling of gratitude for Uncle Bill and his hard work on the farm. He says his morning prayer with a new appreciation and emphasis as he thanks the Lord for Uncle Bill and his farm.

In contrast with learning as verbalization, the latter process is learning as experiencing of truth. Words are essential, for we communicate truth largely through words. But words are articulations of truth only when they are meaningful.

SOME GENERAL OBSERVATIONS
ABOUT THE LEARNING PROCESS

LEARNING PROCEEDS FROM WITHIN

Children are not mere animals, and therefore we may expect that their learning is fundamentally different from that of animals. At least one such difference arises from the fact that human beings are spiritual selves, subjects, created in the image of God. The child has the capability of self-direction (subject always, of course, to God) and cannot be treated simply as a passive object. Rather, he should be treated as one who is self-active, who calls to order his own way of life according to the truth. He can be forced to do things, but he cannot be made to understand, will, and accept or reject the object of knowledge.

Moreover, learning is a *religious act* because the person who learns is a religious being. As religious being the person is rational, moral, social, aesthetic, free, and responsible. Learning by the person as religious being, therefore, involves the understanding, appraising, and accepting or rejecting of truth. Truth understood and appraised with reference to one's own relation to it forms the personality, for truth understood and accepted or rejected by the person becomes the directing power of the person as he orders his way of life in the dimensions of personality. In learning a child taps the resources of his thinking, feeling, and willing with reference to the truth.

LEARNING IS PRIMARILY DEVELOPMENT, NOT GROWTH

The reader will recall that we defined growth as maturation of structure, and development as maturation of function. This distinction applies as well to the psychical as to the physiological aspects of the person.

There is a psychic structure as well as a physiological structure. The relation of sensory experience to the perceptual, of perceptual to recall and thinking, of thinking to generalization in concepts and ideas, and the like, are structural in the same sense as relationship of the digestive process to glandular secretions. And of course there is psychic development, as when a child acquires greater thinking capacity, perfects skills, or gains insight into problems. Sometimes the meanings overlap, as when we speak of a growing insight into a perplexing situation and of developing better insight. The former refers largely to maturing structure; the latter to more effective use of function.

It is important that we keep these ideas as distinct as possible because we are subject to great confusion at this point as we study current psychology and education. If man is only a biological organism as assumed by modern psychologies, then function is a qualitative change based on biological or physiological structure. All function must be referred to physiological structure for its explanation. On this basis growth and development are practically synonymous terms referring to a progressive adjustment of an organism to the environment in which it is to operate.

Man, however, is not merely a biological organism but an organic unity (which includes the biological and the psychic) based on the spirit. Maturation, interaction, learning, and forming are the fruit of a developmental urge of the spirit organically united in the psychophysiological structure. Hence we are not going to confuse growth and development as terms descriptive of a maturing person, though the two terms of necessity overlap.

Learning, then, is a form of development, not merely of growth. A child can learn to speak when physiological organs involved in speech have grown to sufficient maturity to articulate communicatively, that is, in a way that others understand. Speech and speaking are developments in the personality. Learning is development in the whole person. Nothing is learned in isolation. Nor can any structure function in isolation with reference to learning. Development is a three-dimensional process in the person. The whole personality is involved in our teaching whether we recognize it or not. Learning is a personal activity.

LEARNING DEFINED

What is learning? We find a curious reluctance on the part of psychologists to offer a definition of learning, according to Bugelski.[1] He refers to learning psychologists telling us more frequently what learning is not, than what it is. In 1945 Guthrie, a student of learning, said that a scientific theory of learning has yet to be agreed upon and Bugelski writing in 1956 tells us that this is even truer today.[2]

We cannot wait for the psychologists to reach some agreement on a scientific definition of learning. Anyway, suggests Bugelski, we would not want psychologists to teach our children. "We don't even ask psychologists to train our bird dogs," says Bugelski, "We go instead to a bird-dog man. Huw much further are we [he refers to learning psychologists] from telling our kindergarten teachers how to teach our children?"[3]

Shall we conclude that psychological studies have nothing of value to contribute to our understanding of how a child learns? This is not what Bugelski means to say. He is rightly interpreted in the context of his writing, it seems, when we take heed lest we think psychology can give us as teachers a complete and final description of what takes place in learning.

Bugelski himself ventures a definition after several preliminary considerations. Says he, "Learning is the process of the formation of relatively permanent neural circuits through the simultaneous activity of the elements of the circuits-to-be; such activity is of the nature of change in cell structures through growth in such a manner as to facilitate the arousal of the entire circuit when a component element is aroused or activated."[4]

This definition might pass for an answer to the question as to what happens in the nervous system of a person when associations are made in experience. There are other answers, but this is one of several in keeping with recent laboratory studies in learning based chiefly on animal experimentation. And this kind of experimentation and description has its place. But what benefits accrue to a teacher,

1. Bugelski, *The Psychology of Learning*, p. 5.
2. *Ibid.,* p. 3.
3. *Ibid.,* p. 9.
4. *Ibid.,* p. 120.

especially a Christian teacher, from such a definition of learning? The Christian teacher who views the learner as a religious being looks elsewhere for an account of the nature of learning. He will not discard the suggestions projected, but he will look for a more adequate and comprehensive description.

We come a little closer to the true nature of learning when we see it defined as a change of behavior resulting from experience. If one's response to a given situation is different this week from last week, one is said to have learned.

Since the word experience is used here in connection with learning, it is well that we have a clear understanding of how it is used in connection with learning and teaching.

In everyday language we make a distinction between hearing or reading about something and having experienced it. The difference is that between Jackie hearing about milking and farming and Jackie coming concretely into contact with these activities and even participating in them — or between the Jackie who heard his daddy's sermon and the adult in the pew who had a personal encounter with God in choosing for a sanctified life of service. Another illustration: Two people read about getting ready for spring gardening. One is a city man who has never come into personal contact with soil and growing plants, having grown up in a city apartment. The other is a suburban city worker who regularly cultivates his yard for luxurious plant growth. What will the first man learn from his reading?

We must distinguish between two kinds of experience, experience which is concrete and in first-hand contact with the object, and vicarious experience, substitute-contacts. For example, the teacher could not take her pupils to a farm, but sought to reproduce the farm by picture, action, story, perhaps interviews with others, etc. Pupils vicariously lived on the farm. The city dweller might page through a picture volume on gardening, or actually watch a gardener at work without engaging in the activity himself. Sometimes we can hardly experience vicariously what others experience in the concrete. This is being written when Hungarian refugees are arriving in America after their awful experiences in conflict with the Communist regime. We saw pictures in *Life* magazine, read of their crossing into Austria, etc. But have we experienced in any sense the deprivation and anxiety these people were subjected to? Insofar as all humans experience suffering, to greater or less degree we can enter into the lives of the afflicted Hungarians. But how abstract and academic this still is, compared to the reality!

Now the definition of learning as a change of behavior resulting from experience takes on some meaning. Experience has reference to the interaction of a subject and an object in which the subject undergoes a change such that a new relationship is established between the two. In the case of a person this means that his personality has undergone a change. For example, he likes olives now but he did not when he first tried them some time ago. He speaks French now, but he did not understand a word when he first came to France.

To be sure, learning involves a change of personality as a result of experience. One's behavior is an overt expression of one's personality. Momentary behavior, however, may indicate merely what one has learned to do under given conditions. When some responses occur with increased frequency in a repeated situation, there is still more evidence of real learning. One is beginning to give evidence of having accepted in his heart certain standards of conduct. Now it is not merely his behavior that shows his learning, but his very act is disclosing what kind of person he has become.

When one has come to accept truth for self-discipline, one has truly learned. There may be momentary slips into deviations, but they represent what one has learned to do under certain conditions. The evidence of heart acceptance is not in the isolated doing, but in the consistency of integrated action.

It should become increasingly evident how understanding and a feeling of security are related to learning. These constitute the keys to acceptance. As religious beings we are relentless security-seekers, and we find security only through understanding. We commit ourselves only to that which we understand or discloses meaning to us. "Learning is the quest for meaning, and meaning is the link between learning and life."[5]

We ask again, what is learning? We venture at this point a tentative, working definition. It must be explored further as we continue. *Learning,* we might say at this juncture, *is the activity of a person as he focuses his attention upon an object for understanding and acceptance of it in its true nature.*

CRITIQUE OF CURRENT VIEWS OF LEARNING

When we say views of learning, we do not mean *theories* of learning. Let us restrict the term "views" to over-all accounts, i.e., to interpreted descriptions of the learning process as a whole, and use the term "theories" to mean accounts of the learning process that are based explicitly on experimental evidence. In terms of this distinction a view will be primarily a reflection of philosophical perspective rather than the inductive result of factual research.

The first view of learning which we reject is what may be known as the biological view. This view says essentially that learning is the

5. Mursell, *Psychology for Modern Education,* p. 321.

process of transforming mass action of a biological organism into well-defined, organized responses. A child is a biological organism with propensities for becoming human, in the same sense as a little runabout pig is a biological organism with propensities for becoming a mature pig. For example, vocalization of unrelated sounds becomes organized speech; throwing hands and feet at the sight of a red ball develops into catching and pitching with precision in a ball game; scribbling on a large sheet of paper becomes the recording of premeditated ideas in an article on philosophy or politics or business.

Now we do not deny that these organizations of mass action do take place. Body organs grow structurally so that they can function in complex activities such as speech, walking, writing, thinking, and composing. But these refinements of mass action do not constitute learning, though they are involved in learning and even constitute a part of the process. Learning cannot be defined wholly in terms of these refinements, for a child is not merely a biological organism. He is a person who as a phase of his organic unity has biological life. So we reject the view, not the fact of biological structure and function.

The second view we reject may be called the social or cultural view. This view says that learning is the process of stimulating innate, inherent capacity to its greatest possible self-fulfillment by environmental activity in an ever-changing culture. For example: All children vocalize, but some have the capacity for developing the language arts with creative genius, others develop a reading and speaking ability for daily communication only. Furthermore, a child in the United States develops facility in the use of the English language in an American context. Learning is the process of self-fulfillment in a social and cultural context.

Again, we do not deny that innate capacity is developed in a given milieu, and that the opportunities provided either limit or facilitate the development of capacity. And the social and cultural structure will have much to do with the direction this development takes. A child does take on forms of life style of his community as he interacts with them. But learning is not *essentially* a matter of self-fulfillment in a given milieu. It is more than making temporary or more permanent adjustments. Learning is essentially the understanding, appraising, and accepting or rejecting of the milieu as one comes to understand and accept oneself.

THE SETTING FOR THE LEARNING PROCESS

As a story has a setting and as a drama has a stage, so the learning process may be thought of as having a setting or stage. We may

think of the setting as being threefold. There is, first, the self-active
learner, a person-with-a-history; there is also a goal which qualifies
all goals made perceptible to the learner; and there is the medium
in which perceptible goals as directional-process goals are being
realized.

THE SELF-ACTIVE LEARNER

A child comes to school as an immature person with his own life
style. His present life style may prove an asset or a liability to him
as he sets out to learn in school. It generally is both in several ways,
but he lives, moves, and has his being in it. He cannot be reached
for educational purposes apart from his life style. He must feel that
he is accepted in it before he can tolerate changing it. He may feel
ever so insecure in it, but it is his present world which enables him
to function with a measure of integration. He is a learning unit in his
life style. His learning potential, what he can come to understand
and accept at the moment, depends upon the unity of his person in his
present community. He is motivated and must be motivated from
within the twofold unity of his life if he is to learn. This phase of
the setting may be thought of as the developmental urge, or the
inner drive or positive forward impetus to maturity, of a child at
a given level of development.

PERCEPTIBLE GOALS

The second phase of the setting may be called the developmental
goal. It is the goal which qualifies goals made perceptible to the
learner. We shall see in our further study that a learner is motivated
to focus his attention upon an object for understanding by goals
perceptible to him. When Jackie was in church with his mother all
he heard was words, words, words, except for the word "house" which
referred to the church, for that is what daddy and mother called the
church, namely God's house, and "zeal," which had something to do
with those seals mother read about. But zeal for the house of God
sounded frightening to him in the context of "eaten me up." Such
an adult goal as zeal for the house of God can, therefore, never
constitute a constructive goal for Jackie. No, he needs the kind of
goal the teacher provides when she takes the class on a visit to a
farm. That kind of goal, originating in his perceptual field, can be
formulated into meaningful words or concepts that will activate needs
in Jackie to felt needs and thus motivate him to constructive action.

But today's perceptible goals must be realized in order to make
larger goals perceptible. So we go on from lesser goals to greater goals.
Endlessly? No. We have seen that there is a final goal for the
religious being. His personality must be formed to give expression

to what he really is, a son of God, created in God's image. This is the single, all-inclusive developmental goal. It is the goal perceptible to the teacher, who is a mature person. The perceptible adult goal must be translated into perceptible goals according to the level and life style, according to the developmental urge of a child. We may call the perceptible goals of the learner *directional process goals*. That is, they give direction to the learning process as goals. And the directional process goals get their direction in the thinking of the teacher from the ultimate goal.

The medium

In addition to a learner and a goal, learning involves a medium, a something through which a learner reaches a goal. For our purpose this medium is the organized program of the school as we know it today. The program of the school is the medium in which perceptible goals as directional process goals are being realized. We may think of the organization of the school as a series of developmental tasks. Organizing the program and executing it consists of executing developmental tasks. Developmental tasks are defined by Havighurst as follows:

> A developmental task is a task which arises at or about a certain period in the life of the individual, successful achievement of which leads to his happiness and to success with later tasks, while failure leads to unhappiness in the individual, disapproval by society, and difficulty with later tasks.[6]

Learning to read, for example: when a child is ready for it and experience calls for it, it is a developmental task the school is equipped to carry out. The place of the school is in this setting.

For questions for further study and selections for further reading, see close of Chapter 17.

6. R. J. Havighurst, *Human Development and Education*, pp. 1-5. See also Table IV, pp. 174, 175.

Table IV

SOME DEVELOPMENTAL TASKS OF AMERICAN YOUTH OF CHRISTIAN HOMES

PERIOD	Pre-school		Childhood		Adolescence		Transition to Adulthood
	Infancy 0-2	Early Childhood 2-6	Middle 6-10	Later 10-12	Early 13-16	Later 17-20	Adulthood
General characteristics	Dependent to exploratory	Energetic play, more regulated activity	Establishing self in social groups	Major projects in group activity	Differentiation of goals, emerging uniqueness and awareness of choices	Social sex activities, preparation for adult tasks, searching for major commitments	Mating, assuming responsibilities of home, church, career, and citizenship
Physical landmark	Random movements leading to creeping and walking	Walk, talk, body controls, runabout, first growth spurt	Gradual physical growth	Onset of second growth spurt	Puberty and accompanying physical adjustments	Growth tapers off, all-around development more gradual	Physical peak
Social surroundings	Home and family	Family and immediate neighborhood	School and neighborhood	School, expanding neighborhood, church	Widening community through high-school associations, youth activities in church, recreational centers	Job or advanced education	Job, family and home, church responsibilities
Need for affection	Establishing feeding schedule, confidence in care; weaning, toilet training	Acceptance of new brother and/or sister	Transfer of acceptance to teacher	Weaning process and acceptance of love by parents and other adults vie for dominance	Conscious of attention of opposite sex, transfer of acceptance to God and service of God	Close comradeship with opposite sex, growing awareness of God's love	Marriage, sex adjustment in wedlock, love-life of the home a reflection of Christ and His church

Need						
Need for approval by authority figures	Acceptance-frustration of desires, acceptance of family practices	Accept school purposes and procedures. Judgments on basis of right. Control of emotions. Teacher as standard.	Inner demand for control and outer seeking of freedom.	Accept conflict between demands of parents and standards of groups.	Attempt at independence of judgments to standards. Awareness of divine demands upon life.	Accept goals and demands of life. Answer to God's claim upon life of service.
Need for approval by peers	Attention paid to others' feelings, social skills, sharing, taking turns, inhibition, aggression, respect for property rights	Social skills in play, attempt to attain acceptable social standing, care for appearance	Conformity to sex rule, acceptance of group code, leadership skills and following leader	Courtship skills, acceptance by opposite sex, standards for sex association	Sensitivity to group opinion in community relations, choice of groups according to standards	Balance of family relations and community responsibilities.
Need for independence	Acceptance of separation from parents, choice of activities pleasing to others and self, suggestions to groups	Increase self-direction	Demand for freedom and feeling of security	Independent choice and group acceptance, recognition of authority	Decisions of import without relying on adults, acceptance of discipline of institutional authority.	Decisions despite parental or adult opposition, plan for and with spouse, family responsibility
Need for self-respect	Physical skill that calls for attention of others, acceptance of own impulses and responsible action	Adequacy in school task, skills in games, acceptance of skills and aptitudes of self	Approved interests, finding of means of income to increase feeling of independence.	Acceptance of own body, sex role, acceptance of abilities and failures, vocational reflection and search for direction.	Choice of vocational goals, part-time job to strengthen feeling of independence, feeling that religious choice is voluntary	Establish self as spouse, parent, worker, and community person. Active participation in community control.

*Adapted from Table I of L. J. Cronbach, *Educational Psychology*, pp. 94-95.

12

Theories of Learning: The Conditioning Theory

THE QUESTION OF METHOD

INDUCTION AND DEDUCTION

In the preceding chapter we said that theories of learning were accounts of learning that are based explicitly on experimental evidence. In that sense they are derived from facts, and may be called "inductive."

There is no doubt that the inductive method, in which attempt is made to discern laws and theories from observation, has proved its worth and significance many times over. Practically every instrument of modern civilization owes its origin to this kind of theorizing. Inductive reasoning is an attempt to gain systematic descriptions of what actually goes on; and if the experimental method can aid us in describing the learning process we shall have gained much. Learning, after all, is a fact, and it is important that we know as much about it as possible. Indeed, as students of education it is our moral *duty* to gain this knowledge, since the object of our attentions is nothing less than the human personality.

Deduction is reasoning out the consequences of general principles accepted as true, and we must stress that the Christian holds such principles and may not accept any theories that conflict with them. Because of such principles, e.g., we rejected two views of learning in the preceding chapter. But deduction does not give us observational data, and therefore it alone is not adequate to instruct us about the nature of learning. The lines between facts, theories, and views are impossible to draw precisely, and sometimes in our discussion of theories which are supposedly based only on facts, we shall be obliged to criticize them because they actually are based on non-Christian presuppositions as well as observations. Nevertheless, there is a large body of data on learning unearthed by researchers in psychology, sociology, and education itself. We shall discuss these data in terms of four theories which attempt to do them justice, and finally we shall attempt to formulate a theory which is even more adequate because it stems from the perspective of Christian revelation.

THE ROLE OF ANIMAL RESEARCH

The first attempts at observing learning under controlled conditions were made in the study of animal behavior. The reasons for this shed light upon these theories. There are essentially three reasons for this initial approach.

First, psychologies of the latter part of the nineteenth century were still influenced by the thought that mental life and activity are largely a matter of association of experiences. We recognize a familiar person by his voice or his step, though we do not see him. We identify a friend at a distance by his gait. Learning, thinking, memory, imagination, etc. — in short, all mental life — was thought to be the association of past and present experiences. By this time psychology had discarded the soul theory, and likewise the theory of mind as an entity. Mind was interpreted as a stream of experience. In this interpretation of mental phenomena psychologists were following the line of thought introduced by a school of British philosophers two centuries before. These British philosophers were known as associationists because they viewed mind as a functional phenomenon of associations. The concept of association, therefore, was prominent when the first experimental studies of learning were undertaken.

Second, the hypothesis of naturalistic evolution began to take hold of scientific thinking. It was believed that repeated confirmation of this hypothesis elevated it to a theory or even to a law in every field of human study and research. In psychology it was thought particularly fruitful, for one of the phenomena of human development seemed clear from naturalistic evolution, namely, that all life is continuous from the single-celled organism to man. This definitely discredited the soul and mind theories of mental life. It seemed that mental phenomena must be given an interpretation continuous with those of biological life.

As a result, the idea was promulgated that a first-hand study of animal behavior would give us not only the rudiments but the basic principles of human behavior. The human organism, it was concluded, is a more complex structure but not essentially different from lower forms of life. Everything that exists, it was said, exists in quantity and can be measured. There is no essential qualitative difference among organisms; the difference is quantitative, one of degree.

Third, controlled observation could be carried on more adequately with animals than with human beings. The experimenter could starve a rat or a cat for several days to accentuate the hunger urge preparatory to a search for food. But one could not do this to a child without violating higher values of human life. There was hardly a limit to controlled conditions to which animals could be subjected if humans could profit therefrom. No animal is considered an end in himself, but a human being is.

Animal experimentation proved so fruitful in disclosing elements of learning previously not known or vaguely understood, that later studies of infants and children were based on them. Of course, the hypothesis that the infant in his early stage is not far removed from the animal level was the presupposition that colored all observations and their interpretation.

THE CONDITIONING THEORY AND ITS EXPERIMENTAL BASIS

Conditioning is a simple process. How does a dog, for example, learn his name? We hold out some food, call him by a certain name, and while feeding him we pet him and give him attention, thereby giving him a feeling of security. We do this many times, keeping the feeling of security constant while feeding him. The food must of course be palatable and satisfy the hunger urge. The same name is used in each feeding. After several practices the dog responds to the name or even to a sound similar to the name. We say that we conditioned the dog to the name. He now has a name. This kind of learning we have all observed though we may not have analyzed it scientifically.

The scientific laboratory has provided us with some striking studies in conditioning under controlled conditions.

More than a half century ago two distinguished Russian psychologists, Bechterev and Pavlov, initiated animal experimentation in this direction. One of these studies has attained fame as Pavlov's dog experiment. A hungry dog under rigidly controlled conditions was fed powdered meat at the same time that a bell was rung. A small container was connected to the duct of the salivary gland so that when he ate and swallowed the saliva would flow into the container. Each time the meat was presented the bell was rung. After several repetitions of simultaneous ringing of the bell and presentation of the food, the ringing of the bell alone produced the secretion of saliva. What had happened was that the salivary response had been associated with the ringing of the bell.

Since Pavlov's day, hundreds of similar experiments have been conducted to establish like effects. Among them is Liddell's conditioning of a sheep. Liddell sought to establish a connection between electric shock applied to the foreleg — the only one that could be moved, for the others were firmly fastened to the conditioning stand — and the sound of a metronome. The natural response to the electric shock was to lift the leg. After several repetitions of presenting the shock and sound of a metronome together the reflex of the foreleg responded to the metronome alone.

What we get from these and many similar experiments is this:

The unconditioned stimulus
      (natural, original) or UCS — food or shock

The unconditioned response
      (natural, original) or UCR — secretion of saliva at giving of food, or the lifting of the foreleg at the giving of a shock

The conditioned stimulus
      (learned, associated) or CS — ringing of the bell or sounding of the metronome

The conditioned response
      (learned, associated) or CR — secretion of saliva at the ringing of a bell, or lifting of foreleg at the sound of a metronome

These and more complicated experiments establish that many potential connections in the nervous system can be linked to a sensory cue to produce a variety of reactions.

We might turn to a study of infant learning for further clarification. John B. Watson attained considerable fame in his studies of emotions of infants. Among his reports we read of the case of eleven-months-old Albert. We see Albert in a nursery as he is happily engaged in play manipulating, without fear, a white rat, a rabbit, a woman's fur, and a bag of cotton wool. No fear reactions are evident in Albert's behavior except in the case of loud noises and sudden removal of support. The experimenters seek to establish a fear reaction to furry objects in Albert's behavior. Watson reports the following:[1]

1. J. B. Watson, *Behaviorism* (New York: Macmillan, 1912), pp. 159-161.

"Eleven months, three days old.

1) White rat which he had played with for weeks was suddenly taken from the basket (the usual routine) and presented to Albert. He began to reach for the rat with left hand. Just as his hand touched the animal the bar was struck immediately behind his head. The infant jumped violently and fell forward, burying his face in the mattress. He did not cry, however.

2) Just as his right hand touched the rat the bar was again struck. Again the infant jumped violently, fell forward and began to whimper. On account of his disturbed condition no further tests were made for one week.

Eleven months, ten days old.

1) Rat presented suddenly without sound. There was steady fixation but no tendency at first to reach for it. The rat was then placed nearer, whereupon tentative reaching movements began with the right hand. When the rat nosed the infant's left hand, the hand was immediately withdrawn. He started to reach for the head of the animal with the forefinger of his left hand but withdrew it suddenly before contact. It is thus seen that the two joint stimulations given last week were not without effect. He was tested with his blocks immediately afterwards to see if they shared in the process of conditioning. He began immediately to pick them up, dropping them and pounding them, etc. In the remainder of the tests the blocks were given frequently to quiet him and to test his general emotional state. They were always removed from sight when the process of conditioning was under way.

2) Combined stimulation with rat and sound. Started, then fell over immediately to right side. No crying.

3) Combined stimulation. Fell to right side and rested on hands with head turned from rat. No crying.

4) Combined stimulation. Same reaction.

5) Rat suddenly presented alone. Puckered face, whimpered, and withdrew body sharply to left.

6) Combined stimulation. Fell over immediately to right side and began to whimper.

7) Combined stimulation. Started violently and cried, but did not fall over.

8) Rat alone. The instant the rat was shown, the baby began to cry. Almost instantly he turned sharply to the left, fell over,

raised himself on all fours, and began to crawl away so rapidly that he was caught with difficulty before he reached the edge of the mattress."

Can Albert's fear of the white rat be unconditioned? Yes, indeed. The experimenter can take Albert in his arms, cuddle him, play with him to make him feel secure. Then gradually the experimenter can introduce the rat by petting him, playing with him, while entertaining Albert. The rat is brought closer to Albert, even crawls on Albert's leg while the experimenter continues to pet the animal. With the encouragement of the experimenter Albert begins to extend his hand. After several periods of reorientation Albert plays with the rat as before, though any loud noise unexpected at the same time may throw him off. The rat easily enters into the picture again.

On the basis of these examples we may formulate a more precise definition of conditioning: learning by conditioning is the process by which a new stimulus or stimuli are associated with or substituted for the original stimulus or stimuli to produce the same or similar responses as those produced by the original stimulus or stimuli.

Conditioning is learning, because it brings about a change in behavior. But still we do not have before us the conditioning *theory* of learning. This theory holds that *all* learning is *essentially* like the process observed in many conditioning experiments; i.e., it is a forming of relatively permanent connections in the nervous system between stimuli and responses. Thus the theory is usually known as the S-R bond theory. And it claims to describe learning in men and animals alike.

DEFECTS OF THE THEORY

As a general account of learning, including such complex forms of learning as problem-solving in arithmetic or home planning, the conditioning theory has been almost wholly abandoned. There are several reasons for this.

First, the conditioning experiments do not lend themselves to such simple conclusions as were drawn from them. (a) A basic rule of experimentation is that only one variable may be introduced into a situation at a time. But Pavlov's and Liddell's stimuli were introduced into situations that were highly artificial to begin with. Watson's experiment with the baby was more satisfactory on this score. (b) Later experiments showed that experienced animals responded differently from inexperienced animals in a given stimulus situation. This would be especially true with human beings, for whom understanding modifies the character of the situation itself. (c) The S-R pattern itself changes with learning. When the stimulus is first presented, the whole organism responds; but after several practices the response becomes localized to one part of the body. This is evident when a child learns to write: at first the effort brings his whole body and mind into play, but with increased practice he can soon think only about the material and write almost entirely with arm, hand, and fingers.

Second, the theory has met rebuff in the area where it has put the most stress, viz., in the physiology of the nervous system. Physiologically oriented psychologists no longer think of the central nervous system as an S-R mechanism. Instead they now speak of a conceptual nervous system (CNS) in which the brain is a "dynamic, live, complex organ which permits a wide variety of different connections to be made to any stimulus and which permits almost any kind of response to occur with or without stimulus from the outside world."[2] This view is a far cry from the central nervous system as described for us in the 1920s or even 1940s. "It calls for a major reorientation of psychological thinking about the determiners of behavior," according to Bugelski.[3] Rat brains are "stimulus-bound." Not those of men. Herrick saw this back in 1926.[4] And Hebb in his *Organization of Behavior*[5] says that brains of rats are of a sensory type, but brains of men of an association type. All in all we are told by physiologically oriented psychologists today that there is an organism between the S and the R. Some have written the abbreviation SOR. But these psychologists now have a new formula: H (heredity) — A (age) — T (training) — E (endocrine, drug, vitamin conditions, etc.) : HATE.

When we read all this, we see that the simple SR formula has fallen on evil days. This does not mean, however, that these psychologists are looking for the source and motivation of human behavior beyond the physiological structure. On the contrary, they consider it mystical, mythological, and unscientific to do so. They merely say that the theory of conditioning is conceived of in the early days needs revision in terms of a conceptual nervous system. Bugelski's definition of learning quoted earlier is an attempt at such a revision.

WHAT MAY BE LEARNED
FROM STUDIES IN CONDITIONING

Because all learning involves associations and connections of stimuli and responses, the studies reported above and others like

2. B. R. Bugelski, *The Psychology of Learning* (New York: Henry Holt & Co., 1956), p. 38.
3. *Ibid.*, p. 39.
4. Cf. his *Brains of Rats and Man*.
5. D. O. Hebb, *Organization of Behavior* (New York: Wiley, 1949).

them have not been without fruit in the study of learning. Handwriting, number combinations, typing, eye movements in reading, location of cities on a map, and numerous other skills, habits and certain factual information are acquired largely by associating stimuli and responses. First learning of the infant is almost exclusively this. Think of associating a bottle with feeding, mother putting out her hands to pick up baby, and the like. Not even the learning process of these is adequately described by the S-R formula, however, but the understanding of what takes place points up many significant facts about learning as a whole.

LEARNING CURVES

Many studies have been made of the learning process which reveal characteristic patterns of achievement (response) as more and more exposure to the material or practice (stimuli) is given to the learner. If we represent graphically the measure of success on the vertical axis, and amount of practice on the horizontal axis, we can display the process on a *learning curve*. Two such curves, the convex and the concave-convex, are of special interest.

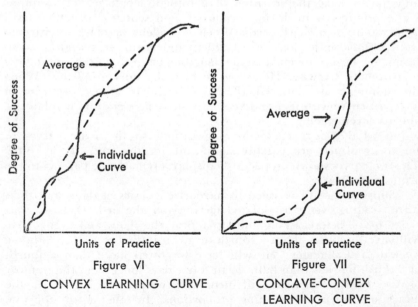

Figure VI
CONVEX LEARNING CURVE

Figure VII
CONCAVE-CONVEX
LEARNING CURVE

The convex curve represents learning of skills, such as handwriting or typing, and rote memory learning, such as the memorizing of dates, correct spelling of words, number combinations, and the like. Notice that the *average* progress of such learning is fastest at the outset, diminishing gradually toward an upper limit ("negative acceleration"). Individual curves, which vary greatly from one person and situation to the next, usually have several periods of steep ascent and "plateaus." The teacher should recognize that such irregularities are entirely to be expected; the plateaus mark points of assimilation and perhaps monotony or frustration, where encouragement may be needed. Toward the end the curve begins rather permanently to level off. A terminal point in progress has been reached. A physiological limit may have been reached, as may be seen in speed typing. Fingers just can't move any faster. Or a feeling of uselessness of further practice may come over one. Just how well need this or that be learned? To an optimum (as well as needed) or a maximum (as well as possible) degree? Not all skills and habits need to be learned to their maximum degree. Why should every one develop handwriting to the maximum? Legibility is sufficient for most of us. Many students fail to reach this or stay there.

The concave-convex curve differs from the convex curve at its beginning only. Instead of an immediate steep ascent, progress in this curve starts out slowly before accelerating. Why? Because this curve represents learning which requires at the outset new concepts and tools. Take the learning of a foreign language, for example. Little progress is made in vocabulary and sentence structure until some essentials are achieved. When a student becomes sensitive to word sounds, inflections, word order, and begins to recognize word forms, he begins to make some tangible progress. Problem solving in arithmetic likewise. Hence we begin with "story problems." When the rudiments are achieved, the curve begins to follow the order of a convex curve with its negative and positive acceleration, its plateaus, and its leveling off.

Just as there are curves of acquisition, so there are curves of *forgetting* which are equally significant for the study of learning. The two curves shown on page 185 display a remarkable parallel to the acquisition curves.

Suppose a child is asked to memorize a series of dates and their corresponding events as isolated facts. After the first recall we wait a day or so before asking him to repeat the dates and events. He will have forgotten about a fourth or a third (Figure VIII). Suppose we wait a day longer. He will have forgotten more than a fourth or a third, but less than half. Wait a few days longer and the number of dates he has forgotten will increase, if no practice is given in the meantime, but in diminishing proportions. In other words the rate of forgetting is the greatest immediately after the first learning.

But now let a child learn important dates and their corresponding events in the meaningful setting of the historical process. Every date and every event to be memorized has acquired a meaningful relation to a larger whole which he can creatively, that is, in his

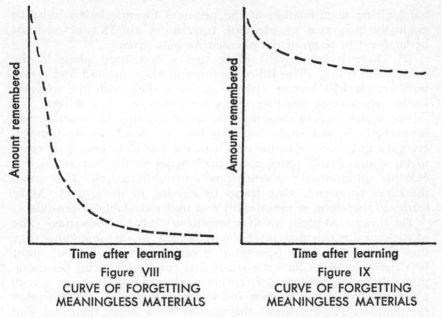

Time after learning	**Time after learning**
Figure VIII	Figure IX
CURVE OF FORGETTING	CURVE OF FORGETTING
MEANINGLESS MATERIALS	MEANINGLESS MATERIALS

own thinking, reproduce. Notice what now happens, as shown in Figure IX. While proportionally the most is forgotten after the first learning, as with meaningless material, much less is forgotten in the over-all. The rate of forgetting is much less and the total forgotten is reduced greatly.

Stating the facts of forgetting positively, retention is greater with meaningful material than with rote material, and retention suffers the most after the first learning.

After a brief description of these phenomena of learning which are closely associated with the conditioning theory, let us note what important facts and principles of learning we come to understand in this connection.

(1) Learning goes on at varying rates among individuals and in the individual. Every learning curve, even a group curve, is irregular. There is a positive acceleration as improvement is made with practice. There is negative acceleration as improvement between practice periods begins to decrease. There is a saturation point at which progress is practically at a standstill. Each one of these phenomena in the learning process needs understanding with reference to difficulties in the material and interferences in the learner. A plateau, for example, may mean that learning the material in hand has lost its early novelty. A new approach may revitalize the process. It may also mean that achievements are being made that do not register as overt progress. Such may be the case when in

handwriting manipulation of the pen and forming letters must be gradually integrated to adequate control. A child's progress must be analyzed in terms of the phenomena here given.

(2) There is an upward phase and a downward phase in the course of learning. The fuller meaning of these upward and downward trends will become clearer in connections with the study of further theories of learning. Here we can note a few things.

The significance of meaning and understanding for learning was noted early in our study and will become clearer as we proceed. Here it can be said in connection with the learning curve that meaningful material will prove more challenging to the learner, as, for example, an unsolved problem whose solution is desired. This causes the curve to ascend. One learns by striving to understand. Make learning, therefore, as meaningful and understandable as possible.

The downward phase involves forgetting. What is forgetting? The physiologically oriented psychologist is apt to say something like this. There must be a perseveration of neural activity which must be allowed to go on for some time. Any interference with perseveration will be destructive of retention. For example, look up a telephone number, dial it at once, and you will most likely not remember the number. Pause, "think" the number for a while, then dial, and you are more likely to remember it. The same is true of remembering names. This physiological process or something familar may be a factor. The important fact for us here is that there are factors that promote retention and reduce the amount of forgetting. We can direct learning so that the rate and amount of forgetting is kept at a minimum.

The upward and downward trends, and especially the curve of forgetting, point to a need for prompt and regulated review of what has been learned. If the newly-learned material is reviewed shortly after the first learning, the drop in the curve will be reduced considerably. Then, if reviews are spaced in short intervals at the outset, and at larger intervals as the work continues, forgetting can be further reduced.

The reader can apply this systematic review to his own studies. After the first learning, say of the conditioning theory, review it before going on to new material, then review it on occasion several times. This will be a practice far superior to delaying reviewing till a test is announced. Sometimes this practice is referred to as "overlearning." It requires a bit of selling to students. For less mature learners it can be achieved by varied approaches and techniques.

Learning suffers more from interferences, perhaps, than anything else. Discouragements and frustrations, repugnant or otherwise unacceptable material, feeling of inadequacy, monotony and absence of challenge, these and many more have already been implied in our study of development. The upward course of the learning curve will be of short duration when such interfering situations enter into the learning process.

(3) Teachers have used a learning curve as an effective incentive for individual and group progress. Take handwriting. A pupil can hold his paper against a standardized chart, mark his attainment according to a score, record it, and keep doing this while he continues to practice. He can plot a curve over a period of time and check his progress. The same can be done for a set of spelling words or number combinations. In case of the latter a group curve can be constructed with which members of the class can likewise compare their individual progress. Am I making progress as rapidly as the group as a whole? These constitute a basis for self-appraisal and competition with one's own record.

For questions for further study and selections for further reading, see close of chapter 17.

13

Theories of Learning: Trial and Error

The trial-and-error theory of learning has been very productive in developing classroom practice. Like the conditioning theory, it is a stimulus-response theory of learning. There is this difference. The trial-and-error experiments which gave rise to this theory disclosed the significance of motives and ends as forms of stimuli and responses that proved very significant in learning. But because the stimulus-response pattern was still considered the constituent unitary element in all behavior, this theory also became known as the S-R bond theory. The S-R then stands for the supposed sensory-connection-motor unit in the nervous system. In the studies of E. L. Thorndike and his students the theory was carried over into the subject-matter field of human learning, especially arithmetic. It gained such prominence in the theory and practice of education that one still hears of Thorndikean "laws" and "characteristics" of learning. Some classroom practice is still based on this theory almost entirely.

EXPERIMENTAL BASIS

Thorndike was one of many students of psychology toward the close of the nineteenth century who became increasingly impatient with the traditional psychology of "soul" or "faculties." These had produced little or nothing useful that could help teachers understand how a child learns. He turned his attention to controlled experiments with animals to see what could be known about learning. His many experiments constitute fascinating reading, and the student does well to refer to several of them. Here we shall merely gather from them what we need for our study.

The experiments included the running of simple mazes and manipulation of puzzle boxes made of packing crates. Hungry animals such as rats, chickens, dogs, cats, and monkeys had to make their way through alleys, get up on platforms, pull strings, or get around obstructions to obtain food which they sensed by smell or by sight or both. Thorndike watched their performance with a stop watch, counted their errors, and recorded their solutions.

From these studies Thorndike concluded that "my observations of all the conduct of these animals during the months spent with them fail to find any act that even seemed due to reasoning."[1] He said this in criticism of those who thought to find intelligence or rational faculties in animals.

Since Thorndike's experiments many psychological studies have been conducted involving the behavior of hens, dogs, rats, monkeys, earthworms, snails, turtles, sheep, etc. The conclusion generally, until recently, has been that animals do not learn either by reasoning or imitation, but by blundering, trying something and then either succeeding or failing. Random, blind, accidental, chance-like behavior resulted, after many trials, in the right response. Frequent practice gradually eliminated wrong responses and finally established the right response in direct line with the stimulus. The animal directly released the catch, loop, or button, or ran the right alleys for the food, etc. Practice curves which were drawn were all of the same general shape, indicating a gradual reduction of errors with very few sharp reductions. A covenient slogan was invented to cover all this random action: it was "trial-and-error." Someone has suggested that it should have been called trial-and-success, for the animals learned the successful responses.

When Thorndike became professor of educational psychology at Teachers College, Columbia University, he turned his attention to problems of human learning. For forty years he busied himself with this important study. He did not begin from scratch in this area. For one thing he had the experience of working with animals. Then too, Bryan and Harter's investigations in human learning (1897-1899) gave him valuable suggestions. He conducted experiments in sending telegraph language, operating a typewriter, tossing balls, number checking tests, writing English words in German script, shorthand, memorizing nonsense syllables, multiplying 3-place by 3-place numbers, learning vocabularies in a foreign language, etc. Notice that limited mental functions such as skills and information were involved, except in the case of learning a foreign language when slightly more complicated processes were required.

DEFINITION OF TRIAL-AND-ERROR LEARNING

According to the experiments referred to above, the trial-and-error theory of learning may be defined as follows: learning is the

1. E. L. Thorndike, *The Psychology of Learning* (New York: Teachers College, Columbia Univ., 1913), pp. 9-10.

process by which a response is selected from among several responses to reach a desired goal. The subject is confronted with a situation in which he is free to select from several channels ways to the desired result. This subject may be a hungry rat in a maze with cheese at the end of a series of alleys; it may be a cat in a cage that has a door with a latch and the desired food just outside the door; or it may also be a person who is challenged to memorize a series of nonsense syllables in a given period of time. In these and similar situations we see learning as trying certain pathways, eliminating unsuccessful ones, repeating successful responses, and finally reaching the desired goal.

Every one of the situations referred to demonstrates certain important features of learning on which the definition is based:

(1) The subject has an urge to achieve. The rat and the cat are hungry. The person finds some purpose in memorizing the nonsense syllables.

(2) There is a goal which satisfies the urge. For the rat and the cat it is the food. For the person it is the achievement of memorizing the nonsense syllables.

(3) The goal is perceived as that which can satisfy. To the rat and the cat the object must appear as food. For the person the nonsense syllables must appear retainable.

(4) The subject must have the necessary freedom to select among responses. The rat and the cat must have choice of movement. The person must have choice of combinations of sounds, letter formations, etc. for association.

(5) Completion of the first effort must end in success to facilitate further trials. The rat and cat must find food at the terminal. The person should be able to repeat the nonsense syllables.

THORNDIKE'S "LAWS" AND "CHARACTERISTICS" OF LEARNING

About a decade after Thorndike had experimented with animal-learning studies he felt justified in formulating three laws and five major characteristics of learning. He stated his findings in a volume entitled *The Psychology of Learning* (1913). This major work of Thorndike became the basis of further study by others and was required reading in courses of educational psychology for many years. He thought his "laws" and "characteristics" to be a sound, though not a final explanation of learning. We should look at them carefully, because they attained such universal significance in American schools and because they do point up pertinent facts pertaining to learning.

Thorndike stated the three laws of learning as follows:

The Law of Readiness: When any conduction unit is in readiness to conduct, for it to do so is satisfying. When any conduction unit is not in readiness to conduct, for it to conduct is annoying. When any conduction unit is in readiness to conduct, for it not to do so is annoying. By a satisfying state of affairs is meant one which the animal does nothing to avoid, often doing things which maintain or renew it. By an annoying state of affairs is meant one which the animal does nothing to preserve, often doing things which put an end to it . . . .

The Law of Use: When a modifiable connection is made between a situation and a response, that connection's strength is, other things being equal, increased. By the strength of a connection is meant roughly the probability that the connection will be made when the situation recurs . . . .

The Law of Disuse: When a modifiable connection is not made between a situation and a response during a length of time, that connection's strength is decreased. (The explanations and qualifications stated in connection with the Law of Use apply here also. The Laws of Use and Disuse are two phases of one law, the Law of Exercise.)

The Law of Effect: When a modifiable connection between a situation and a response is made and is accompanied or followed by a satisfying state of affairs, that connection's strength is increased. When made and accompanied or followed by an annoying state of affairs, its strength is decreased.[2]

We recognize that "conduction unit" and "connection" have reference to the S-R bond in the nervous system.

The three laws of learning tell us in effect that learning has its inception in a satisfying stimulus that sets up a drive seeking satisfaction. The satisfaction comes from a response that completes the conduction unit. The "index" to success in the learning process is satisfaction. Further use of the conduction unit will strengthen the bond established. A hungry cat is ready to respond to food and finds it satisfying to see or smell food. When the satisfying food is attained in a certain way, that way gradually becomes established by successful repetitions.

We now list the five characteristics of learning recognized by Thorndike:

(1) Multiple response. Thorndike observed that in at least nine-tenths of animal and human learning situations the subject makes many responses at the outset and most of these are quite random.

2. *Ibid.,* pp. 1-4.

(2) "Set" or "attitude." Of this characteristic Thorndike said the following: "The responses made are the product of the 'set' or 'attitude' of the animal, and the satisfyingness or annoyingness produced by a response is conditioned by that attitude, and . . . the successful response is by the Law of Effect connected with that attitude as well as with the external situation." Set or attitude, therefore, refers to the anticipatory expectancy of the subject. The subject is "keyed up" to a situation. Whether a response to a situation will prove satisfying or annoying will depend upon the set of the subject. Whether the grasping of the object will result in a satisfyingness of feeding will depend upon hunger expectancy, what the animal can feed on.

We have here, as we shall see, the beginning of a very basic principle of learning. Thorndike saw this and it is well that we hold on to it as we proceed.

(3) Partial activity. "One or another element in the situation may be prepotent in determining a response." Thorndike saw at one time that his own behavior drew the attention of the cats rather than the food. Likewise clawing and pulling at the bars deflected the attention of the subject at times. Elements not pertaining to the situation seemed to enter the field of action of the subject and deflected the attention.

(4) Assimilation or analogy. Thorndike saw the subject responding to similar situations in like manner. A similar, though not identical, situation called forth a similar response.

(5) Associative shifting. For example, one holds up before a cat a bit of fish, saying at the same time, "Stand up." After several repetitions the fish can be omitted, the other elements in the situation serving to evoke the response. This characteristic Thorndike considered the basic concept of the conditioned response.

Though these characteristics have only passing importance to us now, it is well that we take note of them. A beginning student in educational psychology should understand how we have come by the basic principles of learning that we now have.

Not long after having stated his laws and characteristics, Thorndike began to add to the list of characteristics. One of these was belongingness. He did not mean by it what we hold it to mean today. To him it stood for a what-goes-with-what phenomenon. For example, we tend to relate first names and last names together, instead of all first names. He recognized an act of relating a this and that. He believed that it accompanied repetition.

It was to be expected that Thorndike's interpretation of learning should come in for severe criticism by many psychologists. To base "laws" of learning on the limited scope of mental functions with which Thorndike worked, namely skills and information, was presumptuous to say the least. That some important features of learning would be disclosed could be expected, but not of a kind to justify generalization in terms of "laws." What is more, further experimentation by contemporaries of Thorndike began to point up flaws in Thorndike's investigations.

It is well that this should be so, for thus do we make progress in human knowledge. It is well for us, especially as Christians who view man as a religious being, to appraise Thorndike's contribution. Thorndike viewed man as a product of the natural forces of this universe. His pre-scientific commitment closed his vision to the limitation of his own efforts.

DEFECTS OF THE THEORY

Early in Thorndike's studies he concluded, as we saw, that he could find no evidence of what is known as reasoning in animal behavior. Animals, he thought, act upon impulse and blunderingly find their way to the object that consummates the drive. What Thorndike failed to recognize is that even in animal learning stimuli are a part of a larger whole and that responses constitute a part of a larger pattern in the experience of the animal. The Gestalt or configuration theory began to disclose this fact, as we shall see, in the study of learning by monkeys. It became evident that even in animal learning more than a series or chain of stimuli and responses is involved. Trial-and-error learning does not exhaust the learning process even in a chicken, as has been demonstrated. Most psychologists today would agree that we observe thinking in animal behavior — that is, if we interpret thinking to mean relating events into a pattern and facing a new situation in the light of this revised pattern. But we might well hold the line with Thorndike on the reasoning process. Rationality is distinctively a quality belonging to a person. Animals are not persons though they have soul life and consequently manifest mental processes.

Thorndike was altogether too ready to raise animal learning to a principle of interpretation for human learning. By his three "laws" and five "characteristics" of learning he meant to point out that human knowledge is of one piece with animal learning except that human learning is more complex in the conduction units involved. The difference is essentially quantitative rather than qualitative, one of degree rather than of kind. Thorndike's view is atomistic. Behavior to him is a summation of conduction units in the nervous system. Hence he could say, as he did, "All that exists, exists in quantity and can be measured."

Are there different types of learning? Must we think of animal learning and human learning as essentially the same? Yes, replied Thorndike. Yes and no, reply the physiologically oriented psychologists today. "The learning which Pavlov and Thorndike described was basically a mechanical acquisition of connections which left no room for any 'subjective' possibilities such as insight, understanding, intelligence, and so on," according to Bugelski.[3] For Pavlov and Thorndike the connection was between the S (external stimulus) and R (external response), external in the sense that they are external to the sensory-motor process. This leaves no room for action to originate in the nervous system itself. Physiologically oriented psychologists find much evidence for S-R stimuli and responses within the nervous system. Their view is held to be more central, and that of Pavlov and Thorndike more peripheral. So, when we ask, "Are there different types of learning?" both central and peripheral psychologists, being physiologically oriented in their thinking, answer, "No." All learning is in the nature of the modification of the nervous system.

Yet, some are inclined to answer yes at the same time, for they have discovered a distinction that has some merit. It is the distinction between what they call early and late learning, i.e., between the learning that occurs in infancy or early development and the learning that takes place in later life. We note that in early development learning is gradual, a step-by-step process, whereas in later life learning may be rapid and a one-trial perfection. This is explained physiologically in that in infancy certain areas of the brain are involved which in later life appear unimportant or are not involved at all. The brain seems to generalize its functions so that in later development the brain as a whole can substitute for certain areas when they are removed. Learning in later life, as from books and lectures, might follow an entirely different set of rules than learning from experience in earlier life.

A comparatively recent study in learning, however, points up another difference that is of significance between child learning and animal learning. Dr. and Mrs. W. N. Kellogg of Indiana University adopted Gua, an 11½ month chimpanzee, for study in order to compare his development with that of their 14-month-old son Donald. The child and the ape are reported to have been given the problem of releasing themselves from a cord tied with a slipknot around the wrist and attached to the floor.[4] The random trial-and-error procedure characteristic of learning when the subjects are inexperienced and too immature to enter into the situation with understanding was in evidence. Success that did come after "blind struggle," fretting,

3. Bugelski, *The Psychology of Learning*, p. 57.
4. W. N. and L. A. Kellogg, *The Ape and the Child* (New York: McGraw-Hill, 1945).

trying to run away, and the like seemed largely "by chance." The difference came into view when the slipknot was removed from the child's arms to his feet, and in the ape likewise. The now somewhat experienced subjects approached the new situation differently. The ape had to go through the blundering movements practically all over again. The child, however, soon recognized what needed to be done. There was transfer in the child's learning much advanced over that of the chimpanzee. While one study is not conclusive, it points to an early manifestation of a difference between animal and human learning.

WHAT MAY BE LEARNED FROM THE THEORY

THE ROLE OF FREEDOM

The role that freedom plays in the learning process is only hinted at in Thorndike's experiments. While Pavlov and Liddell strapped down their subjects to very limited action to isolate one movement if possible, Thorndike allowed greater freedom of action. The former reduced the subjects to channels for stimuli and responses. Thorndike permitted freedom in a circumscribed area. The animal was free to select his movements as he was impelled by a goal presented to him as a satisfying end.

We said that the role of freedom is only hinted at by Thorndike. Later we hope to see how important this principle is in human learning. Freedom is inherent in man as religious being. To be, he must be free. To develop as a person he must have the opportunity to make choices voluntarily. But as a fish can exercise his level of freedom only when submerged in water, and as a bird is free only when he can throw out his wings in a wide-open sky, so a child is free only when he is disciplined according to the norms of his being. What constitutes freedom for Freddie in the second grade? Opportunity to choose within the range of his ability to regulate his own life as religious being. As he chooses voluntarily for the right he is developing self-control, which is his freedom. Desirable personality forming takes place in a medium where right choices can be made without wrong choices proving too frustrating to the learner.

THE ROLE OF REPETITION

"Practice makes perfect," we hear said, and the Jesuits had a pedagogical proverb: *repetitio mater studiorum est* — repetition is the mother of studies. Aeneas Silvius, Renaissance teacher, expressed the same thought in these words, "Memory is the nursing mother of learning." Thorndike formulated the "Law of Use" to state this age-old idea in terms of his system. But Thorndike himself abandoned the Law of Use when he began to see that what he called *belongingness* played a large role in learning. This had to wait for further development in the insight theory. Yet many a classroom teacher seems not yet to have heard of the fallacy of learning merely by repetition.

But the use of the term "repetition" is ambiguous. It may mean going over the same material in exactly the same way several times. It may also mean a varied attack upon the same situation. In the first sense it certainly contributes little or nothing to learning, but often defeats its own end. In the second sense it establishes a condition necessary for effective learning.

How does a child learn that $8+5=13$? By repeating over and over what the teacher said? This is like words, words, words in connection with learning where milk comes from. He learns by understanding what $8+5=13$ means, that is, he sees the relationships involved. He may have to come back to the statement several times in order to establish adequate relationships before the combination is permanently fixed. In this broad sense repetition does play a role in learning.

REWARDS STRENGTHEN LEARNING

The Law of Effect was barely stated when its application became common practice in classrooms and it has remained a key principle in elementary and secondary education to this day. Unlike the Law of Use, further experimentation has confirmed its essential truth. Thorndike himself modified it in 1931 to read: "Acts followed by a state of affairs which the individual does not avoid, and which he often tries to preserve or attain, are selected and fixated, while acts followed by states of affairs which the individual avoids or attempts to change are eliminated." The first class of affairs were called "satisfiers", the second class "annoyers." In 1932 Thorndike even dropped the concept "annoyers." The "law" has been revised following later experimentation and is referred to today as the principle of reinforcement, which says in effect that rewards strengthen learning. The principle of reinforcement is now a central doctrine in learning theory. It represents a major contribution of recent psychological studies.

We met this principle before in our discussion when we said that feelings of success and failure play a large part in learning. Every learner must experience the feeling of successful endeavor as he strives for a certain goal. The feeling of failure may and often does momentarily spur one on to more intensive effort. But more often, failure is debilitating and leaves a feeling of defeat. This is particularly true of slow learners. They are apt to experience the feeling of success least often, and yet they need it more than bright learners, for their frustration point is much lower, as a general rule.

How a child interprets his success or failure is even more important for his initiative and self-discipline than success and failure themselves. One may fail and view it as a challenge; another regards it a threat to his security. One pupil may succeed and view it as getting away with something with the result that evasiveness, or escape, may be the thing actually learned; another views it as a satisfaction with work well done.

The importance of felt needs in learning

That all learning has its inception in felt needs has been expressed in various ways. Thorndike said this in effect in the "Law of Readiness." The learner is not a two- or three-gallon jug passively to be filled. Nor, by the same token, is teaching the procedure of filling the jug. A learner is a person who in his organic unity has needs which must be met to form his personality. But he must feel these needs if they are to become a source of constructive action. Felt needs are tensions from within in the form of a drive that is activated. When activated they can be directed toward a goal. Presence of a goal can activate needs. A learner experiences readiness when needs are felt. Learning has its inception at this point for it gives him dynamic as a self-active person.

"Set" or "expectancy" in learning

The feeling of hunger leads one to anticipate the presence of food. Whatever is present that even suggests food is interpreted as such because the organism is keyed up to this anticipation. This we call "set" or "expectancy." When the teacher had started a discussion on milk and its origin, a curiosity was aroused in the children which had its dynamic in an expectancy following from a felt need. In subsequent experience the organism selects things and events that carry forward the anticipatory expectancy to a satisfying end or goal. Every successful experience is integrated in the whole such that it constitutes a phase of later behavior.

What a learner perceives in a learning situation depends upon what he consciously or even unconsciously anticipates. His life style may be a "set" or "expectancy." A boy who is bullied and bandied around by adults at home is apt to interpret the exercise of authority by his teacher in the same light unless some special consideration is shown, and such consideration he is likely to interpret as weakness. A learner may interpret every learning situation as an opportunity to draw group and teacher attention to himself, if not by superior achievement, then by less worthy means. The question of what a child is learning is answered in terms of what he anticipates or expects. If it is high grades he works for, competitive achievement is what he learns; every other learning is subsidiary or of little consequence. He may be learning in a clever way to get around a task, though he makes an appearance of having accomplished it. It is the former that patterns, that shapes his personality; the latter will affect his personality only secondarily, if at all. Much of the latter is apt to be forgotten, for he will practice the former in other situations, while the latter he discounts. It should be clear that a learner is formed in his personality by what *he* sets out to learn, not necessarily by what the teacher purposes.

MOTIVATION IN LEARNING

Thorndike opened up the subject of motivation in learning. Felt needs develop set of expectancy. Set and expectancy look forward to a satisfying goal. Thorndike spoke of "satisfiers" and "annoyers" as ends that do or do not meet the needs of the subject. This opens a subject much larger in scope than Thorndike had anticipated. He failed to anticipate its full significance because his view of human drives was restricted to a mechanistic nervous system that linked stimuli and responses.

That motivation affects learning is common knowledge. That there is no learning without motivation is less commonly understood. And that we learn only what we are motivated to learn some would doubt, if not deny.

What is motivation? Some teachers confuse the term with incentives and speak of lesson motivation in the sense of making the undesired desirable. It is assumed that arithmetic cannot be inherently challenging, so they try to find some way of making it intriguing. By a game, for example. Now, incentives of this nature are not excluded, but motivation is a much more personal concept that is implied by such practices. Some psychologists try to avoid the concept of motivation because it appears to them to conceal a conscious or unconscious preoccupation with metaphysical entities such as id, impulse, or universal mind. But these misgivings simply reflect their philosophically naturalistic bias. Viewing man as Scripture presents him, the Christian sees in motivation the developmental urge of a person who is a religious being, not merely biological in nature.

Recently, physiologically oriented psychologists have begun to recognize that there is indigenous motivation from within the neurones. Neurones will "fire" spontaneously, as they put it. Thorndike saw only a connecting nervous system in which afferent nerves send messages over a complicated network to efferent nerves. These psychologists find that stimuli can originate in neurons. One recent physiological approach to motivation finds its primary sources in the electrical activity of the nervous system, and particularly in the brain. The brain is thought to operate analogously to a giant electronic calculator. It is said to be continuously and spontaneously active whether stimulated or not. Changes in brain patterns are constantly going on and any activity from without must seek entrance among these patterns as a visitor among a room full of active people. So it is thought that motivation describes an interior state of an organism rather than the traditional and mysterious biological urges, choices, needs, and the like.

For our purpose, motivation may be thought of as readiness for learning and includes attention, curiosity, set, anticipation, expectancy. Motivation determines how well one learns and how long one keeps on learning. A strongly motivated person tends to analyze. He is challenged to work sufficiently to achieve desired ends. No one learns unless he is confronted with a challenging situation. The true nature of the challenge has a great deal to do with what a person actually learns in a given situation. Antagonistic impulses are overcome by strong motivation. Strong motivation to learning will lead to better and longer learning, and thereby reduce the need for repetition. Repetition such as needed will be more effective. All in all, it cannot be emphasized too strongly that we learn what we want to learn.

Interests have their source in motivation. Goals which are an expression of a person's motivation become interests when they are more or less permanent. Interest is self-perpetuating and makes learning permanent. "The function of the school properly understood," says Mursell, "is not to take a predetermined body of content and trick it up to make it interesting. Its true function is to organize both content and teaching-learning situation with a view to establish vital interests which tend to go forward and develop."[5] And again he says, ". . . it may well be argued that the function of the school is not to find some better substitute for the content of culture, but to bring the content of culture into vital relationship with human living. This can only be done by shaping motives, the determination of goals, the creation of vital interest."[6] These quotations of Mursell are not given to subscribe to the pragmatic bias implied, but to point out that learning has its dynamics in the motivation of the person.

THE ROLE OF INCENTIVES IN LEARNING

Though incentives must not be confused with motivation, they play an important part in motivation. When effort begins to lag because of exhaustion, frustrating failures, loss of allurement of the

5. Mursell, *Psychology for Modern Education*, p. 108.
6. *Ibid.*, p. 112.

goal, and the like, a "shot in the arm" is needed to bring it back to earlier or even greater impetus. The means employed to this end are known as incentives. Teachers use incentives of all kinds, as do parents, good, bad, and indifferent. A gold star on a neatly written paper is a common one. Reading one's paper before the class is another. School marks are often so employed. Parents hang up a chart in the kitchen on which a child checks off his chores to see that they have been accomplished. Pupils are given a day off (teachers too) because of a successful paper drive. And so one might continue to list many more. Several will occur to the student as he reads this.

But are all incentives equally good educationally? They are meant for educational purposes, and do accomplish educational ends, that is, the forming of personality. But what qualities do they form in the personality? This is the question. From the point of view of forming personality we may speak of positive and negative incentives, and intrinsic and extrinsic incentives.

Positive Intrinsic Incentives. When Bill has written a composition that represents real achievement in content and form, and then is called upon to read it before the class for discussion, he is rewarded for his effort by satisfying his need for peer approval. Likewise Jim, who, though his composition is not of the quality of Bill's, made great progress, receives greater group acceptance from a similar reward. But Joe, who does not write well at all, made several drawings of high quality which he discusses before the group. He too gets group approval. Joe is encouraged to put his thinking down on paper in as good form as he can by the acceptance of his drawings.

We see at least two positive incentives at work here with telling effects. They are *recognition* and *feeling of success.* Both are in terms of the area of learning, expression of one's ideas on a subject. We call them positive because they say "yes" to the work accomplished. They are not only positive but intrinsic, that is, they are directly related to the area of learning. They appeal in the learner's consciousness to the very thing that is being learned. Other positive intrinsic incentives are the following: checking one's progress in number work on a progress chart, privilege to help a slower learner with his study, taking charge of a group, and arranging one's work for group exhibit.

In selecting such positive intrinsic incentives one must bear in mind the level of a child's development. It is a great incentive, for example, for a primary child to get up before the group under any circumstances. This recognition is always welcome to him. The self-conscious junior high boy who finds standing before a group uncomfortable needs another appeal. Perhaps he can serve as chairman of a group sitting down in a semi-circle. The feeling of success appeals to all groups. "Nothing succeeds like success" is an old slogan which is psychologically sound because success gives recognition, security, and satisfaction.

Positive Extrinsic Incentives. Teachers put school marks such as A or B or C on papers. Pupils are urged to work for an A or a B. Gold stars or silver stars are placed on papers or on charts behind a learner's name. That these are wholly external to the subject in hand should be clear. Such incentives are apt to take the form of goals. But we do not have schools to work for A's or for gold stars, that is, for extraneous or extrinsic goals, but for goals inherent in the subject matter. How A's in History can be transferred into love for history is a very difficult question. These are positive incentives, but not intrinsic incentives. Hence they are less desirable. When a teacher resorts to lesser incentives, he should know what he is doing and understand that real goals in learning may be far off. On the other hand, extrinsic incentives may lead to intrinsic interest. We cannot do without extrinsic incentives, but must select them with a view to cultivating intrinsic effort.

Negative Incentives. Sometimes teachers resort to punishment and failure as incentives. They are incentives when in a child's consciousness they are closely associated with the subject matter in hand. The connection must be clear or they lose their value for learning what should be learned. These we call negative incentives, for they say "no" to the learner. But to say "no" is not enough. Personality is formed by do's and yes's, not merely by don'ts and no's. Negatives cannot be eliminated from life, as we saw in connection with emotional constellations of fear and anger, but they do not build a positive line of action that forms personality. And not all pupils can profit equally from negatives. The slow learner, for example, profits little from failure. His frustration point is low. A bright learner is often challenged by momentary failure.

How to reduce trial-and-error learning

Though random behavior cannot be entirely eliminated from learning and must be reckoned with, it is disconcerting to the learner. In solving an arithmetic problem many trials at a solution may be made. Some may be almost random attempts. But a learner soon tires of such random activity unless he senses some purpose or direction in what he is doing. We therefore give the learner a key to the problem as we look for what is required, a reasonable answer. Only when a tension-toward-an-envisioned-goal is set up in the consciousness of a learner will he tolerate random activity. Making learning purposeful in the consciousness of a learner requires thorough planning of a highly skillful nature by the teacher. How to reduce random activity to a minimum by purposeful learning deserves careful study on the part of the teacher.

For questions for further study and selections for further reading, see close of chapter 17.

14

Theories of Learning: Field Theory

According to the two theories of learning which we have discussed thus far, learning is an additive process. Concepts, meanings, understandings, beliefs, appreciations, attitudes, information and skills are achieved by adding fact to fact to fact, item to item until a rational whole has been constructed. One learns to write, to read, to swim, to make friends, etc. by drilling on isolated parts which are pieced together to constitute a certain ability. The additive process of learning was common practice long before the conditioning and trial-and-error theories of learning made their appearance in books and classrooms. The theories we studied, however, tend to confirm the practice with their emphasis upon connections of stimuli and responses. The concepts of readiness and effect did nothing to challenge this practice.

Early in the experiments with animals and almost immediately in experiments with humans it became evident, however, that stimuli and responses are not isolated, independent units of behavior, but constitute integral parts of larger wholes. The total situations in which Lidell's sheep and Thorndike's cat were involved defined for them the nature of the stimulus and provoked the response. These facts became clear especially after the German psychologists Kurt Koffka and Wolfgang Koehler published their experiments with apes. Many others, among them Raymond Wheeler and George Hartmann, have been engaged in similar studies with animals and humans for more than a generation, and disclosed like facts. The German word *Gēstalt* was first used to designate this psychology: it means shape, form, or pattern. In this country *configuration* was used. Later the term *insight,* meaning sense of or feeling for pattern or perception of relationships, was employed. More recent development of this study has led to such terms as *field* and *transactionalism.* The last two terms will come up for discussion later in this chapter.

EXPERIMENTAL BASIS

Koehler describes his experiment with the behavior of a full-grown female chimpanzee named Tschego. Of the earlier career of Tschego, Koehler knew nothing. But to set the stage for observing Tschego's behavior under controlled conditions, Koehler kept her away from other animals for 1½ years. She was kept in quarters free from movable objects except straw and her blanket. She could freely observe the pranks of young apes round-about her cage.

On the occasion under study Tschego is let out of her sleeping place into the barred cage in which she spends her waking hours. Outside of her cage and beyond the reach of her long arms is placed a bunch of bananas, a much-desired objective. To one side and near the bars of the cage are placed several sticks. We see the problem. A hungry chimpanzee is confronted with food beyond her reach. The facilities for extending her reach are near at hand, within range of vision.

What does Tschego do? She first tries to reach the bananas with her arm, but in vain. After vain attempts she goes back and lies down. She gets up again, tries a second time, a third, and that for about a half hour. At the end of this period she lies down for good, having given up the effort for a bad job. She shows no further interest in the objective. As far as the sticks lying in her immediate neighborhood are concerned, they might as well not be there.

But gradually some young apes playing outside the cage in the stockade approach the objective. In a flash Tschego leaps to her feet, takes hold of a stick, pokes it through the bars holding it now in one hand, then in the other, places the stick on the farther side of the bananas, and brings them in reach. She clutches the stick much as she does her food, and is able to direct it upon the objective.

This rather simple account, which can be duplicated in more complex forms from many similar studies, is very revealing. The motive (objective) so strongly stressed by trial-and-error learning is here too. The readiness is also present, a hungry feeling. The object, bananas, took on no form of objective until the inner urge was there. And incentive was present. Tschego gave up the struggle until the young apes threatened the objective. But there is something here which was not so evident from Thorndike's studies, namely the establishing of a new organized whole when the stick became part of the total situation. This the Gestaltists call insight or perception of a relationship. Tschego did not see the stick in relationship to the bananas and her own arms until the factor of attack upon her objective was threatened by an object not strange to her but suddenly seen in relationship to her objective.

The term "insight" is a convenient word to describe the behavior of Tschego, but it does not explain what took place. Let us explore this kind of behavior a little further.

Experiments have been made with chicks that might help us. The experimenter trained chicks to feed from the darker of two gray surfaces placed before them. Having established this approach, response to the darker surface, the experimenter introduced a third surface darker than the one the chicks were trained to feed from. They had learned to avoid the lighter surface; but now the second surface, darker than the first, was lighter than the third. The chicks chose the grains on the third surface as the darkest one. The behavior of the chicks was consistent when we consider that they were responding not to a single object but to a relationship, the "darker than."

This relationship response was present in Tschego's behavior. Her adroit action of taking the stick can be explained only on this basis. Many studies of varied kinds are contained in the sources. Experiments with painted food containers, with feeding under lights of varying intensity and the like, all demonstrate the same phenomena. Koehler's own work, in which he put his apes through successive steps of increasing difficulty, are among the most extensive of such demonstrations.

THE FIELD THEORY OF LEARNING

Learning is not merely a random responding to isolated stimuli, not even in animal experience. That there are connections being made in the nervous mechanism in the form of conduction units cannot be denied. And that many futile efforts often precede insight is clear from observing learning even in humans. But to say that these wholly explain learning is to fail to penetrate beneath the surface phenomena of the very expriments on which these conclusions are based. When we observe animal behavior carefully, we conclude that what is going on in the animal cannot be described in terms of mere blundering toward a goal and the stamping in of reaction mechanisms. Gestalt studies have clearly demonstrated that a perceptual wholeness is involved in a learner's experience.

Learning is response to relationships in a perceptual field. The sense organs of the perceiver put him into contact with the field in such a way that he can respond to it. The field has external organization so that it can be perceived as a whole in the relationship of its parts. Learning, as we observe it in the above experiments, shows that the perceiver is capable of relating the parts of an external field to himself. When this stick was brought into line with the food so that the two were seen together, it became a part of the field and was picked up and used correctly. When the stick had once been used, it could be removed farther and farther away without placing it outside of the field. Perceived relationship is, therefore, an important factor in learning.

Helping a learner perceive relationships enhances understanding. Whether we look at the stimulus or at the response, we recognize that behavior cannot be understood as a summation of independent elements. The successful act is the result of integrated experience, of relating both stimuli and responses to one another as integral parts of a whole. The teacher, for example, gives a sentence in which the spelling word is correctly used. This gives the learner a context in which the word is related to a larger meaning. It gives a learner a cue to the spelling of the word. Likewise, a learner more easily recognizes the higher or lower of two tones than a tone by itself. Even few adults acquire absolute pitch.

The significance of motives as emphasized by the trial-and-error theory is reaffirmed by the insight theory, but their role is reinterpreted. Tschego saw the stick as an integral part of the hunger-bars-food field when the tension of a felt need mounted at the sight of the young apes. It is under tension of a felt need from within and a consummating object from without that the whole field is transformed into the perceived relations of integrated action. There seems to be an almost instantaneous reorganization of the perceived field. It is this sudden factor that leads the Gestaltist to speak of insight. What the original goal was not able to accomplish was effected by a further incentive. The enhancement of the incentive led to the emerging of a solution. The goal or objective is not only a mover to action but also a source of further integration when it spurs on to new solutions.

The description of what takes place in learning, according to the configurationists, is something like this:

(1) A learner perceives a situation. This means that the learner relates an externally organized field of objects to himself according to his felt needs. He organizes his perceptual field according to his expectancy on anticipation based on his felt needs.

(2) He acts, and redefines the perception as need arises and potential admits.

(3) Further action leads to extended reconstruction.

(4) Suddenly insight emerges.

It should be noted that certain factors were found to interfere with the emergence of insight:

(1) Lack of sufficient motivation. The animal may not be hungry, or only mildly so. The food may not have eye appeal.

(2) Elements in a situation may be too widely scattered. Sticks at too great a distance or behind the animal may not quickly, if at all, be brought into relationship with the object.

(3) Experience may be lacking. This was found true of younger animals, especially, that had little or no experience with manipulating objects for a purpose.

(4) Old habits may block the way of new perceptions. Animals accustomed to reacting to a given situation in a uniform way find it more difficult to make a change in the perceptual field when suddenly called upon to do so. When the concepts of pattern, configuration, insight and the like are carried over from animals to man, mental life and learning take on another form from the atomism of S-R psychologies. In contrast with connectionism we have a field psychology.

Field-theory psychologists point out that the earliest mental stages of a child are general, non-localized experiences of hunger, warmth, and pain. From these undifferentiated wholes specialized forms of experience are differentiated. These in turn become new wholes which are related with one another into larger wholes. The same principle operates which we recognized in connection with development in general, namely, undifferentiated whole — differentiation — integration. Burton describes mental development as follows:

> The first recognizable experiences are possibly those of general lightness and darkness, followed eventually by recognition of fuzzy fields of differing degrees of brightness — window areas, for instance, differentiated from wall space. Naturally, the baby has no meanings to go with these early ones. Later, large objects begin to be separated from the general undifferentiated field, but animate and inanimate objects are not for some time differentiated from each other. Eventually, the baby has actually to differentiate himself from the total field within which he lives. Whole persons, objects, events, and processes are perceived. These wholes are primary; that is, they are not composed or built up out of simple elements, but exist in their own right. With experience, and as he matures, the learner differentiates the details [parts]. These parts become wholes in their own right; and as learning proceeds, the learner becomes able to transpose these wholes into new situations. Transfer is possible . . . if learning has been truly integrative. The functions and meaning of parts is determined at any given time by the whole within which they appear.[1]

1. W. H. Burton, *The Guidance of Learning Activities* (New York: Appleton-Century-Crofts, 1952), p. 185.

The field psychologist describes mind as mental life which as un-differentiated whole involves further wholes by differentiation. The whole is primary. Understanding, concepts, beliefs, attitudes, and skills are not achieved by adding fact to fact to fact. Swimming, for example, is not learned by drilling upon isolated parts which go to constitute a complete ability. Quite on the contrary, the whole organism is put into action, and from this, drill upon parts follows. Likewise the whole is perceived in experience, be it imperfectly, be-fore the parts begin to constitute new wholes which are integrated into a more perfect whole. Think of Tschego as he sized up the situation and under tension integrated new wholes. Individuation, that is, perceiving parts as wholes, follows. Parts are related to the previously perceived whole in a new relationship. They are integrated as an enriched whole. Mind is not an entity at work assimilating facts, but a function of the organism capable of this kind of behavior.

More recently the word "transactionalism" is being used. It con-notes the dynamic wholeness of man's inner and outer experience as it centers in the phenomena of perception. For example, the sub-jective experiences evoked by a symphony are in active interrelation-ship with the external situation presented such that they together constitute an organic whole. The same holds for a vitalized learning situation in the classroom, a history lesson, for example, in which one vicariously lives the period under discussion.

Students who have done some advanced work in biology, physics, and mathematics, may recognize that the field theory has borrowed from the technical terminology of these fields. We shall not enter into this technical terminology here. But it is worthy of note that these sciences are growing closer together. There can be no objection to this as long as we recognize that the laws of physical and bio-logical behavior do not exhaust the behavior of the person. The field psychologist has much to contribute to our understanding of human development, learning, and teaching, but when he wants to explain all human behavior in terms of physical and biological laws, or of a mathematical whole, we point him to man as a person who tran-scends these laws.

DEFECTS OF THE THEORY

The main defect of the field theory of learning is that it does not recognize the radical distinction in kind between animals and human beings. Because he wishes to be "objective" and philosophical-ly unbiased, the field theorist assumes that he must explain human learning as only a more complex form of animal learning. He re-duces self-consciousness of purpose to the "insights" experienced by

Tschego. In terms of our earlier analysis, he reduces the self to a biological function of the organism.

But this is evidently not true. Though human beings have structures and functions in common with the animals, these are formed uniquely by their participation in the organically whole *person*. For example, the existence of *soul life*, with its capability to form concepts, introduces a new factor into the awareness of a perceptual field.

Analysis, synthesis, and valuing transcend perception. They are marks of distinctively human rationality. Recall, e.g., the slipknot experiment involving the child and the young chimpanzee. As we see the child transfer earlier experience to a new situation, we observe the emerging of analysis and synthesis, of rationality. Relationships enter the field of a child which fail to establish themselves in the experience of the chimpanzee.

Suppose, for another example, that we replace Koehler's chimpanzee back in his cage, but this time instead of some loose sticks we place near him a dead tree with several branches. When the young monkeys approach his bananas we can see him making futile gestures toward the fruit, but all the while ignoring the tree. Why? Because the branches of the tree are seen as part of the whole, and the bananas as part of another; he cannot analyze one part of the field, separate it off, and integrate it with another part. In contrast, a reasonably intelligent six-year-old boy would soon have broken off a branch to gain his prize.

We conclude that the field theory is an improvement over the S-R theories in doing justice to the subtleties of human learning. All of these theories are relevant to human learning at different levels, but none of them gives an account that adequately describes the learning process of a being who is created uniquely in the image of God.

WHAT MAY BE LEARNED FROM THE THEORY

(1) It is true that human learning, like animal learning, has its basis in the perceptual field. It is also true that human learning proceeds by way of differentiation and integration of parts and wholes. As we shall see later, human learning moves beyond the perceptual to the conceptual, but it never loses its anchorage in direct experience. That is why the teacher who relied wholly on words to explain dairying failed to communicate; and that is why a person who has never experienced human love will miss the heart of texts such as "God so loved the world" (John 3:16).

(2) Learning begins with wholes, however undifferentiated they may be. A seventh grader does not develop understanding of the

Revolutionary War by analyzing it into causes, battles, generals, results, etc. at the outset. Help him see the problems that arose among the colonists in their relationship to England and in their own desire for self-determination as colonies. Help them to understand what the colonists sought for themselves and how these purposes became crystallized in their thinking. Did they finally achieve what they set out to attain? What happened along the way to chart their purposes and their course   These and similar views of the whole will call for differentiation and later integration.

Whole-part-whole learning has sometimes been interpreted to mean that we can pass lightly over the part. But this is wrong. For example, when teachers got away from the a-b-c method of teaching reading, phonics was discredited. As a result youngsters read words and sentences, but could not attack a new word to pronounce it. Spelling of words was likewise neglected. A child learns to read sentences and words in context before he calls words and pronounces letters. But in the process of differentiation phonics becomes important as a tool for interpretation of a sentence and later for writing, for phonics is basic to spelling as well as to sounding a word. So, while learning is not a fact-to-fact-to-fact relationship in experience, facts must be understood and remembered.

For questions for further study and selections for further reading, see close of chapter 17.

15

Theories of Learning: Reasoning and Creative Expression

We have now discussed three theories of learning which rely strongly on animal experimentation and thus emphasize similarities between animal and human learning. We have gladly admitted that such similarities exist, and have found these theories useful in coming to an understanding of human learning; but at the same time we were disappointed in each theory insofar as it purported to be an *exhaustive* account of how a *human* being learns. For however closely he be linked to nature, man is at the same time a *unique* creation of God.

The theory to be discussed in this chapter attempts, without adopting an explicitly Christian view of man, to account for distinctively human learning. Like the ancient Greeks, proponents of this theory stress the *rationality* of man as his peculiar endowment: in a perfectly definite sense of the term, man has reason but animals do not. Unlike the Greeks, however, those who hold this theory generally do not think of reason as a separate faculty, but rather as a function of the person in his organic unity.

How does man exhibit his rationality in learning? In two ways: (1) by the solving of problems, and (2) by the creative expression of concepts.

PROBLEM SOLVING

Consider the following problem:

There are three [unmarked] pails with capacities of three, five, and eight quarts respectively. The first two are empty, the third is filled with water. The problem is to divide the liquid into two equal parts without using any facilities other than the three containers.[1]

Stop for a few moments and work out the answer. Then reflect on the *process* by which you reached it. If this theory is correct, the

1. Cole and Bruce, *Educational Psychology*, p. 489.

essential ingredients of learning have been manifested. They are:

(1) *Confrontation.* A state of affairs is met which has new and unfamiliar elements. Hence, at least momentarily, the subject interrupts his normal stream of thought and action.

(2) *Expectancy.* The problem may appear overwhelmingly difficult; if so, it will be abandoned. But more commonly the problem will be received as a challenge. Anticipation will be sharpened; the whole person will be keyed toward a solution.

(3) *Recognition.* We said earlier that the problem contains unfamiliar elements; but at the same time it must contain familiar ones, or else a solution could not even be attempted. The subject must make the terms of the problem meaningful to him by placing them into a perceptual field (e.g., the perceptual field of liquid measures). Clearly the perceptual organization effected by a problem-solver depends greatly on his past experience, his interests and needs, and on his whole life style. But unless there is a meaning-situation in which the subject as perceiver actually merges with the object to form this field, the process will be retarded or actually halted. (Recall, at this point, how perception was necessary to teach the children about dairy farming.)

(4) *Goal-oriented reflection.* This may proceed in several ways: by blind trial and error, by insights gained from imaginative contemplation of the perceptual field, or by a combination of these. At its best, however, the reflection which occurs here involves the use of *hypotheses;* a solution is proposed which has consequences, and these consequences may be tested imaginatively or actually. (E.g., the hypothesis that half the liquid will be in the first pail is easily refuted by simple arithmetic). It should be noted that thinking of this sort does not proceed by straight-forward "recipes"; it often requires ingenuity and sometimes even genius — as is illustrated historically by the introduction of major new concepts of science. It would seem clear that only human beings are capable of such problem-solving activities by goal-oriented reflection.

(5) *Conceptualization.* The result of problem-solving activity is, of course, a solution. But if his thought processes have been deliberate and purposeful, the subject has gained more than a particular solution: he has gained, as well, a richer body of concepts which have been mediated through his own perceptions and thinking activity. Hence he has better prepared himself for further learning and for communication of his present learning.

CREATIVE EXPRESSION

The process of learning, it is held, does not reach its consummation until reasoning has issued forth in creative expression. By creative is meant *authentic* with respect to the experience of the subject; the opposite to creative expression would be mere repetition of unassimilated impressions. The creative product is not merely a copy of the external situation and not merely an expression of the subject's inner impulses, but a result of their merger in the subject's experience.

REQUIREMENTS FOR CREATIVE EXPRESSION

(1) Negatively, creative expression avoids the fixed and specified pattern. This fact should discourage the teacher from insisting overmuch on formalized "recitations": when material is genuinely assimilated rather than merely memorized, its expression will take on a personal character appropriate to the learner. It is easy to stifle individual initiative, originality, and even unique special aptitudes by insisting upon wooden formulas of expression.

(2) Though a fixed pattern is to be avoided, creative expression does follow *principles* of form: (a) there must be *organization* — an integration of parts into a dynamic whole; (b) there must be *economy* — that is, succinctness, a sense of direction and focus; (c) finally, there must be *functionality* — the expression must meet the need of the student for communication, as the art production meets the felt need of the artist.

(3) Finally, the creative expression must exhibit personal integrity and genuineness. The process involved is not merely "intellectual"; the person has experienced a change, and now has an *investment* in his product. He wishes to express himself in *his* way, "as he sees it." The product is expressional rather than representational.

TECHNIQUES FOR ENCOURAGING CREATIVE EXPRESSION

(1) Activate a need for expression in the learner. The impulse must come from within, but frequently the teacher or parent can bring a certain need to conscious awareness.

(2) Encourage an atmosphere of freedom. A learner must feel that he may express himself without undue restraint. What he says and the way he says it may need much improvement, but his right to say it must not be questioned. The learner must also develop a feeling of obligation. Freedom always implies obligations, otherwise freedom becomes license and the individual cuts off his own freedom. The obligation to express oneself acceptably should be felt by the learner. Communication must be mutually satisfying.

(3) Promote a feeling of security. The learner must feel at home in a situation if he is to express himself without being threatened by a break in that relationship. One may make a greater contribution than another, but if they all count and are assured of recognition

when creative expression is attempted, effective expression is promoted. The fulfillment of primary needs must not be threatened by free and responsible expression.

(4) Encourage some improvising in the beginning stages. First attempts may be rather awkward and lack finish.

(5) Provide suggestions of improved techniques as necessary. Failure to give necessary help at the right time may encourage early frustration.

(6) Help the learner to be critical of his own product. "Am I saying what I want to say?" Self-criticism leads to self-discipline. Self-disciplined expression makes for progressive adjustment.

(7) Finally, to express oneself creatively one must have something to express that calls for resourcefulness. Hence the curriculum should provide for rich experiences, both first-hand and vicarious.

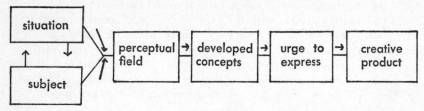

Figure X

SUMMARY OF REASONING-EXPRESSION THEORY

DEFECTS OF THE THEORY

(1) Precisely because it attempts to describe man and human learning as unique, we may press the charge of inconsistency against this theory. The presuppositions of the theory are not Christian but naturalistic; the distinctively human is explained as the composite product of biological and social influences upon the adjusting organism. But such a "this-worldly" view cannot account for the uniquely human.

(2) The theory overemphasizes creativity in the sense of subjective authenticity, and thus does not take sufficient account of objective standards and norms. Creative expression according to the aforementioned principles is good, so far forth; but unless it proceeds according to the divinely-ordained norms of truth, beauty, and moral goodness it fails to cohere with reality as it truly is.

(3) There is more to learning than problem-solving, though life does often seem to be one problem after another. The problem-solving approach, when overemphasized, tends to make of education a training in "know-how" rather than a pathway to the truth of God.

WHAT MAY BE LEARNED FROM THE THEORY

(1) First of all it must be said that this theory fills a gap left by the theories of conditioning, trial-and-error, and field relationship. A person's ability to penetrate a situation in thought and form generalizations or concepts, and subsequently to give expression to his thinking meaningfully and resourcefully, so that communication is effected, these are not adequately comprehended by the other theories. Reasoning and creative expression cannot be explained in terms of neural connections or organized wholes of field relationships in experience. In conceptualizing we recognize a soul-function in operation that transcends categories comprised by previous discussions.

(2) The theory of reasoning and creative expression helps us get a clearer understanding of how learning takes place by pointing out how a person conceptualizes. Reasoning is a process of relating concepts into meaningful organic wholes. This is possible because concepts are not abstractions, but have a perceptual basis in experience. A learner is to develop concepts from perceptual fields, give expression to his experience meaningfully, and through expression enrich his conceptualizing. A major task of the school is the organization of a body of concepts. For example, as the facts of history are interrelated into a perceptual field the learner forms concepts which become his tools of interpretation for further facts and relationships. Learning is a process of conceptualizing. The teaching process in school is to be focused upon conceptualizing and creative expression. Learning is not transmitted by verbalization, but developed by directing the conceptualizing process.

(3) This theory correctly points to creative expression as an integral phase of learning. We have seen how representational expression and creative expression differ. The former will not suffice, for it is no more than a reproduction of unassimilated impressions. To be genuine, expression with integrity must be more than representational; it must be the expression of the person, it must be creative. Schools and teaching should cultivate creative expression to be educative.

For questions for further study and selections for further reading, see close of chapter 17.

16

Theories of Learning: A Christian View

RECAPITULATION

We have now considered four theories of learning. Of each of them we may say that while it brings out important facets of the learning process, as a *total* theory it is an oversimplification which could lead to a one-sided and unbalanced teaching approach. Let us first develop the latter point.

OVEREMPHASIS OF A SINGLE TEACHING METHOD

We all recognize that one must use certain theoretical concepts to describe learning. In any scientific theory it is important to use as few such concepts as possible. Then everything else is explained in terms of these concepts. All theories agree, however, that learning is a complex process, and no few terms and principles adequately describe learning. Learning theories which fail to take into account the true nature of man are bound to oversimplify. Man is much more complex than known methods of scientific investigation can disclose. Therefore, only a learning theory which takes as its basic principle man as religious being, according to the Scriptures, can rightly interpret observed facts of the learning process.

We might take the overemphasis on exercise as an illustration. "Practice makes perfect" or "what is practiced is learned," it was thought. But when practice becomes monotonous drill, pupils rebel. And when other undesirable or distasteful consequences follow practice, practice likewise results in the very opposite, a learning to avoid what is being practiced. Practice must end in goals meaningful to learners and be constructively helpful in meeting felt needs. If a pupil understands what he is doing and can interpret the process as he goes along, need for drill is reduced greatly. Grasping meaning, rather than drill, is the key to learning, though practice or repetition has its place when carried on in meaningful situations.

The same may be said about reward and punishment as "reinforcement" of learning. They have their place, but are woefully inadequate in developing meaning in learning. They may tell pupils what to avoid, but not why to do so. As a matter of fact punishment may have the opposite effect, as in a spelling bee. Sitting down as punishment for making an error may prove very satisfying. A pupil may feel relieved that he is no longer "on the spot."

Again, problem solving is an excellent technique in many learning situations, but it does not serve the purpose of all learning. Drill is very necessary for fixing knowledge. Merely securing a right soultion is not sufficient to retain the necessary facts and their relations, or to achieve the necessary skills.

INSIGHTS GAINED FROM THE PRECEDING THEORIES

Though learning is not *simply* what any of these theories proclaim it to be, nevertheless a satisfactory overall view of learning will incorporate many insights which these theories have severally contributed. We have noted these insights as we went along; now, as a summary, we will list them together as a set of propositions about learning.

(1) All learning involves the *connecting* or *associating* of experiences.

(2) Learning is essentially an *activity* of the *learner*.

(3) Learning presupposes a measure of *freedom* for the learner.

(4) Learning depends upon the existence and character of the learner's *motivation*.

(5) The learner must be allowed to make a certain number of *errors*.

(6) *Incentives* expedite learning.

(7) Relevance to the learner's *present interests* expedites learning.

(8) The feeling of *success* expedites learning.

(9) Learning is promoted by the feeling of *social acceptance*.

(10) All learned concepts are derived ultimately from the *perceptual field*.

(11) Learning proceeds by the *discernment of general relationships* within the perceptual field.

(12) The formation of useful concepts is a *dynamic process;* hence a major function of the school is to develop a graduated body of concepts in the various learning units.

(13) As the learner develops meaningful concepts, he spontaneously *expresses* them in communication.

A RE-EXAMINATION OF THE LEARNING PROCESS

Three classroom situations

Miss Jones is about to start a unit of work that leads up to a proper celebration of Thanksgiving Day. She is teaching a fourth grade. As approach to the study she brings to class a large print of the painting "The Pilgrims Going to Church." We have all seen it and recall the setting and the figures. In questioning about the scene, Miss Jones draws out a discussion about Indians, log cabins, desolate country, and the Pilgrims leaving their homes to find refuge in a strange land.

Compare this with a similar scene in a kindergarten. Miss Hayes uses the same print to draw out a discussion. But what does she hear? Such words as hunting, shooting, long skirts, big hats, and turkey.

Now let us look in on Mr. Smith's ninth grade history class. He too uses the Pilgrim scene, but this time to develop ideas pertaining to early colonization of American shores. What response does he get to questions based on the print? We hear the words persecution, religious freedom, Mayflower Compact, stockade, ravages of disease, starvation, and massacre. Some feeling for the plight of the persecuted and their attainment of freedom comes into evidence.

Why the varied responses to the same scene? The external situation shown by the print is the same. But each group approaches the situation with a different set or expectancy. As the learners and the external situation merge, varying perceptual fields emerge because of the difference of set.

Concepts expressed vary according to the understanding that the perceptual organization makes possible. The ninth graders have gone a long way to enrich their perceptual field in comparison with the fourth graders, and the fourth graders in comparison with the kindergartners. The kindergartner thinks of shooting and hunting when he sees a man with a gun; to him it is an isolated experience. The fourth grader talks of Indians trying to kill the Pilgrims. The ninth grader discusses the desire to worship and to protect one's family from marauding Indians. The graduated bodies of concepts vary greatly because perceptual fields vary in organization and in content. Each group views the scene in the degree of enrichment of his personality. A unity within enables him to approach the situation with a feeling of security, and a unity in external relationships helps him extend himself further in a broader area of relationships.

If Miss Hayes expects to develop a feeling of genuine Thanksgiving from a historical situation, she will have to begin with what a kindergartner can see in the scene and associate with it. Mr. Smith finds a historical continuity of facts and events in the experience of ninth graders that have given them a body of concepts as a basis for interpretation. Persecution, freedom of worship, frontier, etc., have a perceptual significance for ninth graders. If Miss Hayes or even Miss Jones should talk about persecution with some feeling, she would be leading a child into a territory so strange that it may affect her pupils as Jackie was affected by has father's sermon. They may develop irrational fears and prejudices.

WHAT ACTUALLY TAKES PLACE IN LEARNING

The act of learning may be viewed as a journey into the unknown. The learner is called upon to enter new territory more or less resembling territory of his acquaintance and in which he has come to move and order his way with a large degree of security. The novelty of a new experience is always challenging. The developmental urge in its indigenous motivation is a self-starter to action. Random trial-and-error movements may be the first evidence of this motivation. But the unfamiliar also holds the threats of the unexpected. The learner must be able to handle himself in the new situation. When he can order his way with a reasonable feeling of security, he will continue his exploration. When he can maintain himself no longer because primary needs are threatened, however, he begins to feel frustrated and develops a feeling of hostility toward the situation as a whole. In the face of mounting threats to his security, a learner does one of these things (which we all do in similar situations) : he violently attacks the situation to make himself feel momentarily that he is master of it, or he tries to circumvent the problem in a felt need for self-defense, or he pauses, analyzes, and reorganizes himself and the situation in which he is involved. In learning, a person is asked to extend himself in the dimensions of his personality into an external situation. If he fails to understand his going, he feels as threatened as one who journeys in a strange land. He begins to wander around, and when pressed for action he does one of the three things mentioned.

Developmentally speaking, what actually takes place when a child learns? A child extends himself in his organic unity into an external situation. His anticipation and expectancy will determine how he will view the situation into which he enters. His view of things in relation to himself will determine his feeling of security or insecurity. The degree of security with which he seeks to organize the merged field of self-and-the-external-situation, will determine what he does about it. If in the exploratory merger he is threatened, that is, primary needs are not met, he will run away from or circumvent the situation. He may also make violent attack upon the source or what he considers to be the source of his problem. If, however, the merger creates a feeling of security, though challenging, he accepts it and truth is disclosed that forms him in his personality. In any case he learns, whether it be to formulate a satisfying goal of escape, or the satisfying experience of positive achievement along lines indicated. A developing child always learns, even in his escapes. He is an indefatigible learner. What he learns in the merger of self and a situation is our concern in teaching.

Descriptively this is what takes place in learning. We don't say that this is what ought or ought not to take place in learning. There is no ought involved here. It represents our best contemporary understanding of what actually occurs.

As Christians we remind ourselves of the fact that a child is a religious being and that human learning as we described it is the learning process of a religious being. The Scriptures tell us, and we see it evidenced in human life, that the religious being, made in the image of God, finds his final and deepest security in what he feels to be true. Notice that we say what he *feels* to be true. This is said advisedly. As rational-moral-social-aesthetic-free-responsible person a learner merges with a situation in understanding. As he forms concepts truth is disclosed to him which he relates to himself. It is a primary need of every learner to commit himself to truth when he can embrace it as relevant to himself. Truth understood in relation to felt needs cultivates a feeling-tone of identity, of being one-with. Truth felt is accepted as that to which one surrenders for control. It is in this surrender that one's personality is formed.

ACCEPTANCE OF TRUTH: THE CENTER OF LEARNING

It should be clear that the learning of a person as religious being is essentially a coming to grips with truth. To what one feels to be true about an object presented for understanding, he gives his allegiance. Truth is disclosed to the person as he forms concepts from a perceptual experience and as concepts merge with other concepts to develop more inclusive and extended concepts. It is of the essence of the religious being to feel secure in the presence of what he can accept as true. This forms him. This shapes him as a personality.

The root of "good behavior," or in scriptural language, of living in this world in heavenly places in Christ Jesus, is the acceptance of truth as revealed to us in the Word and in the work of God. "If pupils say what they should when a teacher asks a question but do not change their behavior outside of the class, the school has not improved a pupil's adjustment to the world," according to Cronbach.[1]

1. Cronbach, *Educational Psychology,* p. 40.

One might object to Cronbach, "But it might make a difference later." Cronbach would reply, and rightly so, that the change then came because in a later situation the adjustment was made as he grasped the meaning of a situation. A person's values determine which of many answers to a problem he regards as best. And values are geared to truth that we have come to understand and accept.

The Christian embraces the value system of the Christian faith, because faith is knowledge (grasping of meaning) and trust. His values do not shift. They remain constant. How to make constant values relevant to the flux of life, however, is and remains a major problem in education and in all human development. Our pioneer forefathers, for example, prized independence and self-reliance. And well they might. The freedom and initiative that motivated them should ever be sought and retained. But today we are more in need of cooperation because we are economically so dependent upon one another. The shift is one of emphasis, not of values.

Only a teaching process that recognizes the need for understanding or grasping meaning as a key to learning and that discloses truth to the consciousness of the learner can develop a value system for the person by which to order his life.

The learning process is essentially the same for all situations. There is only one kind of learning in the sense that we have viewed it. The facts of the learning process are the same for all learners, in all situations. And lives are changed, personalities are formed only as truth is disclosed to a learner's consciousness and accepted in his heart.

KINDS OF LEARNING

The fact that ultimately there is only one kind of learning should not keep us from making some important distinctions in learning according to the dimensions of the personality. So we may speak of four kinds of learning: cognitive, memorizing and rational; motor; social; and emotional. Let us consider each in the order listed. They correspond to the areas of human personality development.

COGNITIVE LEARNING

Cognitive learning has reference to the learning that goes on in the knowing dimensions of life. It is generally known as intellectual learning. There is no objection to this terminology as long as we remember what intelligence is. There is abstract intelligence, mechanical intelligence, and also social intelligence, as we saw earlier in our study. To avoid confusion on this score we shall speak of cognitive learning.

Both memorizing and thinking are cognitive forms of learning. We memorize in order to deal with a future challenge. It may be for momentary and immediate recall, as when we "learn" a telephone number or a house number. It may be to recall names of certain persons one meets at a party. Some students memorize notes dictated by a professor, expecting that in an announced test or examination the questions will be based on these notes. Pupils are taught arithmetic and mathematics by formula, trusting that the memorized formula will help them know arithmetic or mathematics. And to be sure, in many cases learning in school and in college amounts to little more than passing tests rather than thinking through a body of evidence.

There is, of course, a place for memorizing, both rote memory for immediate recall, and a more logical memory by which meaningful material is retained. But in all memorizing, insight, a grasping of meaning or understanding, is a potent factor. For momentary recall of a telephone number or house number little insight is needed. Mere repetition may do it. But when several numbers, or lines of literature, or dates are involved, meaningful associations facilitate memory more than mere repetition. The best way to memorize for longer retention is to think through or structurize the material to be memorized.

Cognitive learning consists largely of thinking or reasoning. If we mean by thinking the relating of parts to a whole for anticipated results, we find evidence of it in animal life. Animals can show amazing insights. But if we mean the ability to reflect upon one's past experience in order to select approaches to a present situation, and to reflect upon their present relationships with anticipated results, yes, even to experience anticipated results vicariously, then we are thinking of a process distinctively human. And this is what we mean by thinking or reasoning. It is given man as religious being to form concepts and by conceptualizing to ferret out truth. And he can take abstract ideas and relate them to his way of life and gain new meaning for his experience. This is cognitive learning.

We recognize at once that cognitive learning is one of the supreme functions of the school. The school is established to organize and guide cognitive learning. We should think of the curriculum as a storehouse of concepts for thinking, and the school as a workshop where young people learn to use these concepts to ferret out truth. A learner gains insight into truth by understanding and using concepts employed in the curriculum. Mere abstract concepts memorized for recall do not form the personality. One "knows" mathematics, for example, only when one understands the concepts employed as insights into truth. Guided by these concepts, the learner ferrets out truth as a discipline for the forming of his personality. Likewise to "know" United States history is to have acquired a body of meaningful concepts to guide the learner toward disciplined judgments.

In general, then, one "knows" a subject when he has acquired a meaningful body of concepts (understanding) that help him ferret out truth for self-discipline. A concept is a generalization, based on perceptions of various kinds, that one can bring to bear on many situations, e.g., multiplication, industrial revolution, providence of God, and redemption.

The formation of concepts is a dynamic process, as we emphasized before. One forms concepts in dealing with situations he wants to deal with, and trying to find out how to manage situations. To understand a concept is to be able to use it. Words can be very deceptive. As a matter of fact words do not constitute concepts to a person unless they are meaningfully related to his experience. Think of what Jackie experienced in response to his daddy's sermon. We do not learn merely by verbalization, yet words are important. Words define and relate meanings in thinking, and enable one to manipulate meanings, once those meanings have been acquired. The learner grasps meanings best when he is able to work with numerous simple illustrations and applications.

If the formation of concepts is a dynamic process of grasping meaning, not a memoritor process, it follows that subjects should be taught with a challenge to inquiry rather than as a memorizing of abstractions. History, for example, is not to be taught as a body of facts to be "learned by heart," but as a body of meanings consisting of insights and interpretations that bear on felt needs in thinking, valuing, and action. Then facts are related in meaningful relationships. And meaningful material needs very little repetition for retention. It can be reviewed in other meaningful situations leading to new understandings.

The acquisition of concepts as a dynamic process is of central importance to all learning and teaching, for in conceptualizing the learner comes to grips with truth. As truth is ferreted out for acceptance personality is formed. Most of what children should get out of their studies therefore, is made up of concepts.

MOTOR LEARNING

Motor learning is essentially the finding of a way to meet a situation by co-ordinated movement. It involves largely the body mechanism. Typing, handwriting, driving a car, and the like are largely of this type. Practice or repetition will have to establish the responses necessary in the successive movements. In the development of these skills understanding can facilitate right action. Explanation of how a mechanism (a car, for example) operates will   facilitate one's manipulation of it. When skills have been acquired, thinking about them will interfere with their operation. Walking, for example, is automatic until we think which foot comes first. But in the development of motor learning the grasping of meaning can be important.

SOCIAL LEARNING

The force of the social in human life is great, as we saw, for man as religious being is social. Social learning consists largely of the acceptance of models which give the learner the prospect of successful and acceptable ways of living. It, too, starts with a challenge based on felt needs. No one can go through life successfully without a feeling of acceptance by the group of which he is a part. Parents, teachers, pastors, group leaders in scouting, and the like are prestige-endowed for the younger. Their very actions as successful persons become models for youth in trying to meet their problems. Here too the grasping of meaning is the key to effective learning. The interpretation a youth places upon his chosen model or models in relation to his own felt needs will be determinative in his actions. Teaching, then, is not merely a setting of good examples for children, but also helping youth interpret their own needs aright.

EMOTIONAL LEARNING

We have seen that we should think of emotional life in terms of constellations. We do not define emotional life by pointing to apparently isolated emotional experiences such as fear, hope, hate, and surprise. Emotions are woven into the warp and woof of life to the extent that the demarcation of feelings, emotions, and moods only leads to confusion. There are dominant patterns in our emotional life. They are the constellations of love, fear, and anger. The predominance of one or the other determines how we feel about our experiences and what attitude to them we are going to adopt. Being woven into the warp and woof of life, emotional constellations are affected by the grasping of meaning and in turn affect meanings.

Emotional learning, like emotional life itself, is a very complicated and elusive kind of thing. When we speak of cognitive learning, motor learning, and social learning we can point to some definite object of apprehension. Not so in emotional learning. It can better be understood as an integral part of all learning in the sense that it qualifies all learning.

Emotional life is important in learning. We seek not only insight into truth for the forming of personality, but also acceptance of it. Learning finally is heart acceptance. This kind of acceptance comes through feeling for truth and against error or falsehood. The grasping of meaning is never without a feeling-tone. The understanding of what a given task involves, for example, will fill the thought of one with delightful anticipation, but of another with a crippling anxiety. The external situations are the same, the varying aspects are related in the same way and lead to similar concepts, but the personality fields differ because of the past experience of the persons involved. Learning will take a different course in each case. What presents a challenge to one constitutes a threat to the other.

What, then, is emotional learning? It commences with a challenge based on felt needs, as does all learning. As these needs attain meaningful direction toward anticipated ends or goals that can prove satisfying, the love constellation is at work and generates a feeling of security. In the context of a feeling of security the constellations of fear and anger are not eradicated, but they find their sthenic, supporting, place. Authority is accepted without threatening anxiety, for it spells out kindness and warmth of personal interest. Thwarting is accepted as a momentary deviation rather than a threat to one's feeling of independence. Learning which has challenging goals and develops meaningful material in the attainment of these goals calls forth zest and enthusiasm. The entire learning process, in other words, becomes good emotional learning.

The very opposite can likewise become the case. An external situation may fail to activate needs in the life of a learner, other than the feeling to get this over with as soon as possible, or escape it if one can. It may be a drab routine of duty. The constellations of fear and rage take on greater proportions. A feeling of guilt may further complicate matters. There may be external conforming to escape consequences, but this gives no abiding satisfaction. This too is emotional learning. But truth is distorted and rationalization will strengthen error and falsehood.

SUMMARY

When proper learning is seen as a unified progress on all these fronts, classroom procedure will take on a vitality which turns formal learning into dynamic living. The whole teaching process takes on a vigor which enlists a learner's indigenous motivation. For, we repeat, a child is an indefatigable learner. He would rather learn than do anything else. His developmental urge is the drive in all learning. The teacher, however, must understand how to direct the process to right ends.

Let no teacher say, "It cannot be done." It has been done. It is being done. And many are learning more about doing it every day. One may conclude "I cannot do it." This is a different matter. We will discuss barriers in a teacher's personality later.

THE CHRISTIAN SCHOOL AS A SETTING FOR LEARNING

In an earlier discussion we set forth three "givens" in relation to which the learning process takes place. They are the self-active subject, the goal, and the medium (i.e., the subject matter). In Christian education the learner is viewed as a child in Christ, the goal is formed personality as a son of God, and the body of subject matter is the learning material appropriate to the subject and the goal. Now the question is, how does the learning process we discussed and summarized function in this setting?

(1) A learner comes to school as a religious being, more specifically as a child in Christ. Of the former we are certain, for this is the very nature of a human being. His entire development has been that of a religious being. The second we assume on the ground of Scripture. Children of believing parents have the promise that their children are holy, they are the Lord's, they are children of the covenant promise. Parents send them to the Christian school to comply with their covenant obligation and their promise at baptism to secure the help needed for Christian instruction. The learner comes to school in the developmental pattern or design characteristic of him in his life style. The life style is in general that of a Christian home in the culture and civilization which in general is Western, and more specifically American. The developmental pattern is individualized within this broad frame of reference. The primary needs, developmentally speaking, are those of a child developing to maturity. The secondary needs are those of his developmental pattern and level and of his life style generally.

(2) The school presents an external situation in the organized activity taken from our culture and civilization appropriate for the maturing of a child in Christ. There is an educational program appropriate for a child in Christ. To nurture a child in Christ on an educational program appropriate for a child not in Christ is to malnourish a child in Christ. For a child in Christ all education will ultimately nourish him as a Christian, but in the process he is nurtured on an inadequate and poorly balanced diet. Balanced development can hardly result. The Christian school selects and organizes subject matter as appropriate for the nurture of a child in Christ.

(3) The learner motivated by directional process goals extends himself into the school program, selected and organized for a child in Christ in keeping with child development. Developmental levels and developmental patterns of children spell out basic needs. Directional process goals seek to satisfy these needs. Learning has its motivation in this source. Mursell has said this well for secular education: "All in all," he states, "it should be clear that the practical problem of motivation in school is not a problem of small tricks, pleasing devices, and

amusing antics. On the contrary, it is the problem of organizing all school activities, both in and out of the classroom, as the agencies for the satisfaction of basic needs."[2]

Indeed, when school work is organized in such a way that it satisfies basic needs, and opens up compelling goals through experiencing success, it tends to develop integrated personality.

(4) In learning activities the learner conceptualizes in the perceptual field of experience and relates the concepts he forms. In forming and in relating concepts, truths are formulated in his understanding and related to larger areas of truth.

(5) The truths a learner understandingly relates to his needs acquire for him a feeling tone of necessity and moral obligation. In this feeling tone the will-function is given direction and purpose. He exercises self-discipline (obedience) according to the goals he accepts for himself and is formed in his personality by this acceptance.

(6) As religious being motivated in the renewal of his person and forming personality, he expresses himself with integrity and in accepted form.

This is education of a child in Christ in a Christian school. Perhaps some would suggest that we should say "ought to be." Both are true. As we approximate this education we have better Christian schools.

For questions for further study and selections for further reading, see close of chapter 17.

2. Mursell, *Psychology for Modern Education*, pp. 61-62.

17

Transfer of Learning

THE MEANING AND IMPORTANCE OF TRANSFER

"Transfer of learning" is an academic term for the "carry-over" effect of past learning on present behavior. Did the courtesy of the fifth grade youngsters to their visitor in the classroom have an effect on their manners on the playground and at home? Does the "A" on a sheet of three dozen arithmetic problems guarantee that the child will know how to make change for a dollar? After the student has "learned" correct English usage in school, does he let it modify his speech and writing out of school?

Not necessarily. It often appears that learning makes no real difference at all. Consider, e.g., the story of the fifth grader who had the habit of saying "I have went" instead of "I have gone." The teacher had drilled the right usage in exercise upon exercise, but in this lad's writing the form "have went" occurred again and again. At a loss what to do, the teacher said to Harold one day, "I am going to get you over that mistake if it's the last thing I do. This afternoon you stay after school and write 'I have gone' five hundred times." (Is repetition the mother of learning?) Harold commenced his strenuous task ardently at 3:30 P.M. He wrote "I" five hundred times in one column; then "have" five hundred times. At five o'clock he was well on his way with "gone". The teacher, eager to go home, said, "Harold, when you finish, you place your paper on my desk. I'll find it in the morning." Harold finished at about 5:30. Wanting to be courteous, he wrote a little note at the bottom of the last sheet (he filled several). This is what he wrote. "Dear teacher. I have write I have gone 500 times and now I have went home."

No one would disagree that there had been a failure of learning here — or, for that matter, in any case where transfer is utterly lacking. Our whole foregoing discussion of learning leads us to believe that transfer is an index of learning: if learning is the genuine article, it *will* make an impact on behavior outside of the immediate situation where it was gained.

It follows that transfer is an important concept in the theory of learning. The teacher will wish to understand how it works, the best means for effecting it, and the degree of success he may reasonably expect. To assist us in answering these questions, we have the benefit of extensive empirical studies made in the past few decades[1] and several theories which attempt to explain them.

THEORIES OF TRANSFER

FORMAL DISCIPLINE

The theory of formal discipline arises primarily out of a philosophical doctrine of the human soul rather than experimental studies. This doctrine, which originated with the Greeks and was reinforced by 17th century dualists such as Descartes, teaches that the soul is an entity which has parts, called faculties. Traditionally there are three such faculties, viz., reason, emotions, and will, though some suggested the addition of imagination, memory, and the like. A person thinks with his reason, decides with his will, and mourns or delights with his emotions.

According to this theory, learning is the exercise of each faculty according to its way of functioning. Intellectual learning means to take in facts and ideas and to exercise the mind in the use of them. Volitional learning means to take on difficult tasks and exercise the willpower in performing them. The more distasteful the exercise the more willpower is required, so difficult and distasteful performance has the greater merit.

And what happens to one's view of transfer of learning on this basis? If the influence of past experience on present behavior is governed by the strength of a given faculty, then exercise of the faculty is primary. Power of thought and power of will are primary, and the what in learning is determined by its capacity to strengthen these powers. So Plato chose for the motto of his Academy, "Let none ignorant of geometry enter here," for he believed that geometry particularly trained the mind and the disposition for the study of philosophy. Medieval educators held that grammar, rhetoric, and dialectic (logic) were a necessary groundwork for the study of theology. If the intellect can handle difficult problems in mathematics, it can do so in international relations, for mathematics provides the intellect exercise in certain forms. We hear it argued today that we must develop critical thinking by studying "ten great books" and asking questions.

1. For accounts of some of these studies, see References at end of this chapter.

It is this theory that filled arithmetic books with problems in mental gymnastics, spelling books with "jaw-breakers," history books with dates and battles, geography books with states, provinces, capitols, rivers, and products.

But is this theory a true description of the effect of past experience on present behavior? Education as a process assumes the fact of transfer of learning. We have argued all along in our discussion, both in human development and in this section on learning, that a child's learning in one situation makes a difference in the next situation. But how does it take place, and what is the nature of it? Does formal or mental discipline describe it? The difficulty is with the first concept, that the mind or soul is an entity. The second concept, that the mind is compartmentalized into faculties, is a further difficulty.

The truth about transfer of learning should be understood in another framework of reference. We think of the person as an organic unity in which the spirit as life principle is infused in a psychophysical structure. There are physiological, emotional, social, and knowing dimensions to the functioning of the person, but every dimension involves the whole person. Past experience and its effect upon present behavior should be viewed in functioning of the person as organic unity. Knowing, feeling, and willing are not to be thought of as faculties or powers, but as names designating functions operating in certain ways.

IDENTICAL ELEMENTS

The identical elements theory has its origin in Thorndike's and others' quantitative theories of behavior. Recall that Thorndike thought of mind not as an entity, but as a quantitative accumulation of S-R bonds in the nervous system. In this, as we saw, Thorndike was interpreting the earlier association theory of human experience in terms of the physical structure of the body. For every response there is a stimulus. The same or similar stimuli produce the same or similar responses. Past experience is deposited in the nervous system as connections among neurones, and it takes certain stimuli to activate a chain of connections to produce certain responses. Every learning situation involves a set of stimuli that activate responses. The learning process consists of seeking desired responses to given stimuli, or achieving certain S-R bonds. Learning situations resemble one another as far as anticipated behavior is concerned in that they involve similar or dissimilar sets of S-R bonds. Suppose learning situation A involves S-R bonds a-b-c-d-e-f-g. Learning situation B involves bonds c-d-e-f-g-h-i-j. Learning situations A and B have bonds c-d-e-f-g in common. Now if a learner is carried from situation A to situation B, he encounters familiar experiences c-d-e-f-g. The new experiences will be h-i-j. It can be expected that he can use bonds c-d-e-f-g in a new situation when he sets out to learn bonds h-i-j.

We might think of this sort of thing taking place in column addition. Addition of a single column has similarities to two- or three-column addition. Hence, single-column addition transfers to two-column addition in accordance with identical S-R bonds involved. The same holds for the study of English grammar and English usage, Latin and English, geographic facts and principles from one continent to another, and citizenship in the classroom and that in the community at large. That there are identical elements involved goes without saying, but that these explain transfer is another matter.

The principle of transfer of learning was understood in terms of identical elements for some time. Transfer is determined by similarities or dissimilarities of the stimuli evoking responses, it was thought. What a child learns in school carries over into life according to the elements identical between school situation and community living. The theory appeared promising enough so that several textbooks and learning exercises were organized to take care of similarities and dissimilarities of previous learning and present learning, and of school and life. Continuity of learning was sought in this fashion.

The following statement presents a challenge to this theory:

> Some time ago habit training was introduced into prisons on the assumption that good habits make good citizens. The prisoners were taught hygienic habits, vocational habits, and were paid wages that they were forced to share with their families. During a long period of incarceration the prisoner received an impressive amount of such habit training, which was designed in such a way that identical elements outside the prison should cause these salutary habits to function when the prisoner was freed . . . . The policy did not work out. The study of S. and E. T. Gulick shows that eighty percent of the men discharged from a reformatory where many approved methods of habit training were in use, were not reformed five to fifteen years later, but continued in their course of crime. The gradual training of habits and reconditioning, with reliance upon identical elements within and without prison walls to effect the transfer, produced few reformations, if any at all. To the prisoner with a dominant anti-social outlook, or other antagonistic traits, such habit training is worthless, for he is in no frame of mind to put it to use. On the other hand, in those rare cases where dominant attitudes and goals are altered, habit training is of secondary importance. The reformed prisoner will find ways of learning to live more hygienically, of taking care of his family, of fulfilling his responsibilities, provided only that his interests

and ideals are altered. And they are not altered by mere routine drill.[2]

The theory of identical elements has all the weaknesses of the conditioning and trial-and-error learning theories which we summed up as being mechanistic and atomistic. The quotation from Allport should indicate that we are not dealing primarily with a quantitative kind of thing in experience, but with the functioning of a unity of being. When a child attacks a new arithmetic problem by analyzing its component parts as given, required, and process of solution, then anticipates possible mistakes and even estimates his answers, or when he in imagination creates for himself a situation which further concretizes the problem, drawing a figure, for example; when a learner does this we see how a mechanistic-atomistic S-R bond theory of any kind breaks down as descriptive of what takes place in his experience. Especially when we consider that the learner is a person, and that a person learns by understanding and appropriating truth or alleged truth as a forming power in his personality, the identical element theory is worthless. This does not mean that similar behavior patterns are not involved. Our study of the perceptual field and the forming of concepts has amply demonstrated that they are involved. But as "the reformed prisoner will find ways of learning . . . provided only that his interests and ideals are altered," so behavior patterns as S-R bonds or any other structural units in the organism are subordinate to who the learner is in the organic unity of his being.

But how far are we in school practice removed from the identical elements theory? May we not say that with a few changes of words here and there, the statement of Allport applies to much learning and teaching in school? Let us raise the question in the words of Mursell:

> We want to produce thinking people. Science, mathematics, and history contain a great deal of the stuff with which people think; and without available material people will never think very much or very well. Quite true! But we set up learning experiences in science, history, and mathematics which emphasize the memorization of content and perhaps introduce some "thought questions" and "original problems" which are nothing but empty verbal puzzles.
>
> We want to produce people who have a wide range of living interests. Literature, music, and art can be priceless lifelong interests. True again! But we teach the historical framework of literature and only the techniques and abstract fundamentals

2. G. W. Allport, *Personality: A Psychological Interpretation* (New York: Henry Holt, 1937), p. 263.

of music and art. We want our young people to develop an integrating philosophy of life. Every subject in the curriculum can contribute to and reflect upon such a philosophy. But we organize the learning of sheer memory content. We want children to adhere to normal social conventions, among which presumably is neatness. So we drill them on being neat in their paper work. We want the various subjects in the curriculum to bear upon one another, so we set up comprehensive survey courses in which little bits of various subjects are put together in an arbitrary way that we find convenient. We rely, that is to say, on identical elements. But good people, good citizens, strong and effective personalities are not developed by such procedures.[3]

How do we develop thinking people, strong and effective personalities, good citizens, and the like? We have tried to answer this question in the chapters which preceded. But the identical element theory cannot explain the transfer of learning that takes place in genuine learning.

GENERALIZATION OF EXPERIENCE

There is a third theory of transfer of learning more commonly accepted among students of the psychology of learning today. It is not associated with a single school of psychology. Several physiologically oriented psychologists subscribe to this theory, as well as do the more organismic and dynamic groups. Few question the fact of generalization, but they would explain the basis for generalization differently. For our purpose it is enough to state what is generally meant by generalization of experience.

Perhaps we can best understand this theory by referring back to our discussion of the thinking-creative expression theory of learning. We learned that man can conceptualize, that is, generalize his perceptual experience and with the concepts achieved go on to further generalization for new concepts. Concepts become a part of the mental structure and function as attitudes, ideas, and ideals. The reformed prisoner, spoken of above, has developed concepts of hygiene, responsibility, workmanship and the like that become generalized in his experience as interests and ideals; they become goals in his life. He now goes about finding ways of realizing these goals. The concept of addition has been developed in the second grade, say. This means that the process of addition in the perceptual experience has been generalized. Column addition, addition of fractions, etc. are further steps in the generalization. Addition as a concept now begins to stand for a process of accumulation. Or, again, the concept "noun"

3. Mursell, *Psychology for Modern Education*, pp. 299-300.

is arrived at by experiencing places, persons, and things. Once having generalized his experience, he can use the concept "noun" in Latin, French, etc. as well as in English. Do we want courtesy of the classroom to carry over into life? Then we must help the child to generalize it into a concept of ideal living. Generalize classroom experiences into attitudes and ideals and they will affect behavior everywhere.

What actually takes place in the structure of the person as he generalizes his experience, and thereby directs subsequent behavior, is a debatable question for psychologists. He does generalize, and the recognition of this constitutes a major contribution to the psychological studies of our time. "Caesar crossed the Rubicon" may be learned as an historical fact or merely as sounds to be repeated. It will change behavior as it is applied to similar situations in the learner's experience and he generalizes the expression into an attitude, interest, or ideal.

Several things follow from the principle or theory of generalization. Motivation and insight are potent factors in generalization. We are more apt to generalize our experiences into attitudes and ideals when we have a measure of understanding of them and seek them for a purpose. Then too, improved methods of learning have a salutary effect upon one's power to retain. Practice itself accomplishes little along this line, but content understood and earnestly sought will reduce need for practice and make needed practice effective.

We recognize that with this theory we are much closer to a right understanding of how learning in one situation carries over to another. As in the thinking-creative expression theory of learning we encountered a distinctively human way of learning, so here in the generalized experience theory of transfer. It recognizes the unity of the human being as a fact and sees all function as an expression of the whole being. But as Christians we cannot rest in this account of the transfer of learning. We are not merely interested in the organismic unity that makes generalization possible. We see in man a son of God, and this view requires another account.

TRANSFER IN CHRISTIAN PSYCHOLOGY

The generalized experience theory is perhaps the best we can expect from a secular psychology. One wonders whether the generalization spoken of doesn't go beyond what an organismic energy system of secular psychology can really allow. Here, as in connection with the thinking-creative expression theory of learning, secular psychology speaks of man as though he is a son of God, without admitting it. Be that as it may, as Christians we have another point of departure and outlook.

We saw that the person as religious being forms concepts in a learning situation meaningful to him. As he grasps meaning, truth is disclosed to his consciousness. What a learner accepts as true, whether it be really true or allegedly true, forms him in his personality. Past experience will influence present behavior to the degree that a learner has accepted truth in his heart, in the very core of his being. He will approach every new situation from out of this accepted truth.

Let us try to make this concrete in terms of a classroom situation. A teacher who understands primary and secondary felt needs of a third grader with reference to his level of readiness, and knows how to activate these needs and anticipated needs, is prepared to undertake the teaching of, say, single column addition in arithmetic. The process must be understood, not merely performed. As learners go through the process meaningfully, as they grasp the meaning of the process, they become ready for broader application of the concept of addition. The teacher introduces two-and three-columned addition. Truths of accuracy, good workmanship, and established order of number relations are disclosed to the consciousness of the learner. These truths become further generalized as they are meaningfully disclosed to them in other perceptible situations. But the realization of accepted truth is predicated on a learner's pursuit of goals that meet both primary and secondary needs. Without these drives other drives will take over, and the very ideal of accuracy becomes distorted in terms of other needs, as, for example, get this thing over with.

It should be clear that rote performance and formal accumulation of information will only incidentally, or accidentally, if at all, lead to any degree of desirable transfer.

What, then, is the basis of transfer, that is, making past experience effective in present behavior? It is truth accepted in one's heart. Call it the disposition of the heart, if you will. Disposition of heart forms, orders the ways of one's personality in every dimension. We may say that Christian education seeks a disposition of heart in the learner. A person who has accepted the truth of authority of government, of the dignity of human life and the protection of life, of courtesy and respect for one's fellows under all circumstances, is a safe driver on the modern highways, for example. But this way of behavior is not acquired by precept alone, nor by developing some habits and skills, nor by mere information. It is the result of personality development in which a youth in the felt needs of his person actively pursues goals that generalize experience into conceptual understanding and thus disclose these truths progressively according to his level of readiness.

To conclude our discussion of theories of transfer, we observe that each of the first three makes positive contributions but that none is wholly adequate. The mental discipline theory understands correctly that learning can be generalized and can strengthen powers of thought and action. The identical elements theory is right in pointing to patterns of behavior as similarities in various situations. The generalized experience theory correctly points to the fact that experience conceptualized issues forth into attitudes and ideals that carry over into broader areas of living. Each of these, however, is inadequate to the degree that it fails to recognize man for what he really is, a religious being. He comes to grips with truth as he conceptualizes experience, and in the acceptance of truth disciplines himself in right living. Disposition of heart is the dynamic of right behavior. And disposition of heart follows from accepted truth.

QUESTIONS FOR FURTHER STUDY

1. In animal behavior and in the behavior of infants, learning by conditioning is more in evidence than in later childhood and thereafter. Why?

2. Think of some ways of behavior in your own life which can be ascribed, at least in part, to conditioning; for example, certain foods you like or dislike, certain fears you seem to have, or certain places you seek to avoid.

3. Perhaps conditioning is never completely absent from learning. Why?

4. List specific learning and teaching techniques that follow from a careful study of the facts of learning demonstrated by the curves of learning and forgetting.

5. Are you a slow reader? A rapid reader? Have you reached the maximum speed of which you are capable? It is estimated that a freshman should be able to read approximately 250 words per minute of material as difficult as this text.

Test yourself by reading a chapter you have not seen before, selected from a book of comparable difficulty to this text. Divide the number of words by the time (in minutes) you spent in reading. This gives you the number of words per minute. Now try to recite to yourself the essential content of the chapter. How well can you repeat the major thoughts? This gives you an indication of how thoroughly you read.

Speed and comprehension belong together. Do you need to build up your reading speed and increase your comprehension? How will you proceed to do this?

6. Learning inevitably involves a try and try again. Trials will be accompanied by some successes and some failures. Failures should not be avoided. Why not? Successes should be experienced. Why? How can a teacher determine the amount of each, appropriate to the developmental task of a child?

7. It has been demonstrated many times that we learn meaningful material more quickly than the meaningless, and retain it longer. This has often been shown by comparing the learning of nonsense syllables and words. For example, draw up a list of 25 nonsense syllables such as baf, puc, kiv, nar, vap, etc. Also draw up a list of 25 words, such as top, fat, cup, gun, sell, jar, etc. Learn one set at a time and plot your progress carefully. Compare results. Better yet, use a subject not aware of what you are planning.

You may extend this a little further by drawing up a new set of nonsense syllables and a new set of words. Now add this direction when you give the set of words: Make associations with your words, as a hunter uses a *gun* to shoot; he killed the *fatted* calf, etc. Compare results with the former, especially the difference between the progress made without directions for associations and those with directions. What do you conclude with reference to teaching?

8. We frequently see a sign posted in an office or classroom which says, "Think." What does this sign mean to convey? Is this good advice? What is the implication of this advice?

9. Appraise the following forms of thinking: Wishful thinking, rationalization, defensive thinking, appeal to authority, stereotypes and cliches in thinking, rational thinking, thinking based on faith.

10. What is group thinking? Does it raise or lower individual thinking? To what extent is class discussion group thinking? Does it help or interfere with individual thinking? To what extent should a teacher influence group thinking in his class?

11. What kind of thinking is taking place in a classroom when a textbook assignment is accompanied by a lecture by the teacher and the pupils are expected to repeat what was included in both? Appraise this kind of thinking as a way of learning.

12. We sometimes read of a social mind. What is meant by this term? How is it developed? It is developed in the classroom too? Appraise it as a way of thinking.

13. Can attitudes be changed by thinking? Explain.

14. Should a learner in a classroom say what he is supposed to say or should he say what he thinks? Explain.

15. Examine an editorial in a newspaper or in a magazine. Analyze it carefully with reference to clear thinking. Do you find "loaded"

words or phrases? Does it play up prejudices in readers? Is it directed to guide the reader in clear thinking? Do the same for your college paper.

16. Appraise the statement often heard, "It is more important to learn how to think than what to think."

17. A distinction is sometimes drawn between representational thinking and creative thinking, and the former, it is claimed, must precede the latter if we would be formed by the truth. Is the discussion in this text concerning thinking, reasoning, creative expression, and learning in general in line with this contention?

18. At the time of the writing of this material there is a strong agitation for more emphasis on "intellectual training" in the schools of the nation, and a "return" to what are called "fundamentals," meaning organized and formalized subject matter. It is being charged that we have spent too much time on "life adjustment" in elementary and secondary schools and have failed to secure mastery of essential knowledge and skills.

a. How do the understandings, meanings, and concepts of child development and learning we have studied stand with reference to this criticism? Is this criticism pertinent to the learning process we have developed in this discussion?

b. How is the development and learning process we studied critical of the above criticism?

19. What limitations are set upon the learning process in a secular school, a school that does not make God's revelation in the Bible and in nature and culture central in learning?

20. Several times throughout this discussion we have said that the school seeks to develop a graduated body of concepts. Not that this is the end-goal of education, but the end-goal is not attainable without it. But isn't this true in all of life? Of course it is. Then how does the process constitute a special task of the school?

21. How can your study of learning improve your own study habits?

SELECTIONS FOR FURTHER REFERENCE*

Blair *et al.*, Part 3, "Learning."

Coladarci, Chapter V, "Learning: Motivational Aspects"; Chapter VI, "Learning: Maximizing Transfer."

Cole & Bruce, Part 3, "The Psychology of Learning in a Free Society."

Cronbach, Chapter IV, "An Introduction to the Learning Process"; Part C, "Acquiring Ideas, Attitudes, and Skills."

Crow & Crow, Part 4, "The Educative Process."

Gates *et al.*, Chapters IX, X, "The General Laws of Learning";
Chapters XI, XII, "Principles of Guidance in Learning"; Chapter
XIII, "The Development of Meanings"; Chapter XIV, "Reason-
ing and Problem Solving"; Chapter XV, "Transfer of Training."

Jordan, Chapter V, "General Principles of Learning"; Chapter VI,
"Conditions of Learning: Motivation"; Chapter VII, "Transfer of
Training."

Morse & Wingo, Chapter VIII, "Learning Experience"; Chapter IX,
"Learning in Groups"; Chapter X, "One Foot in the Past"; Chapter
XI, "Guides for Learning."

Mursell, Chapter VI, "How we Learrn"; Chapters VII, VIII, "The
Course of Learning"; Chapter IX, "Emotional Learning"; Chapter
X, "Transfer of Training."

Peterson *et al.*, Chpater VII, "Case Studies in Teaching and Learning"; Chapter IX, "Individual Learning"; Chapter X, "Learning Motor Skills"; Chapter XI, "Retention."

Remmers *et al.*, Chapter IX, "What Are the Influencing Factors
and Functions of Learning"; Chapter X, "How and Why We
Learn."

Skinner, Part 2, "Learning."

Sorenson, Chapter XVI, "The Progress of Growth and Development through Learning"; Chapter XVII, "Principles and Theories
of Learning"; Chapter XVIII, "Interest, Attention, Incentives,
and Motivation"; Chapter XIX, "Memory, Remembering and Forgetting."

Stephens, Chapter IX, "Theories of Learning"; Chapter X, "Utilizing
Motivation and Experience"; Chapter XI, "Providing Guidance and
Reinforcement"; Chapter XII, "Meaningful Relations in Learning
and in Problem Solving"; Chapter XIII, "Reducing Interference
and Confusion"; Chapter XIV, "Teaching for Permanence and
Trnasfer."

Witherington, Chapter VIII, "General Principles of Learning."

*References here are cited by author's name. See Bibliography for title and
complete publication data.

Part Four:

What Is Teaching?

18

Teaching

"As the child learns," said Pestalozzi, "so must one teach." And nothing could be more true. There was a day when learning was misunderstood, when the principles of child development were derived from philosophic general principles rather than from careful observational study. This was the time when the symbol of teaching was the hickory stick, when adult ways were imposed by coercion upon children who "should be seen but not heard."

Happily, these days are largely in the past. But the gain has not been unmitigated; just as in the "old times" there were teachers who genuinely understood children and maintained wholesome rather than arbitrary discipline, so in recent years there has arisen a "modern" school practice which encourages child-expression to excess. So-called "progressive education," which bases itself on the primacy of individual interests and needs in learning, has often led to a permissiveness and lack of organization which the Christian finds equally unpalatable.

By addressing ourselves to the formulation of sound principles regarding child development and learning, we have sought to lay a firm foundation for the analysis of teaching which will occupy us in this final section of the book. We will begin by dispelling some misconceptions about the nature of teaching.

WHAT TEACHING IS NOT

NOT MERELY THE TRANSMISSION OF IDEAS

Ideas are sometimes represented as entities in the mind that one can share with others. They are held to be a something that can be divided and distributed among others, and in the division do not decrease but actually increase, for the subject who shares his ideas begets ideas by sharing. Knowledge is the accumulation of these entities. Association theories of earlier days spoke in terms of entities or units of thought. The teacher was said to have ideas, not the pupil. The latter was to receive ideas, assimilate them, and share them. The haves give to the have-nots without the haves decreasing their holdings. Thus knowledge is transmitted. And these ideas have power. Therefore knowledge, consisting of a fund of ideas, is a powerhouse. Knowledge is power.

Now of course it is true that something often goes on which can be *called* the sharing of ideas, just as ordinary speech still uses the expression "the sun goes down." But neither conception has scientific accuracy.

The fault of this view lies in the supposition that *words* are the sufficient vehicles of ideas, and that hence the impartation of words is adequate for the impartation of the associated ideas. But we have already learned that concepts and groups of concepts ("ideas") cannot be conveyed merely with words. They are, rather, generalized perceptual experiences. Without perceptual basis, the concepts simply do not arise in the learner's mind.

The number six, e.g., is an idea or concept based on a perceptual field involving six discrete objects. The distance of 93,000,000 miles to the sun has no meaning for us until it is related to a perceptual field, say how long it would take for a space ship flying at a perceptible rate to get there. And even then one develops only a vague concept of the actual distance. And the light years describing the distance of the stars is beyond all comprehension. When the Lord tells us that it grieved him that he created man, or that he repented, or that we grieve the Holy Spirit, what is this but God speaking to us in human language, that is, in the perceptual experiences of which we are capable? This is what we mean when we say that God speaks to us in anthropomorphic[1] language. As a matter of fact the entire Bible is revelation of God, not in divine concepts, but in human concepts. In human perceptual fields the Lord directs us in the development of true concepts of himself and his work. He does not merely transmit ideas to us, but he activates in our experience perceptual fields for understanding.

Not the molding of passive objects

Several times we have had occasion to note in our study that the learner is a self-active subject, and all learning is the self-active process of the learner. You can lead a horse to the water but you cannot make him drink. "Learning is done by the learner, and not

1. Or, anthropopathic.

by some kind of transmission process by the teacher."[2] This may be set down as a major contribution by psychological studies that should be written large in the thinking and planning that goes into teaching. The learner selects from the perceptual field of which he is a part. The external situation, in form and content, is presented to him as a given. The set of the learner, his anticipation and expectation, determines how and what he selects in the process of converging. The learner is impressed by the external situation through the channels of perception. He becomes part of the field as he actively selects from it to form his personality field. In his motivation, according to accepted goals, he develops concepts. In conceptualizing, truth is disclosed to him. In the acceptance of truth he directs or orders the dimensions of his personality accordingly. Thus he is formed and forms himself.

Only in the hands of the Lord, in his providence, are we as clay. He is the potter; we are the clay. He molds and makes us according to his will. But even the Lord deals with us as active agents as he molds us. We read, "Work out your own salvation with fear and trembling, for it is God who works in you to will and to do according to his pleasure." As subjects we mold ourselves by our self-active choices, even in the providence of God. How we remain free, responsible agents in the providence of a sovereign God, is not for finite concepts, let alone for sinful hearts to grasp. We have perceptible areas of experience that correspond to God's work in us, but they do not coincide with God's thinking. Hence, we cannot fully understand how God works. Isn't this precisely what Jesus taught Nicodemus when he inquired how a man can be born again? Recall Jesus' words, "If I have told you of things on earth and none of you believe me, how will you believe me if I tell you of things in heaven?"

NOT THE DISSEMINATION OF ADULT ORGANIZED SUBJECT MATTER

Not long ago the author stepped into a classroom and heard the teacher hold forth on the United States Constitution. He was trying to outline it for his pupils and verbalize about each part, giving an illustration or two. Before leaving the author inquired whether the pupils had observed local government, including the sanitation department, parks, city commission, etc. "No," was the reply, "we are coming to this later. Do you think we should begin there?" "It isn't so much where you begin," the author replied, "but more important what the youngsters understand."

Apart from the fact that the United States Supreme Court cannot

2. Bugelski, *The Psychology of Learning*, p. 457.

agree on the interpretation of the Constitution, the verbalizing in the classroom in terms of adult ideas in the Constitution assumes that teaching is the handing out in small portions and in reduced complexity of adult organized subject matter. It is no such thing. And many behavior problems in the classroom and ineffective outcomes in learning result from this fallacy.

Adult organized subject matter is the logical summary of earlier perceptual experience of adults. A child's understanding of the powers and duties of the United States Congress does not come from a logical presentation of them by the teacher for later testing for recall. It comes first of all from earlier contact with government in the home and in the school, in the local community, and from the interpretation of these in adult life about us. If these represent government that commands respect and devotion of the child, the powers and duties of Congress acquire meaningful content. Apart from these and similar perceptual experiences, the powers and duties of the Congress remain hollow phrases subject to a child's interpretation according to his limited and often distorted experience with government.

Adult subject matter is the strange land we spoke of earlier by way of analogy. A child cannot extend himself in the dimensions of his personality with a feeling of security into a strange milieu. He feels threatened, not challenged. The unknown holds anxiety for him. Familiarity and acceptance amidst the novel and strange provide initial security for progressive exploration of a new situation.

WHAT TEACHING IS

Let us begin with a simple analogy. Suppose I take a two-year-old to a cage which contains a small white rabbit. He is not familiar with rabbits, nor has he acquired a fear for furry animals. The very sight of a bunny intrigues him. He reaches for the bunny but suddenly the little animal throws his front paws on Bobby's hand. Bobby pulls away. Now he goes at it more cautiously, perhaps even with a bit of fear. I proceed to pet the bunny, let him crawl over my hand, bring the bunny close to Bobby, and talk to Bobby about the bunny. At the same time I get hold of Bobby's hand and hold it near the bunny. I encourage Bobby, show him how to treat the bunny, and even become firm about keeping Bobby from poking his finger into the bunny's eyes or ears. I am teaching Bobby to know the bunny.

In teaching Bobby to know the bunny I did three things, consecutively and also concurrently. (1) I presented an external situation, form and content, with which he can merge. I activated him in a need for a knowledge of animal life and how to live with animals.

(2) As he entered a perceptual field I communicated with him. I altered and recognized the external situation as I proceeded to give it increasing perceptual significance. That is, I instructed him. (3) I supported him in his approach to the bunny. When momentarily he was thwarted, I helped him reassess the situation. I firmly resisted and redirected his attempts to manipulate the bunny to the bunny's hurt. That is, I disciplined him. To sum up, I did three things which developed a counterpart of self-activity in each case in Bobby. I inspired Bobby; Bobby is motivated. I instructed Bobby; Bobby explored. I disciplined Bobby; Bobby obeyed. In a word I directed the learning process of Bobby to a well-formulated, prescribed end. Bobby in turn was formed in his personality as he understood and accepted the bunny for what he really is. This is teaching. Bugelski states that so far as is known, no teacher has ever been able to "knock sense" into anyone. Mursell puts it this way: *Teaching is the structurating of personality through learning activities meaningful to the learner. The teacher can structurate personality by helping the learner discover ways of thinking, feeling, and acting constructively to satisfy basic needs. To do this a teacher is to reveal needs to the learner and need-satisfying goals, and help him discover ways of reaching these goals.

Now let us analyze each of these activities more closely.

ACTIVATION AND MOTIVATION

Obviously this does not mean that a teacher gives life and energy to a child. A healthy child has a boundless amount of it. Neither does it mean that a teacher starts a child at learning. He is an indefatigable learner. Felt needs seek consummation. Learning is inevitable as felt needs are realized in perceptual fields of experience and concepts are formed. So a child does not become a learner. He is that by nature.

But there is lacking a self-conscious direction of true needs toward true goals that can meet these needs. It is here that a teacher has his task. Learning as a natural process of development must be directed toward goals that can form the person as religious being. This direction begins by activating felt needs that find their consummation in right goals and making goals perceptible and attainable

The first obligation of the teacher is to create a feeling of unrest, curiosity, a level of anxiety in the learner. The learner must "pay attention." The felt need so aroused must be related to a consummating object which is calculated to develop him in his personality. Striving for and attaining this goal is the reinforcement in learning; it allays anxiety. For example, a teacher may develop a nicely calculated anxiety about the dropping or rising of the level of water in the Great Lakes, or the reign of Charlemagne. This may be difficult, but it is psychologically necessary for learning.

To inspire a learner is to activate him toward ends which are in harmony with a child's religious nature. To inspire a child and to arouse him are not the same thing. He may be aroused without establishing an accepted goal. This may result in random activity which accomplishes nothing positive except by accident. In our study of learning we saw that a certain amount of random activity can hardly be avoided, but by establishing attainable goals in a perceptible situation the teacher is reducing wasteful random activity to a minimum. He makes all learning purposeful.

INSTRUCTION AND EXPLORATION

It is not enough to make a learner goal-conscious, to whet his appetite for something. The wherewithal to reach the goal must be forthcoming too. Without it the learner soon feels frustrated and the goal itself loses its impelling force.

The learner, set to do, needs the source material which he must employ to reach the end-in-view, the goal. He has the resources for action within. These resources now need to be focused on certain objects for selection and manipulation. In school the external situation, including all the source material, is provided in the curriculum: the curriculum of the school includes all material and activity organized for the educational objective, namely forming personality in the medium of our culture. The teacher selects from the total curriculum according to what a child on a given level and in a given area of learning needs to achieve this purpose.

This is instruction. It means to furnish the wherewithal for a child's self-activity toward an accepted goal. We must divest ourselves of the idea that by instruction a teacher gives the child something in his mind or molds his mind. Kunkel has well said that all education is self-education. By instruction the teacher provides the external resources on which a learner with his internal resources can go to work.

Instruction involves two classes of activities on the part of the teacher. First of all *he* sets up a learning situation, using stories — spoken or written, books — textbooks and reference books, bulletin board, blackboard, excursions — imaginary or actual, demonstrations, experiments, maps, etc. These are all source materials directly providing perceptible content in a perceptible form. We may say that through these sources the teacher is communicating with a learner indirectly. All genuine teaching is effective communication.

The teacher does more to communicate effectively. In the second place he exchanges concepts with the learner. He cannot give a learner ideas, but he can from his own fund of ideas activate ideas in the learner, enrich and appraise them. In this sense he can tell the learner. What does a teacher tell a learner? Concepts which the learner finds perceptible according to his own perceptual field of experience. Communication by words is possible when the speaker or writer uses concepts, not mere words, from his own understanding and activates in the hearer or reader similar concepts. Within limits it may be said that the effectiveness of teaching is inversely proportional to a teacher's talking.

Yet, direct communication by the teacher is very important. It carries the weight of a teacher's personality much more than does indirect communication. There is a direct communication in the teacher's very presence. His personality is constantly communicating to the learner. But always he is interpreted by the learner according to the latter's set or expectancy. Here, as in the acquisition of information, how a learner feels about a teacher is more important than what a teacher says, or even does.

How directive must a teacher be? How nondirective? "Telling" or "talking" method (lecture) has its place as well as discussion. There is nothing wrong with the lecture. Its effectiveness depends upon the lecturer and the readiness of the learner. Guide, "show the way," but give the learner opportunity to make mistakes. Imitation also has its place. But it must be accompanied by meaning and appreciation.

DISCIPLINE AND OBEDIENCE

Exploring source material toward an end-in-view is a difficult task and requires constant support. The end-in-view, the perceptible and attainable goal, is very likely not the end the learner would himself have chosen. When the teacher has activated real and true needs in the learner in relation to an external situation, the end the teacher formulates comes in view for the learner. The desired end is gradually accepted by the pupil. He must now mold himself, and when he wavers, be held to his task. The support the learner experiences from within and from without in sustaining him in his task is discipline. There must be constant reinforcement of learning for self-discipline.

If the teacher has succeeded in inspiring a learner and furnishing him with source material that he can manipulate understandingly with relation to the end-in-view that he has come to accept, the discipline or support will come largely from the relationships in the personality field of the learner. It will be largely self-discipline. But some hurdles may appear which are too great even for the most impelling force from within. Help for the learner must be forthcoming in the form either of incentives, preferably positive and intrinsic, as we saw, or in the form of suggestions for manipulating the material. It may also occur that competing forces from within or without or both become dominant and distract the learner, thus weakening his motivation in the right direction. Some firm handling by the teacher may become necessary. Negative and extrinsic incentives may be invoked. They all constitute forms of discipline or reinforcement, and must be appraised in terms of what they accomplish educationally.

This may be called the broad concept of discipline. A narrow concept is more in terms of punishment. Though punishment as a negative incentive is not excluded, discipline as such must be viewed positively as directing the will function of a child to right ends. In instruction the teacher addresses himself largely to the understanding and thinking functions of the person; in discipline largely to the will function. What rather naively is called a discipline problem in the classroom is more accurately recognized as a learner who fails to respond to the inspiration and instruction of a teacher. Some measure beyond the usual techniques must be taken to help a learner to respond in a desirable way to effective teaching.

Discipline in the classroom has been classified usefully as constructive, preventive, and remedial.[3] The control that follows from a well-planned teaching-learning situation as a by-product may be called constructive discipline. The will-function of the learner is directed by the motivation indigenous to the learning process. The learner is engrossed in the activity of attaining the end-in-view in a given situation. That this is the most desirable form of discipline is obvious from what we have studied concerning the forming of personality. It brings about the most harmonious functioning of a learner's resources to a well-conceived end.

A teacher must, however, at times resort to a second type of discipline which is aimed at avoiding anticipated infractions of classroom control. He keeps riding his eyes over the classroom during a discussion or study period, or he checks some developments in the rear of the classroom by having a pupil move to the other side of the room. He employs certain "tricks of the trade" to keep things in line. He has a box of "aspirin tablets" available for quieting initial and momentary disturbances. This may be called preventive discipline. It aims at avoiding incidents that may get out of hand. That this must be handled with much discretion should be clear. Youngsters should not get the impression that a teacher expects the wrong of them. Then a teacher may get what he expects. But learners are

3. R. Schorling and H. T. Batchelder, *Student Teaching in Secondary Schools* (New York: McGraw-Hill, 1956), pp. 90-99.

apt to interpret failure to anticipate infractions as weakness in the teacher, and this in turn generates a feeling of insecurity in the class.

Even preventive discipline will not prove fully effective in directing a learner's will function to right ends. What has not been accomplished by constructive discipline is not accomplished by preventive discipline as such. Preventive discipline is only a means to increase the effectiveness of constructive discipline, for the forming of personality in the final analysis takes place in the way of constructive discipline.

The lack of finality in preventive discipline is even more true of remedial discipline. For this reason it is called remedial discipline. In preventive discipline the infraction is anticipated, has not occurred, and does not occur, at least not to a degree that may be called an infraction. But in the third form of discipline the infraction has occurred.

Now what to do? Children should recognize that infraction of classroom control is a confronting of rightful authority with overt rebellion, and they should learn what this means. A teacher's position in the classroom is an authoritative one. Is it retributive, that is, does it mete out justice according to the crime committed? Is it the arm of justice which demands punishment? No. This is not the authority of a teacher. God vested this authority in government, according to the Scriptures. It alone exercises the sword of justice. A teacher's authority is first of all moral, for he has been designated to form personalities. This task has an absolute ethical ideal and is therefore a moral task. Infraction of classroom control is therefore open rebellion against moral authority. And, whereas all authority ultimately rests in God, it is open rebellion against God himself. Failure to bring this to a child's understanding so that he may have a feeling of guilt and may learn penitence is to fail in the educative process itself. But not only is a teacher's authority moral, it is also judicial, that is, he must determine and mete out punishment, not in a retributive or punitive sense, but in the total structure of an educational program. Hence the term remedial discipline.

What then is remedial discipline? Remedial discipline aims at correcting a wrong relationship of a learner to the classroom organization. But this must be done educatively to direct the will function to right ends instead of to ends that became evident in the infraction. This requires first of all a recognition on the part of the teacher of the dignity of a child as religious being and his development along ways that God has ordained for development to maturity. It requires, furthermore, a developing recognition by the learner according to his perceptibility that he is rebellious and therefore needs forgiveness. Forgiveness is obtained in the way of penitence. The teacher does

not merely work toward a feeling of guilt, but more toward feelings
of penitence and forgiveness. But feelings of penitence and subsequent forgiveness do not completely eliminate the judicial aspect
of authority. Sometimes the feelings of guilt and penitence may be
considered enough to effect the direction of the will function to
right ends. At other times it may be necessary to add punishment
appropriate to the offense, that is, as closely related to it as possible.
Rather than punishment, it is chastisement, aimed at bringing back
the wayward to the straight and narrow way. So the Lord deals
with his own. He chastises them.

It is especially remedial discipline that should convey to a child
the loving heart of the teacher. How to make love felt by a child in
the process of punishment requires a large measure of penitence on
the part of a teacher who himself has only a small degree of complete
submission to God's will.

A child's counterpart to a teacher's discipline is obedience. Obedience is not compliance with arbitrary command. It is voluntary
surrender to constituted authority. In the classroom this authority
of the teacher is exercised constructively in the learning-teaching
process, preventively in the use of techniques to avoid the actualizing
of potential sources of infraction, and remedially in feelings of
guilt, penitence, and forgiveness, and in punishment. So a teacher
disciplines; a learner obeys. And it is in the way of obedience to
rightful authority that true freedom and self-fulfillment are found.

For questions for further study and selections for further reference,
see close of chapter 19.

19

The Teacher

Teaching is a very responsible task. Though the words of James 3:1-2 were not written immediately with the modern teacher in mind, the words are very applicable. The Revised Standard Version renders this passage as follows: "Let not many of you become teachers, my brethren, for you know that we who teach shall be judged with greater strictness. For we all make mistakes, and if anyone makes no mistakes in what he says he is a perfect man, able to bridle the whole body also." In a day of teacher shortage and when ever greater demands are being made upon the classroom teacher, these words are not too encouraging. And one would hesitate to undertake so great a responsibility if it were not that the Lord himself calls to service and promises to qualify when he calls. Let a teacher be assured of a call to service.

Teaching is an art based on a growing science, educational theory and practice. The teacher is an artist. His art is the directing of the learning process of immature learners to right ends. We saw briefly what this means, namely, to inspire, instruct, and discipline learners. To carry out his task effectively he should understand the medium in which he is to direct the learning process and the ends which it is to serve. He should also understand the learner in his total development and the learning process as it functions in a given medium. It is the latter, namely, development and learning, with which we have concerned ourselves largely so far. We have seen briefly what teaching as an art involves in the way of doing. But in all of this the teacher himself as a person in the dimensions of his own personality is very much involved. He does the teaching. Furthermore, he is beset by barriers of many kinds. In these too the teacher must be realistic and must face his problems with courage.

In this chapter, then, we deal with some personal matters pertaining to the teacher.

TEACHING INVOLVES A DYNAMIC
INTERPLAY OF PERSONALITIES

We note that how a teacher feels about children is more important than the professional learning he has attained. This is not said to minimize the latter, but to emphasize a psychological fact. For parents and teachers alike, it is true that the patterns in their own personalities are more determinative of how they treat children than the rules and regulations they learn from books. Sound rules and regulations are often misappropriated by wrong attitudes of the teacher. Teachers as well as parents see themselves reflected very often in their handling of children.

Earlier in our study we spoke of the primacy of love in learning and teaching. To the degree that one can love and accept love he can enjoy security needed for normal development and effective communication. This is true in every relationship of life. But we are apt to mistake certain feelings about others as love reactions when they actually are expressions of conscious hostilities. Of this a teacher must be aware.

Let us illustrate in terms of two concrete situations.

Teachers A and B have learned and are convinced that an attractive, well-arranged classroom with materials pertaining to the work in hand all around, facilitates pupil interest and initiative. It adds to the inspiration and instruction we spoke of. They also agree that the learners should participate in setting up such a classroom appearance and keeping it so. Student committees are constantly at work making preparations for new displays and rearranging them. And all of this is an integral part of the subject matter fields under study. Teachers A and B have learned what it means to enrich the perceptual field of experience for greater understanding and developing of concepts.

A closer acquaintance with the classroom situations of these two teachers reveals some interesting facts. Among the boys and girls of teacher A there is more spontaneity, more creative effort, more resourcefulness, and teacher A finds himself busy trying to direct all the energy expressed. The members of teacher B's class manifest far less ingenuity and resourcefulness. On the contrary, they wait for the teacher to take the initiative and frequently fall below the expected.

Why the difference? When we study the situation more closely, we find that boys and girls in teacher B's class manifest anxiety about the teacher's approval of what they are doing. They seem to fear lest they meet with rebuff of their attempts. The teacher invites initiative, even assigns tasks in that direction, and shows his disappointment when nothing has been done. But the boys and girls never feel quite secure in what they are trying to do. In teacher A's group there is a superabundance of activity and material. The groups freely consult teacher A about their differences and problems. Teacher A injects suggestions and helps here and there, and invariably they are followed out as though the children themselves had devised them. The anxiety evident on the group of teacher B is entirely missing in the group of teacher A. The group of teacher A manifests an acceptance of responsibility and a freedom to execute it.

How are these different situations related to the respective teachers' personalities? Teacher A loves children, accepts them on their level of development, recognizes that they need direction (sometimes firm), but when he directs he manifests no anxiety or misgivings about them. Teacher B has his chief interest in the subject matter and in right performance. Being a near perfectionist in standards of performance, he finds a child's immaturities and consequent mistakes irritating. He communicates this irritation, often unconsciously, to his pupils. They feel insecure in what they are trying to do. In addition to this, teacher B is the type of personality who feels insecure when it is not overtly evident that he is in control. Teacher A exercises much control in an indirect way, making pupils feel that they are functioning in their self-control. Teacher B is a *dominant* type of personality; teacher A as a *social integrative* type of personality. Teacher A is more mature and understands himself much better. Teacher B may make himself believe that he loves children when he makes them "toe the mark." Actually he harbors much hostility to children in their ways of development. Unconsciously he communicates this hostility. Teacher A can subordinate momentary irritations to greater purposes.

From these and many similar situations we may learn much pertaining to the psychology of the teacher.

WHAT DYNAMIC INTERPLAY DEMANDS

MATURITY

In general it should be said that teaching demands personal maturity. Maturity, we have had occasion to observe several times, means for a Christian that he accepts life responsibly in the service of God. He strives humbly for the beauty of Jesus to be seen in him. Professionally this means that he is trying to communicate to children in the dimensions of his own personality the beauty of Jesus. To do this he must understand himself. An immature person hesitates to reveal himself in his true nature because he fails to understand himself. He uses all kinds of escapes and compensations. And all these reflect his true feeling about himself and others.

What are the marks of maturity as they are evident in a teacher?

A teacher should be able to practice self-analysis without morbid introspection. As a Christian, he is constantly asking himself three important questions and facing the answers honestly.

(1) Am I coming to understand myself in the dimensions of my personality in the light of the Word of God?

(2) Am I capable and eager to grow in my professional task?

(3) Am I capable of exercising the self-control needed for positive guidance of child life?

To understand a child a teacher must understand himself. To understand a child in his development it is sometimes necessary to be able to probe into one's own childhood a bit. Earlier we saw that a child must accept himself and feel accepted to develop normally. He must feel accepted by his teacher, too. To feel rejected is frustrating and no one of us surmounts it in an integrated way. Neither does a child. To be understood and to be accepted are prerequisites for a child's progress. Only a teacher who has achieved a large measure of self-understanding can give a child these needed feelings.

A mature teacher develops a constructive program of activity. He accepts his professional task as primary. This requires long-range planning of his own professional development and of the work in the school and classroom. He accumulates a working library consisting of books, work materials, and such references as enhance his professional resources.

He keeps well-chosen fellowships. His profession keeps him associated with people schooled in the arts and sciences. This is a benefit that accrues to one as a teacher. But his fellowships should extend to many walks and services of life. A teacher should be a community person too. Some service in the community is beneficial to him as a person.

Recreation and hobbies wisely chosen bring good returns in terms of restfulness and relaxation. When a hobby or recreation becomes a source of income its value as a form of relaxation is reduced, if not entirely eliminated. The same is true for community service.

Judge a professionally minded teacher by now he plans all activities in terms of the profession to which he gives his life.

A mature teacher acts with resolve. Procrastination is a liability to any person, but especially to a teacher. And so is rash action. To be alert to every opportunity for appropriate words and deeds needs constant cultivation. A teacher should be capable of following a wisely-chosen course and holding to it until convinced of a better way. Inaction, in some situations, is worse than momentary action from which one can return. For example, when a class is disrupted by some aggressive pupil, some action is imperative. At other times inaction may be desirable. But even inaction is to act, and must

soon be replaced by well-considered action. A teacher must be able
to make up his mind in critical situations.

A mature teacher sets his mark high. Note that we say *his* mark.
With reference to the mark for the pupil the teacher is guided by the
principle of readiness. With reference to himself he is guided by the
ideals for his life and for his profession. And these ideals are ever
of the highest order. In the Christian life we follow Paul when he
said, "I press toward the goal for the prize of the upward call in
Christ Jesus" (Phil. 3:14, Weymouth). The "upward call in Christ
Jesus" may be interpreted in terms of a teacher's professional task.
What he says and does he is constantly appraising in the light of
whom he ought to be. And when he becomes discouraged, he recalls
the words of Paul, "In nothing be anxious, but in everything by
prayer and supplication with thanksgiving let your request be known
unto God. And the peace of God which passes all understanding
shall guard your hearts and your thoughts in Christ Jesus" (Phil.
4:6, 7).

Avoiding escapes

In his self-analysis a teacher may be guided by these marks of
maturity which we have discussed. But we are all given to avoid such
self-analysis. Often we harbor a hidden fear of what we may find.
We find ways of escape. Every profession seems to have its own escapes
from being honest with oneself. Teaching does. Let us mention a
few, so that as teachers we can recognize them when we experience
them. Escapes are palliatives that lull one into complacency only to
find that the disease breaks forth in unguarded moments with new
fury, and in unexpected ways.

*Contentment in conforming to accepted patterns of life without
normative appraisal.* How common this escape from thorough self-
analysis is may be illustrated by the following. John goes to church
with a fellow Christian. Following the worship hour the fellow
Christian invites him to have a coke at a nearby drug store. John
is horrified at the suggestion and replies, "No, thanks, I do not
buy on Sunday." The fellow Christian accepts his friend's objection
and does not go in for a drink. But as they continue on their way,
John pulls out a cigaret to light a smoke. "Have one," he says to his
friend. "No," answers he, "I do not smoke. Should a Christian be
found smoking?" Each has accepted a pattern of life, rather uncritically, without normative appraisal.

A teacher's way of life must consist of more than uncritically accepted patterns if it is to inspire learners and give rise to community
leadership. To feel that "I think profane language is an awful thing"

is not sufficient to communicate the sacredness of God's name to
pupils.

Seeking rationalized justification of emotional attitudes. A teacher
keeps children after school hours and is heard to justify his action
by saying, "What are you going to do with them when they don't
behave. You've got to punish them somehow." This teacher cannot be
bothered with careful study of child development and why the
children behave as they do.

"The school doesn't have a thing. Textbooks are poor, and they
don't give me workbooks." This is hardly a way of developing one's
own resourcefulness as a teacher-artist. Workbooks have their value,
as do textbooks. But how often are workbooks the handbooks of a
lazy teacher?

The anesthesia of work. "No time for anything but school work.
School keeps me busy every moment." This attitude is sometimes
referred to as the anesthesia of work. There is a perfectionistic attitude in it. One hears the following, for example. "I correct all
the papers myself. I think that is the only way to make sure every
pupil does his work." Or again, "I get all the materials ready for
a day's work. You can't leave this to children and expect to get
it done."

Teachers who speak this way fail to understand that they are really
extremely self-centered. Everything must be done to please themselves; therefore, they do what is to be done. The result is that
their deeper needs remain unsatisfied. The inner life of the spirit
is submerged.

It is grand to be absorbed in one's task, to carry the play spirit
into one's teaching. But to shut out all other activities is to become
oblivious to the needs of others. Rather than be guided by his own
needs, a teacher should let himself be guided by the needs of his
learners. Things will not always turn out perfectly, but better education will be accomplished.

The anesthesia of fun. "Teaching is often a bore, but one does
get good long vacations." Like any other occupation, teaching *can*
become boring; and in the right measure, recreation is a salutory
thing. But such remarks often betray an immature and unprofessional
attitude. The wise teacher will examine his own practice; perhaps if
he approaches the "boring" activities more constructively he will
find a new challenge in them.

Shifting responsibility. The teacher may be having discipline problems, so upon the slightest provocation he sends the pupil to the
principal's office. If asked to justify this, he responds that all the
other teachers do it too. But the principal wants pupils to think of

his office as a place for help, not a courtroom; and the teacher is responsible for his charges.

Dreaming of better days. How many teachers enter the profession for secondary or tertiary reasons? For many, teaching is still a stepping stone, as it has been through the years. There are some that are waiting for "the perfect love" to come along. Others say to themselves, if not aloud, "I'll teach a little while, but . . . ."

Let it be said that many women, especially, who serve the profession for a short period of five to ten years, make a vital contribution and several return in their later years. Without their services the schools could hardly keep going. And there are others who serve for even shorter periods. But while one is at it, teaching demands one's all in consecration and purpose. Teaching cannot fulfill its task as mission when a teacher is waiting for better days.

Complacency. "I don't see that I don't do as well as others." The writer has heard teachers say this when their work called for some reappraisal. Or, "what more can you expect under the circumstances?" Circumstances can account for crippling limitations, but a resourceful personality is no victim of them. And to use them as alibis for inadequate teaching points up a serious lack in the teacher himself.

A large part of the battle for continued self-improvement is won when a teacher recognizes one or more of these escapes in his life, should they be present. He might slip into one of them unconsciously when threatened in his personal or professional security. A positive program of action is the best way to avoid escapes. Such a program, regularly reappraised as occasion requires, organizes and integrates the resources of the teacher's personality in terms of a well-conceived goal. Escapes divide his personality and weaken his effectiveness.

While a thorough academic preparation for teaching is essential, teaching depends for effectiveness largely upon the maturity of a teacher's personality. A prospective teacher may be actually brilliant intellectually, win graduate scholarships on academic records, and fail to mature proportionately in his personality. To direct the learning process of a child requires a maturity that generates confidence in the life of a child. An adequate schooling coupled with personal maturity accomplishes far more than academic erudition. As a matter of fact an erudite person may be unable to communicate because he lives and thinks almost exclusively in a world of abstractions.

To thorough academic preparation we should add professional insight. This is more than passing through a few professional courses in education. It means the understanding of the learning and teach-process with relation to the program of the school. To inspire, instruct, and discipline young lives in the medium of our culture requires that a teacher understands how young learners develop in their personalities through their manipulation of them. But this insight depends as much, if not more, upon a teacher's maturity as it does upon being schooled in educational theory and practice. Some teachers possess much of this insight with little or no formal study of education as a science, though all can profit from reading and study in this area.

BARRIERS TO EFFECTIVE TEACHING

A teacher with the best professional preparation and of mature personal stature meets barriers that are at times very formidable. Awareness of them is a first requisite for overcoming them, or at least for reducing their impact upon the learning process.

THE INNATE RESISTANCE OF THE LEARNER

What can this mean? As stated above, modern education frowns on it. It reminds the secular educator of the theological doctrine of total depravity. And for him this is the most pessimistic view of man. Education, he thinks, is based upon the assumption that human nature is neutral morally, neither good nor evil, but can become either and both in development. Innate resistance or total depravity would indicate that there is inherent evil in human nature.

Innate resistance of the learner does not mean that he is naturally averse to learning. On the contrary, we saw that the child is an indefatigable learner. It is not learning as such that a child resists, but accepting truth and surrendering himself to it in humble obedience. Man, dead in trespasses and sins, resists the discipline of truth because he lacks righteousness (Eph. 2:1-10). Being without righteousness means that man is without right relationship with God, without the fellowship of God's love. This gives rise to the dissipation of his motivations in directions contrary to God's law of love for his life. It is the innate resistance of the broken person we studied earlier. In the disharmony of his functions a person resists all attempts at integration as a religious being in the service of God.

Psychologically, then, we may put it this way. The resistance in the soul life is expressed in unwillingness to accept goals that seek to form one according to true norms. Desires are in conflict with the desirable. The teacher tries to make the desirable real in a child's understanding and to direct the learning process accordingly. But as Christian teacher he recognizes the resistance for what it is.

What can a teacher do in the face of the awful reality of sin in a child's life? Is he the pessimist modern education thinks him to be?

(1) He is no unrealistic optimist. Education is no panacea; it cannot accomplish everything. At the same time, he recognizes that God in his wisdom uses human agencies to accomplish his work in men. He looks upon his task as a ministry to the needs of children. Dependent upon the Lord for wisdom and a blessing upon his humble efforts, he labors patiently and prays earnestly for his work and the children entrusted to his care.

(2) The Christian teacher is very conscious of the scriptural teaching that all men, children too, must repent and be saved. We are saved to serve, but we must be saved to be of service. Conversion of a child is first of all the concern of a parent and a pastor. But conversion involves a daily directing of one's functions from sinful desires and practices into channels of righteousness. And schools are engaged daily in establishing righteousness in a child's way of life. Teachers have many opportunities to undergird the work of parent and pastor in seeking the conversion of boys and girls.

(3) The Christian teacher should recognize that a child of Christian parents is a child of the promise, "I will be a God unto thee and thy seed after thee . . . ." How and when God works in a child we are not told. But we trust God's promise and act upon it. We assume, all things being equal, that a child of Christian parents is in Christ and as such is educable, that is, can form himself in his total personality as a son of God.

OUR CULTURE

How can our culture constitute a barrier to effective teaching when it is the medium in which all learning takes place? Not in the way that Rousseau believed. At the beginning of his *Emile* he writes, "Coming from the hand of the author of all things, everything is good; in the hands of men everything degenerates." But this is a false disjunction which can be traced to Rousseau's disbelief in original sin. We know that natural beings (including man) are not unspoiled at birth, and we also know that human culture is not *in itself* evil (recall our earlier discussion of alleged evil in some human functions).

Our difficulty as Christian teachers with human culture is that at once it is tainted by sin and it is the inescapable medium of education. This is especially true of schools, which exist to orient youth to our culture.

What should be done? The problem is a major one with the widest possible ramifications. It is the problem of every redeemed person in a world where he has a calling. He must be in the world but not of it. The teacher can at least do this: he can so organize the perceptual fields of his students that moral concepts can be apprehended unambiguously. Then, by encouragement and example, he can lead the pupil toward the truth as God has revealed it. This is not an easy formula; in fact, it is really only the barest sketch of what needs to be done. And as we have said so often before, the personal influence of the Christian teacher is the factor that will almost always determine the results.

THE LOW STATUS OF TEACHERS IN THE UNITED STATES

When we speak of the status of the teacher, we are thinking of the regard with which he is held in the hearts of those whom he serves. In his ministry the teacher serves the young people whom he teaches. He also serves the parents whose work he carries on in a specific sphere of child development. He serves the organized church when the learning process undergirds and extends the spiritual work of the church in a child's personality. He serves the community as a whole, for children are participants in a broad community life. The long-range effectiveness of a teacher's ministry will depend upon the place he holds in the esteem of each of these constituents of his service.

Unfortunately, many if not most teachers fail to receive the esteem they deserve. They do not usually earn a salary equal to other professional people — sometimes not even equal to the average income of their constituents. And because many citizens — even Christians — measure their respect according to a person's bank account, the teacher is usually the object of half-envy ("short working hours") and sometimes even semi-disdain ("those that can, do; those that can't, teach").

Now, teachers are expected to be immune to this conflict, for they must find their feeling of success in their "spiritual" call, the call upon their hearts to a sacred ministry. Ideally they should rise above this situation, and many do. But in practice it is difficult for even the most consecrated teachers. They frequently develop a feeling of inferiority, and either get out of the profession into a more lucrative line of work, or lower the standard of teaching as a profession by resorting to outside compensation of one kind or another. No doubt the teacher shortage in this day of plenty can be attributed largely to this situation. Many young people of ability look forward to more lucrative and more respected lines of work. Some of less ability, who have professional ambitions and who cannot qualify for other professions, drift into teaching in the emergency.

How should a teacher face this situation? There are many teachers who rise above this situation and command the respect of the community in spite of the adverse situations to which we referred. How do they do it? It requires, of course, a level of competence and resourcefulness. By consecrated, competent, sacrificial service these teachers evoke a feeling of admiration among the constituency. They are not indifferent to the inverted sense of values that becloud the perspective of many people, but they do not permit themselves to be adversely affected by it. The teachers that become disgruntled add to the problem. Especially pupils feel that such teachers are bored and hostile. The zeal of a consecrated ministry is the answer.

But the zeal of a consecrated ministry is born of the conviction that teaching is an art based on a science. A teacher-artist is a skillful worker who knows his science and is deeply convinced of his great task of directing learning toward well-defined ends.

POOR SCHOOL FACILITIES

While it is true that a teacher largely makes a school, adequate facilities are a great asset. The modern school needs learning aids of many kinds and varieties.

Perhaps one of the greatest barriers to effective education today is large classes, often necessitated by the current teacher shortage. Attempts are being made to meet the need by supplying non-professional persons as teacher aids. At best this is a makeshift and may be used as an alibi for not securing well-prepared teachers for all children. Large classes necessitate mass education. Mass education is not education as we have come to understand it in our study. To bring up a child according to his God-given talents and opportunities in God-ordained ways of child life, and to a God-appointed destiny, requires a learning process that takes account of individual needs. In mass education learning is at a minimum because understanding is at a minimum. Regimented repetition must of necessity prevail. Mass teaching reduces Christian education to an accidental minimum.

What can a competent teacher do when textbook material is poor, furniture is screwed to the floor, blackboard and bulletin space are at a minimum, and the like?

Notice that we said a *competent* teacher. A mere performer who lacks the art based on a well-understood science is stymied. He resorts to practices which he recalls as he viewed them when he was taught, or as he saw others teach. He imitates blindly, and therefore unintelligently.

A resourceful teacher who is energetic is not easily floored by circumstances. He knows how to avail himself of what is given by enlisting pupil initiative as well as his own to construct for themselves many things well-prepared learning facilities provide. Without movable furniture, this teacher can encourage group activity of a productive nature. The class makes its own bulletin board. Workbook material flows from a simple duplicator. These and similar activities make learning even more fascinating for children, for they have added opportunity to experience a feeling of personal achievement. The ceiling of teaching material may be ever so low, but a competent teacher looks upon it as an added challenge to personal resourcefulness.

UNCERTAINTIES IN CHRISTIAN EDUCATIONAL PRACTICE

The modern elementary school is about one hundred years of age, and the modern high school about fifty years. Educational theory and practice appropriate to the school of today have been developed while educational programs became well established. As school attendance increased, a greater spread of learning capacity came into evidence. Many children could not profit from the ready-made courses of study. As understanding of how a child learns and how personality is formed increased, curricula, methodology, and school organization were gradually changed to meet the needs of more learners of a greater variety. The function of the school became more comprehensive as urban life began to deprive children of valuable chores that gave them rich experience in living. Our growing schools cannot wait while issues in educational theory and practice are being debated and appraised. They need action. So they profit the best they can from what is known and generally accepted in educational theory and practice.

Christian schools are also caught in this rapid change. Distinctive educational theory and practice oriented to the Word of God as the light that gives light are very much in the making rather than actualities. We can say so little about them with confidence. In the absence of a distinctive theory and practice, Christian schools are found doing one of two things. They either adhere to a prescientific or more traditional theory and practice with some slight peripheral modifications, or they begin uncritically to absorb secular thinking through the use of modern textbooks and the enthusiasm of teachers for "new" ideas in modern education without foundational appraisal. We are in the process of exploring Christian thinking with reference to educational theory and practice, especially on the elementary and secondary levels. But we are only beginning. In this study we are bringing a few of these beginnings together.

The greatest contribution to education in the next generation will come from psychology and psychotherapy. Teachers should be alert to developments in these areas of thinking and practice. Christian teachers can reappraise the effectiveness of their work as new insights are achieved. To appraise these areas as Christians, however, teachers should be well schooled in Christian theology and Christian philoso-

phy. College seminars and teachers' institutes can help teachers
to keep abreast.

WEAKENING OF THE FAMILY UNIT

Bringing up a child to maturity is the responsibility solely of
parents. God has ordained that the home be the cradle for the
development of youth. This is no artificial assignment. Home and
family life afford a developing child his first and basic security.
When the family fails to any degree in this its most natural function,
there is no institution that can take its place with equal effectiveness.
A God-ordained way of life and institution cannot be replaced by
man with impunity.

Of the Christian home the above can be said with even greater
emphasis. It has pleased the Lord to build his church largely in
the family line. He has promised to be a God unto parents and
their children. The Bible speaks of children from Christian homes
as being holy. And Christian education, as we have seen, is first
of all education of Christians, of children in Christ. Christian education, therefore, has its source and foundation in family relationships. The integrity of the Christian home is essential for Christian
education.

We know, however, what is happening to American home life,
even among Christians, especially in urban centers. Luxurious living
makes all members of the family, especially young people, crave for
more and more of goods and comforts. Indulgence and permissiveness
are rampant. The gap between what young people want and what
they can, at certain levels, use profitably for self-discipline is widen-
ing. Undisciplined, permissive living is on the increase.

As far as the school is concerned a dilemma or impasse is the
result. On the one hand the school must take up the slack where
the home fails. Permissive and indulgent living at home calls for
increased restraint at school to maintain and develop group life as
well as to develop the individual. Child needs are not met by permissiveness and indulgence. These only cultivate feelings of insecurity and unrest. The school, by seeking to meet real needs of
child life, frequently enters upon tasks which the home should
assume. When the school thus takes over duties of parents by extending its sphere of service, it tends to weaken home control still
further. The school is asked to carry more than its just and equitable
load. It cannot replace the home with impunity. It can only supplement and extend the work of parents, no more.

What can teachers do about this tragic situation? The Christian
home and the Christian school should be able to work in united
effort by mutually assuming their rightful tasks. In the face of

the current trend much consultation is essential. Parents who are willing and able to do their full duty need the support of their children's teachers. Parents who fail to assume their responsibility as Christian parents need contact from the school to help them understand their problem. Sometimes this can be done by teachers dealing directly with such parents — which is another reason why teachers should be mature persons who can counsel with parents. Sometimes pastors and other church officers should be acquainted with the situation. In any event, Christian teachers should confer with parents frequently as need arises. Many problems in child development arise from, or are at least closely associated with, family life. Teachers should be fully aware of this in order to deal in an understanding way with children.

The task of a Christian teacher is a glorious one because he is building for eternity. Education as heart acceptance of truth is an abiding effect in the persons and personalities of learners. Teaching is correspondingly a difficult task under the most favorable conditions. In our discussion of teaching and the demands made upon the teacher in the modern school it has become evident that a teacher's work is many-sided. Fortunately we are on the threshold of a more enlightened understanding of child life and the forming of his personality. Teachers can profit greatly from this advance. This deepened insight is only one phase of a teacher's equipment, but a very important one.[1] Christian education especially needs this insight, for it views a child as precious in the sight of God.

QUESTIONS FOR FURTHER STUDY

1. What changes, if any, has your understanding of teaching undergone as a result of your recent study?

2. What further preparations do you consider essential for yourself before you assume the responsibility of a classroom?

3. Try to recall one of your teachers who, as you now understand it, succeeded to awaken in you a desire to learn. What factors seem to have contributed to this teacher's successful influence upon your endeavor?

4. The school being what it is, namely an institution that employs our culture and civilization in organized form for child development, instruction constitutes a major function of the teacher, though not all of it. What activities of the teacher are involved in the work of instruction? How can your study at college prepare you for this major task?

1. This is no time to discredit the need for professionally educated teachers. It is always in order to re-evaluate a professional educational program.

5. What change has your view of classroom discipline undergone, if any, as a result of your study? With what meaning will you now speak of a discipline problem, and how will you approach such a problem?

6. Both parents and teachers are in danger of an attitude of self-righteousness in the act of punishing a child, at least as the child interprets it. Why? Why is this interpretation of our punishing him apt to have undesirable results? How can we avoid such interpretation? Surely not by eliminating punishment, for punish we must. Why?

7. In view of what you have studied concerning child development, what forms might punishment take to accomplish remedial results in a child's life?

8. Throughout our study we have made frequent reference to maturity as a goal of child development and learning, and maturity of a teacher. Some forms of behavior we speak of as immature, and others as evil. Is this merely a matter of terminology, of semantics, or is there a real distinction? Explain.

9. What child development problems may arise from immature actions of parents and teachers? Illustrate.

10. How can Christian education help developing youth to face our culture, and even to try reforming those parts of it which are barriers to effective Christian living? Illustrate.

11. How can you account for the abuses to which children have been subjected in the name of "total depravity"? Are we in danger of this abuse today? Explain.

12. Ask several teachers in elementary and secondary schools who have taught for several years what they consider to be their greatest hurdles to effective work. Do they coincide with some of the barriers mentioned in this text?

SELECTIONS FOR FURTHER REFERENCE*

Beaumont & Macomber, Chapter XIII, "Psychological Principles and Their Implications for Teaching."

Blair et al., Part 6, "The Psychology of Teaching."

Cole & Bruce, Chapter XVI, "The Teacher's Task and the Barriers"; Chapter XIX, "The Teacher as Mature Person."

Cronbach, Chapter XV, "The Teacher as Classroom Leader."

Crow & Crow, Part 6, "The Role of the Teacher in Education."

Fullagar et al., Section IIIC, "The Teacher's Role," Selections 44-47.

Gates et al., Chapter XXII, "The Mental Health of the Teacher."

Lane & Beauchamp. This entire book is helpful for interpersonal relations in teaching.

Morse & Wingo, Chapter XIII, "Learning and Discipline."

Mursell, Chapter XVI, "Teaching and Evaluation in Relation to Personality."

Skinner, Part 5, "Teaching and Guidance."

Stephens, Chapter XXII, "The Teacher and His Own Adjustment."

Stroud, Chapter XVI, "The Profession of Teaching."

*References are cited here by author's name. See Bibliography for titles and complete publication data.

20

Appraising Learning

TRADITIONAL APPRAISAL

"How is Charles doing in school?" asked Charles' mother of his teacher. "I noticed that his recent report card left much to be desired," she continued. "He had an E in history, I recall. That is barely passing. And the other marks were not much better. Effort was marked up a little, so he should be improving. Or is he just plain stupid?"

"I think Charles' marks will be coming up for the next marking period," replied the teacher. "Of late he has been trying very hard. And he seems to take more interest in his work. So, I think you will see some improvement in most or all of his subjects the next time."

Until comparatively recently this was about the extent of a teacher's reply to a mother's inquiry concerning his child's progress in school. It is still the kind of report some schools and some teachers give. Schools and teachers alert to more adequate tools of evaluation or appraisal, however, can give the inquiring mother a more adequate reply that can help her in dealing with her child's needs.

Learning consists of specific achievements by the learner that contribute cumulatively to his total development, we said earlier in our discussion. These achievements are outcomes of the learning process. Can we state the outcomes specifically, and having described them, can we measure them? Can we designate the progress a learner is making along directional process goals to final and more ultimate goals? Not merely in some vague fashion, as "I think Charles is doing better," but in terms of an objective standard that can be universally used, as we use a yardstick or a pound weight?

RECENT DEVELOPMENTS IN THE APPRAISAL OF LEARNING

The age-old practice, which still prevails in many classrooms, has been to give periodic quizzes, tests, and examinations of a more or less factual content to ascertain what a pupil has learned. Some questions may have called for the organization of information, but even then the answers consisted largely of giving back to the teacher factual material previously presented or found in sources. The teacher arbitrarily determined a scale on the basis of which a mark was assigned, 95, or 9, or B, depending upon the graduations of the scale. Sometimes the mark amounted to no more than a vague impression of the test as a whole upon the mind of the teacher. At other times it consisted of specific values assigned to each item. Several of these marks were accumulated over a period of time. These were averaged when the marking period arrived, and the average was recorded as the mark in a given subject for that period. The mark for the semester or year became the basis for judging whether Charles was to pass or fail. Pupils have been known to pass with a grade of 70 and fail with a 69, or pass with a D average and fail with something less marked F. Fred may be known as a B student according to the average of his marks, but no one could tell specifically what this meant except that it is an average of test scores and daily marks.

At the turn of the century, when the learning process and the learning outcomes were being subjected to critical examination, some interesting phenomena turned up. Among these phenomena was the discrepancy in teachers' marks. It was found, for example, that Fred might be rated as a B student in history in School X, while his work would barely bring a C in School Y. A composition paper in English might bring a 90 in New York, but only a 75 or even less in San Francisco. Teachers' marks were not merely found to be fallible, but arbitrary judgments based on opinion. Reports of studies that disclosed these facts multiplied rapidly.

The conclusion was that a teacher's appraisal of learning was largely based on arbitrary standards, each teacher in each school determining for himself how to mark a pupil. The question arose whether a more objective standard could be devised that could constitute a common basis for judgment. Could an objective standard be found by which Henry's papers would be scored approximately alike by different teachers?

REVISED APPROACH TO APPRAISAL

The interest in the appraisal of learning outcomes coincided with the critical investigation of the learning process itself. The theories of conditioning and trial-and-error were developed to explain how learning takes place. According to these theories, learning is essentially a process of connecting stimuli and responses. Learning outcomes can be stated, it was thought, in terms of responses to given stimuli. Responses are the performances of a subject. The attempt was made to construct measuring devices to ascertain objectively the rate and quality of performance. Investigators set to work. Thorndike himself was one of the first to construct objective measurement devices.

Skills and information as learning outcomes were the first performances that were subjected to objective measurement. Handwriting scales, for example, were constructed giving samples of handwriting at various school grade levels or on a scale of number values. A child's writing could be compared with these levels to ascertain his progress. Reading tests, both speed and comprehension, vocabulary tests, grammar tests in English and in foreign languages, and the like, were constructed. By giving these tests on a wide scale throughout the land, norms were developed by which a teacher and a school could compare performance with standard.

Scales and tests thus constructed sought to accomplish three things:

(1) Provide a quantitative approach to appraisal. Learning outcomes were expressed in terms of performance of skills and information that can be measured on a quantitative basis, how much or to what degree. In this way the subjective element in appraisal could be reduced to a minimum and more uniformity could be achieved.

(2) Provide a key by which the performance can be judged. Answers could be judged right or wrong. Thus two persons widely apart geographically and with diverse background could arrive at the same score.

(3) Provide a scale of equal units. To measure a plot of ground we use a standardized unit such as the acre. It was thought that in measuring learning a similar unit must be found. For example, if most fifth graders scored 125 on a scale of units in a geography test, we can call this the fifth-grade level of achievement. To know whether Charles, who is in the seventh grade, is up to grade level in geography, one can follow the scale. Charles scores 127. He is approximately at fifth grade level. Special work in geography is called for to bring him to, say 162, which is recorded as seventh grade level. When tests are thus laid out in units, we can have a uniform basis of marking progress in learning.

What shall we say about these developments in the appraising of learning? Do they help us chart a pupil's progress in genuine learning? The wholesale use of objective, standardized tests in schools, even today, would indicate that this was thought to be the answer to the vague appraisal that preceded.

Appraisal based on the atomistic bias is in error, even more than traditional appraisal based on the unitary character of mind as an entity.

Recent developments in psychology as well as in educational theory and practice have pointed out the inadequacy of a quantitative and objective appraisal of learning. The rediscovery of the wholeness of the person first reflected by the insight theory of learning and more recently in the thinking and creative expression theory, has led to a reappraisal of the process of evaluation in learning and teaching. The quantitative aspect of measurement began to give way to more qualitative modes of appraisal. Development and learning were increasingly viewed as unitary processes involving the whole person. While psychology once again set out in search of a center of reference that unifies the person, educational theory and practice went in search of a self-conscious subject in terms of whom learning activities could be given a unified meaning. There was no return to earlier terminology of mind, soul, faculties, etc. These proved too nebulous and were based on philosophical dualism. New terms came into being, such as organismic, integrated personality, oriented personality, personality dynamics, group dynamics, personality field, not to mention more. Each of these terms is illustrative of the present attempt in psychology and education to get back to a unified whole, more comprehensive than earlier mind and soul theories.

In our discussion of development and learning we have sought a scriptural answer to this search. We found that this necessitated a restatement of the meaning of such concepts as person, personality, development, learning, and the medium of learning and development. We also need a revision of current ideas of appraisal and evaluation of learning outcomes.

Before we enter into this discussion, we should ask two prior questions: Why appraise learning? And what are we to appraise?

WHY APPRAISE LEARNING?

Let us note three reasons why appraisal is important.

(1) Learning, being the activity of a subject, needs appraisal by the subject. We saw that all learning follows in the pursuit of a goal. As learning activities and learning outcomes give a learner the feeling of attaining a desired goal they acquire meaning for him. And meaning is the key to genuine learning. It is important, then, that a learner constantly appraise and reappraise learning outcomes and goals so that he may have the feeling of progress and attainment. A learner is constantly appraising his progress. What he needs is criteria for appraisal. As in teaching we activate needs and make learners conscious of perceptible goals to consummate these needs, so we must develop criteria for continuous self-appraisal. Adequate appraisal by self is a strong incentive to increased effort.

(2) The teacher needs to ascertain whether the learning outcomes

point to progress toward a well-defined goal. The teacher knows the
end from the beginning. He planned the learning process. Directional process goals lead to more comprehensive goals. Techniques
of appraisal equip the teacher with means for assessing a learner's
readiness every step of the way to well-conceived goals. Learning
outcomes must constantly be appraised for their cumulative effect
upon child development. Appraisal is not a spasmodic something that
helps a teacher get scores for marking, but a well-considered technique
in the process of teaching.

(3) The parents call for constant appraisal. The question asked
by Charles' mother at the opening of this chapter is upon the
lips of all parents. They look for it in the report card. They seek it
at P.T.A. meetings and at grade mother meetings. Are they getting
the information from the school which they need in order to co-
operate with the teacher and the administration? Teachers and
principals are professional workers. They have the know-how, or
should have, of appraisal. Parents do not have this professional
information. Schools must translate professional appraisal into a
form of communication parents can understand.

WHAT IS TO BE APPRAISED?

When we raise the question what we can appraise, we should
distinguish between learning and performance. Performance may
not match learning. Learning, we said, is heart acceptance of truth.
Performance may or may not reflect genuine learning, that is,
whether one has accepted truth and is ordering his life accordingly.
In many cases it will fall far short of indicating what has been
learned. In several cases, too, performance may fail to exhibit real
learning.

Can we appraise genuine learning? To raise the question is to
answer it. Learning outcomes are observable to us in performance
only. "By their fruits shall ye know them" also applies to learning
outcomes. Learning outcomes, then, are to be appraised in terms
of performance. When we examine performance as expressive of
learning outcomes, we recognize six distinguishable forms. We may,
for our purpose, think of these as six kinds of learning outcome.

(1) Skills and habits; for example, handwriting, word recognition,
column addition, using a map to locate places.

(2) Information; for example, Chicago is in Illinois, Washington
was the first president of the United States, Jesus arose on the third
day after his burial.

(3) Concepts and meanings; for example, farming, revolution,
Old Testament dispensation, linear measure, qualitative, scientific
method.

(4) Attitudes; for example, self-assertiveness on the play grounds, self-esteem, leadership, co-operation, willingness to accept secondary role for good reason.

(5) Appreciations; for example, of good literature and music, of help rendered by another, of handicaps suffered by playmates, of righteous living.

(6) Ideals; for example, honesty, accuracy, tolerance of weakness, love of the truth.

Every one of these constitutes a performance from which we may infer learning outcomes. When a child writes a story, for example, certain skills and habits are observed such as posture, holding the pen, and letter formation. Information and meanings are observed in the content of the story. Legibility and neatness display attitudes and ideals. Ideals and appreciations may also be evident from the content of the story. The consistency with which these performances are evident in a variety of classroom activities will further establish the evidence that they represent genuine learning.

It is these various performances from which a teacher can infer learning outcomes. He is not to mistake performance for learning, but he is to appraise learning as he comes to see it in the performances. A consistent, steady progress in these performances is a reasonably safe clue to genuine learning.

Now the question arises, can we chart the progress of a pupil in these performances? Can we develop units by which we can block off steps of progress so that objective measures are available to gauge a learner's achievements? We have no way of appraising learning except through performance. We can infer learning from performances, but in so doing must always remember to distinguish between genuine learning and what we observe in performance. Among performances are those which are more peripheral to the learner than others. Others involve the learner more in his total personality. Slant in handwriting, for example, is a skill which does not involve a learner's feeling unless it is the fruit of the attitude of neatness together with muscular co-ordination. Accurate spelling, likewise, is a peripheral skill which does not involve the whole person unless it is a product of an ideal of accuracy in expression. And so we might continue. When we go down the line from one through six in the above performances, we see that the first two are by themselves peripheral performances, the third is more personal, and the fourth through the sixth get deeper into the structure of the total personality.

Charting the progress of a child in these performances according to well-defined units becomes increasingly difficult and wellnigh impossible as we go down the list from one through six. We can develop a handwriting scale to gauge a child's letter formation, slant, spacing of letters, and even size of letters. We can construct spelling scales, comprehension and speed tests in reading, factual tests in history and geography, and the like. Mastery in these and similar areas can be clocked off into units of achievement as children develop to maturity. Grade level norms can be calculated by wide sampling of test material. In other words, we can measure these performances by an accepted standard, and with universally valid results.

But how can we measure a child's enjoyment of a poem or a play, his sense of responsibility in the preparation of a paper, his respect for authority? And these are more indicative of genuine learning than the performances we can measure. These we must appraise to infer genuine learning. But we can have no scale of universally valid units by which to gauge them. We shall have to satisfy ourselves with less objective and tangible modes of valuing. Learning outcomes that contribute the most to the ultimate goal of a child's education cannot be measured in terms of performances. A teacher needs more than tests and scales to ascertain progress in the development of his pupils.

APPRAISAL TECHNIQUES

It should be obvious that the techniques of appraisal are adequate tools only in the hands of a skilled professional worker. As a stethoscope is a comparatively useless instrument to one who has not learned to relate sounds of the body to a syndrome, so a test in history or a spelling scale is of little value to one who does not understand child development and learning. The ease with which some teachers make tests and form judgments about learners is indicative of how little they understand of how a child learns and of learning outcomes.

Oral and written quizzes, tests, and examinations seeking to measure pupil achievement in the usual school subjects are the most common in use among teachers. And it is well that they occupy an important place in appraisal, for subject matter as we defined it earlier in our discussion is the medium in which child development takes place. Techniques that measure or appraise understanding and mastery of subject matter give us a clue to child development.

Oral and written tests

We generally classify these tests as short-answer objective tests and subjective essay tests. The former are also called "new-type" tests because they are of more recent origin.

We shall not take space here to illustrate and describe short-answer or "new-type" tests. Students are familiar with them in general, having taken such tests at various times. A more detailed account of them can be obtained from sources mentioned in the reference list at the end of this chapter.

Short-answer or "new-type" tests have certain advantages over the more conventional essay tests:

(1) They make a larger sampling of performances possible. More items of information and skills can be covered in a given period of time, consequently a wider selection can be made from the subject matter covered by the test.

(2) Scoring can be more objective. If a test is constructed with care, the answers are either right or wrong, or at least largely one or the other. Some ambiguity and overlapping can hardly be avoided in certain tests, especially when a test seeks to measure more than factual information and skills, but even then answers can be judged largely right or wrong by comparison.

(3) These tests are easily scored when a key is constructed. If it is not possible to construct a key that enables almost anyone to score a test item right or wrong, the test in all probability lacks objectivity. With a good key in hand, almost anyone can score a short-answer test by following directions.

But these tests also have their limitations:

(1) Opportunity for guessing is increased greatly. On a true-false test, for example, it has been found that with a minimum of information one can approximate correct answers for half the test by guessing. Guessing has been counteracted by subtracting the total wrong answers from the total right, but this is rather arbitrary practice. It may discourage guessing, but does not rule out the fact.

(2) It takes much more time to construct a good short-answer test than to write an essay examination. The counter-argument is that it takes much longer to score an essay examination. And this counter-argument is right. But essay examinations can be constructed to overcome this disadvantage to an extent.

(3) The cost of administering these tests is greater when prepared in typed, duplicated, or printed form. An essay test can be written on the blackboard. "New-type" tests can be given orally, it is said. Some studies seem to indicate that the outcome is not much different from the same test given in printed or duplicated form. While this may be true for the group as a whole, for certain learners it would present added difficulty, for they grasp the meaning better when seeing the statement before them.

(4) These tests can give a teacher very little information about a child's ability to organize his thinking with reference to a certain problem or issue. Concepts and meanings as learning outcomes are not easily inferred from performances called for on these tests.

When we compare the advantages and limitations of short-answer tests, we must conclude that they fill a need by providing a technique by which teachers can gauge a child's performance in terms of skills and information on a more comprehensive scale than can be had from essay tests. They should be used for this purpose. When used almost exclusively however, a teacher should recognize that he is failing to appraise performances that contribute far more than habits, skills, and information to child development. Almost exclusive use of "new-type" tests is resorted to sometimes because of the large number of pupils involved, and help can be used to score papers. When this is done, let not a teacher suppose that he is reporting genuine learning or any approximation of it when he gives a student a mark based on these tests.

In many cases the value of essay tests has been too readily dismissed. While it is true that they are scored subjectively, teachers can construct questions and topics so that a sort of key can be constructed by which the adequacy of answers can be gauged. The score assigned to each answer may by itself seem quite arbitrary, yet in relation to the entire test it has real significance. The greatest value that accrues both to the learner and to the teacher is the organization of informational content in terms of concepts and meanings that go to make up understanding. This can hardly be achieved by any kind of short-answer test. While a teacher may, in going over the tests with a class to discuss answers given, uncover helpful information concerning meanings and understandings attained, "new-type" tests disclose little of these.

But even of essay type tests it must be said, as of all pencil-paper techniques of appraisal, that a teacher learns little about attitudes, appreciations, and ideals that a learner has achieved. Performance in these areas is not readily gotten from the usual test routine. Other means of appraisal must come to the aid of the teacher to know whether a child is developing understanding or acceptance of truth that forms his personality.

Some valuable suggestions have been made for the improvement of essay type tests and examinations. Let us take note of a few here.

(1) Use essay tests only to appraise performances that cannot be measured more specifically and objectively by short-answer tests. Do not use essay tests to measure factual mastery, for example. This would mean that in many tests a teacher would use both types.

(2) The formulation of questions should call for specific answers. Vague questions, such as "Discuss . . ." "Write one hundred words explaining . . ." "How do you interpret the following . . ." and the like should be avoided. By what standard would you score a "discuss" question? All the student is asked to do is "discuss." Here is a more

specific question: "How did the opposition to the League of Nations mount following Woodrow Wilson's return from Europe?" A rather specific answer can be anticipated and the organization of factual and judgment content can be appraised. The student knows the basis of appraisal from the very question.

(3) Avoid optional questions or "extra credit" questions, whatever one may call the questions appended as not required for satisfactory work on the test. They make comparative scoring quite impossible. By comparative scoring we mean that a teacher takes account of the distribution of individual scores. Whether a score on a certain paper is to be considered a high or average score depends in part on what the class as a whole was able to do with a test. While this should not be the only determining factor, failure to take account of it betrays lack of sensitivity of the teacher to the results of the test as a teaching device as well as a testing device. When an entire class, or the largest number in a class, fail or nearly fail a test, a teacher should take inventory of his own ability to assess the readiness of his pupils. Optional questions make desirable comparison of scores impossible.

(4) Formulate anticipated answers before scoring and compare them with several pupil-formulated answers before determining what to look for in the answers. Teachers may consider questions clear, while even the best students have difficulty in determining what is wanted. Teachers may also overestimate or underestimate the student's ability to handle certain questions. A comparison of a tentatively constructed set of anticipated answers will help a teacher be realistic about his scoring.

What place has an oral test or examination? We do not refer to administering a test orally by reading the test items and having pupils write the answers, but to oral response by the pupils. Obviously comparative scoring becomes impossible. Every pupil is scored on the answer he gives to a certain question. For the class as a whole wide sampling of content can be used, but in a class of twenty or more students each student will have comparatively few opportunities to demonstrate his performance. Each student is tested on a very limited range of material. There is an informality about oral testing which often sets a stage of ease and self-assurance.

But we cannot stop at appraisal based on tests and examinations involving subject matter, important as they are. We must appraise child development. This means that learning outcomes must be found cumulatively to contribute to this development. What techniques has a teacher available for this broader scope of appraisal? Must he rely upon casual observation and opinion, or are more precise and objective tools available? There are tools available that a classroom teacher can use with good results. We shall merely refer to some of the more common here, leaving details for supplementary sources.

TOOLS FOR BROADER APPRAISAL

The anecdotal record. This consists of a cumulative set of notes recording a learner's activities in various situations. It is a descriptive account of what one observes, not a formulation of judgments. For example, "John slumped in his seat when called upon to answer a question in arithmetic." This statement merely describes John's action in a given situation. "John proved stubborn this morning" is a judgment statement. In an isolated case this may prove to be a wrong judgment.

How can the anecdotal record be used? At the beginning of the year a teacher prepares a note card for each pupil. On it he records certain information available at the office such as IQ, general progress of the pupil, etc. As days pass, additional information is called for in certain cases as a teacher's attention is drawn to pupil needs. A descriptive account over a period of days will begin to disclose a pattern of behavior from which a teacher who understands child development will be able to draw helpful conclusions that constitute cues for procedures in teaching them. Obviously not every pupil's record calls for an anecdotal account. But unless a teacher commences with individual records and follows them through, he may never get to closer observation of certain pupils and will form premature judgments based on inadequate data.

Questionnaires, inventories, and interviews. These can be used very unobtrusively during class session. An interest questionnaire, for example, can be injected into oral English lessons for the purpose of stimulating discussion. Personal talks with children at opportune moments can constitute a source of valuable information that can help a teacher understand a child. The formal interview often accomplishes less than the incidental discussion of a child's problem or personal interest. A teacher should be willing to listen more than speak to a child. Admonition and instruction have their place, but they take effect only when a child has accepted a teacher as an influence in his life. Willingness to listen often accomplishes this rapport.

Sociometric methods, such as the rating scale, who's who approach, and the sociogram. Consult sources for their use. This example gives a clue to the value of a sociogram and how to develop it. A teacher planned to divide his class in history into group projects for several days. How was he to determine the membership of his groups? He also had a sociogram in mind as a source of individual pupil study. He passed a card to each pupil and asked the class to write their first, second, and third choice of pupils with whom they would like to work. From the cards he readily organized the groups. But he learned more. Here is Joan Deters; she was third choice on only two cards and had no first or second choices. And Wilbur Huitsing's name did not appear on any card. On the other hand, Ralph Hall's name was either first or second choice on twenty-three out of the thirty cards. Similar information was secured about all members of the class. The teacher saw his work cut out for him as he planned the development of Joan, Wilbur, and others. But it is also of interest how Ralph Hall exercises his apparent popularity and how he is developing in it.

Autobiography and accounts of special experiences such as vacation tours. At given intervals these can be very revealing and give a teacher valuable clues for helpful measures. A teacher should be cautious in the interpretation of motivation when reading or listening to an autobiography. This often requires insights not developed by one not oriented in psychotherapy.

Check lists and rating scales. They may be found valuable to disclose pupil interests and problems that a child is trying to surmount or for which he is seeking compensatory measures. When used, these should be interpreted with care and analyzed with a child for the degree of self-appraisal of which he is capable.

In the use of all these techniques a teacher must be aware that he is not to pose as a psychotherapist. He is a teacher. But directing learning is not some isolated intellectual enterprise, as we have seen again and again in our study. It is a phase of child development, and only as learning outcomes contribute cumulatively to the forming of personality can they be deemed educative.

Because a teacher is not a psychotherapist or a psychiatric social worker, the more technical tools are not for his use. To these projective techniques belong such tests as the Rorschach Test and Thematic Apperception Test, and the case study technique. It is well that a teacher be informed of what these tools are and what information they give in order that he can follow reports by experts based on these techniques.

Finally, *the cumulative record as a school project* should be available to every teacher and every teacher should make his contribution to its content. The pupil's cumulative record is the composite of information gathered in the school office, office of the principal, or personnel officer if distinct from the principal. Teachers should have ready access to this record and make their contribution to its growth. Information contained therein is confidential and should be guarded against abuse. It is a source of information to the teacher, rather than of other teachers' judgments. Teachers should try to form their own judgments on data from several sources.

USE AND CONSTRUCTION OF TESTS

Testing, construction of tests, scoring tests, interpreting scores, and following up the results are important phases of teaching. As a matter of fact, testing is a teaching device and never an end in itself. When divorced from teaching, as, for example, when used as a device to derive marks for a report card, it ceases to be of educational value. Because testing is an important teaching technique, the use and construction of tests is essential equipment for the teacher.

STANDARDIZED AND NON-STANDARDIZED TESTS

Standardized tests are tests constructed by experts schooled in the statistical and psychological aspects of testing. These tests are given to a large number of pupils representative of school population. This is called wide sampling. The mid-point of the scores from highest to lowest is considered the statistical norm of the test. This score represents the average ability as reflected by the test. Mid-points for grade levels can be found and grade averages determined. Thus a given school and class can be compared in mid-point scores. But this says nothing about the distribution of scores above and below the mid-point. How high do they reach or how low do they fall in a given school or grade? How many scores cluster close to the average? How widely scattered are scores? These too can be compared with the distribution on the test for all pupils. For both mid-points and distribution we have technical names with which a teacher should familiarize himself. In the former we speak of mean, median, and mode. In the latter we use quartiles and deciles.

Standardized tests have chiefly administrative values. The teacher can compare his class with national norms as to mid-point and distribution. The latter is often more important than the former. The principal can make comparisons within his school and compare his school with national norms. When doing so, however, teachers and principals should allow for the cultural status of the constituency. National norms represent a wide sampling of great cultural divergencies. If school A is located, for example, in a community composed largely of professional people, business executives, and skilled workers, the national norms are too low. Likewise a school located in a community of semi-skilled and non-skilled workers should not expect to exceed the norm, or even attain to it, depending upon the constituency.

The key used in scoring a standardized test is uniform and can be used accurately by any one who can follow directions. Hence, scoring can be done by non-professional personnel. Papers can be scored by machine when answers are recorded on appropriate sheets for this purpose. Recording of scores likewise can be carried out on appropriate forms by any one who can follow directions. But interpretation is the work of a professional worker. What outcomes on a test mean for a given class or school must be determined by men and women skilled in analyzing the total educational situation.

Use of standardized tests

Standardized tests are not a passing fad, but with improved construction and more intelligent use they have found an abiding place in the educational program of schools. Upon their first appearance they were abused, often being made ends in themselves by accumulating scores with no functional interpretation. At the time when they were so widely being used to satisfy curiosity or to appear in the forefront of educational development, a pamphlet appeared entitled, *After Testing, What?* Both title and content challenged schoolmen to rethink tests and testing. Standardized tests cost money. One should be able to justify their use educationally to warrant the expenditure. A standardized test must fit into a well-planned program of teaching and administration and should be able to contribute what a less expensive and less time-consuming technique cannot furnish. When selected with care and given at appropriate times, standardized tests are valuable tools in promoting instruction.

Standardized tests can be secured in separate subject-areas such as reading, arithmetic, history, etc.; in specific skills such as speed and comprehension in reading, problem solving in arithmetic, location in geography. They can also be had in groups of subjects called test batteries. A battery of tests can give a general survey in the subject matter field.

Not all printed tests are standardized, as some have surmised. Diagnostic tests, for example, seek to analyze specific weaknesses in learning. When difficulties have been located and analyzed, remedial devices can be used to help a pupil over his hurdles. Some tests are constructed to check a learner's knowledge of a certain chapter or textbook. These, and like tests, have their value, but not for comparison.

Construction of classroom tests

Tests of a teacher's own construction are, of course, not standardized, though a teacher can develop norms and distributions of his own over a period of time. He can give the same test or similar tests to several successive classes on the same grade level and arrive at mid-point scores and distributions. These can prove helpful when used for comparative purposes, bearing in mind individual and group differences.

In the construction of a test a teacher should follow a design as much as he follows a design in all planning. A test is a teaching device, not an end in itself. It must contribute to the directional process goals of child development by providing a basis for and interest in self-appraisal by learners. How can this design be accomplished? A few practical suggestions are in order.

(1) Whether to use a short-answer, objective type of test, or an essay test, or a combination of the two will depend largely upon the content of test material. If the material to be tested consists largely of skills and information, a short-answer test serves the purpose best. If meaning and understanding are to be tested, the essay type is to be used. In many cases a combination is to be preferred. In the construction of a short-answer test do not mix types, such as true-false and completion. Mixing types of short-answer tests complicates matters for learners. Two or three sets of short-answer types can be used profitably.

(2) A test is constructed to appraise performance, and test items should be constructed to encourage the best performance by the learner. Performance and learning are not to be confused, as we have seen before. It is through the testing of performance that a teacher tries to appraise learning. But it is always a question whether performance at any time reflects genuine learning. Other forms of appraisal should supplement testing in order that a teacher may discover more about a child's development. But right tests can help a teacher gauge genuine learning through the testing of performance. For example, begin a test with items that give a pupil confidence in his own ability at the outset. To begin with difficult items will frustrate at the outset a child who is not too confident of himself, with the result that his best is not forthcoming.

(3) A test should be valid if it is to be used as a device for appraisal. A test is valid when it measures what it is supposed to measure. Suppose a fifth grade teacher prepares a test in social studies to measure the learner's ability to understand how improved transportation has helped us enjoy the products of distant places. Test items should be constructed to bring out a learner's knowledge pertaining to this fact. Test items must be drawn up in language that is clear and creates no hurdles of interpretation. A difficult phraseology in a sentence would mean that more than knowledge of

social studies is being tested. The test should be designed to measure social studies, not English language or creative writing.

(4) A test should be reliable. This means that the outcome of a test should measure as accurately as possible a learner's actual achievement. One enhances reliability of a test by making it a natural part of a learning-teaching situation in which teacher and pupil try to ascertain what has been learned. A teacher is not likely to increase the reliability of a test by saying, "You'd better get this, for we'll have a test on this next Monday. Those who get less than a C will find themselves in trouble when the term mark is drawn up." A learner's best effort is achieved by constructive motivation. Cramming and last-minute effort are not designed to reflect genuine learning.

(5) Construct a key to a test before giving the test to the class. By so doing a teacher checks both the validity and reliability of a test. If a teacher has difficulty deciding on a clear-cut, specific answer to a test item, pupils will find it still more so. To construct a key after the test has been given may mean that certain test items have to be discarded, and scoring becomes the more difficult. Scoring a test without a key reduces appraisal to momentary impression and opinion.

AN ADEQUATE PROGRAM OF APPRAISAL

When all is said and done, a teacher can be guided in his appraisal of genuine learning by four criteria.

(1) *Is the design for appraisal all-inclusive?*

A teacher must appraise the whole of learning. Testing is a necessary device to ascertain the performance of a pupil. A well-constructed test furnishes data about child development that must be related to data obtained from other sources of appraisal. The testing of habits and skills, information, and meanings and understandings will reflect progress when subject matter selected and test construction are designed to accomplish the final goal.

(2) *Is the change taking place in the total personality of the learner the basis for all evaluation?*

While it is true that the chief function of the school is to develop a graduated body of concepts that disclose truth to a learner's consciousness, how he feels about these concepts is as important in the forming of his personality as the concepts themselves. So we say that the total life or personality of a learner is affected by every learning experience. A teacher is very much concerned, then, how a given experience affects a pupil. We do not merely accept "with the head," but with the heart, that is, with the whole person as motivated from within. An adequate program of appraisal, then, concerns itself with the entire personality.

(3) *Are all possible data for appraisal adequately organized for interpretation?*

All data for appraisal should be organized to form a pattern of behavior that describes the pupil's personality. This can be done when a teacher as a professional person accumulates data for this purpose and continually reinterprets them. School records and a teacher's findings can be integrated into a portrait that is very revealing.

When a patient calls at the office of his physician, the nurse takes out the cumulative record. Before the physician makes any attempt at examination, he consults the record. Examination may disclose new information that suggests a syndrome. Now the physician can begin to appraise the situation.

Teaching, too, is a diagnostic process of constantly reassessing the readiness of learners for new experiences and of appraising past experiences. Only a professionally educated person is equal to this task.

(4) *Is the program of appraisal a continuing activity as part of directing the learning process?*

Evaluation as appraisal is as much a teaching device as the selection of textbooks or the planning of an excursion for enrichment of perceptual experience in learning. If used as a device to arrive at marks, and the like, it fails of its educational value. When planning a unit of work some thought should be given to anticipated test items and to other forms of appraisal that can be used appropriately.

CONCLUSION

Our ability as teachers to appraise a child's progress in the development of his personality as it takes place in the school, or anywhere else for that matter, is extremely difficult. How can we evaluate the impact of truth upon the heart of a child, and the surrender of the heart in humble obedience to truth? The road to freedom is the road of voluntary obedience to the God of truth. Difficult as appraisal of this attainment may be, we must make an attempt at it to know what we are doing and where we are going in Christian education.

We may ask about Charles, for example, to what extent he as a ninth grader has attained the right disposition of heart. The A in history says that he has the right information and skills, and, if the testing has been adequate, that he has developed concepts and meanings that disclose truth to him. But does it say that Charles has developed ear and eye for historical events such as the providence of his Father in heaven, who directs his life all the way? Let us not say that a teacher's appraisal does not concern itself with this except in a very general way. One is reminded of the words of Chapman and Counts that appeared in their book *Principles of Education* more than thirty years ago:[1]

Greeting his pupils, the master asked:
What would you learn of me?
And the reply came;
How shall we care for our bodies?
How shall we rear our children?
How shall we work together?
How shall we live with our fellowmen?
How shall we play?
For what ends shall we live? . . .
And the teacher pondered these words, and
sorrow was in his heart, for his own learning
touched not these things.

A teacher's learning must touch the meanings and motivations of the Christian life to appraise the maturing of Christian youth. If his learning has its dynamic in these meanings and motivations he is prompted to a broader appraisal than an A in history.

Let us not forget that the most effective appraisal is self-appraisal. This applies to the learner as well as to the teacher. A teacher's constant appraisal should activate in the learner a felt need for self-improvement. There is a place in the lives of all of us for a positive, constructive feeling of adequacy. We should constantly feel that we can do better without discrediting our feeling of satisfaction with present attainment. A characteristic of maturity is a constructive self-appraisal that is followed by a sincere effort at progress, and that frowns on complacency.

QUESTIONS FOR FURTHER STUDY

1. Some schools have set marking periods when report cards are prepared to be sent home. It is not uncommon for teachers, especially in junior and senior high schools, to plan their testing periods accordingly. They speak of these tests as quarterly tests, for example. Appraise such a testing procedure according to the learning process.

1. J. C. Chapman and G. S. Counts, *Principles of Education* (Boston: Houghton Mifflin, 1924), p. ii.

2. Examine some standardized tests and the manuals that accompany them. What should a teacher know in order to give them, score them, and interpret them?

3. Examine some diagnostic tests and the manuals that accompany them. How do they differ from standardized achievement tests? How are they to be used?

4. Classroom tests should be teaching devices for self-appraisal. How should a teacher plan his teaching to make this effective?

5. As a student preparing for teaching you should familiarize yourself with important tests that can be used in your classroom teaching. If you are to be an elementary school teacher, you should acquaint yourself with elementary tests available. If you plan to teach on the secondary level, you should know of some useful tests in your teaching fields, such as English, history, biology. You will find the following source helpful: Buros, O. K. (ed.), *Mental Measurements Yearbook*, The Dryden Press. This source adds a supplement biennially to bring the list up to date. Libraries often carry sample packets of tests, and test publishers prepare sample packets at small cost.

6. How can a quiz be used effectively?

SELECTIONS FOR FURTHER REFERENCE

Blair *et al.*, Part 5, "Measurement and Evaluation."

Coladarci, Chapter VIII, "Assessment of Pupil Status and Progress."

Cole & Bruce, Chapter XVII, "Appraising Development and Learning Measurement in Education."

Crow & Crow, Part 5, "Evaluating and Reporting."

Gates *et al.*, Chapter XVI, "Appraising Progress by Means of Tests and Other Devices"; Chapter XVII, "Appraising the School Program through Study of Pupils as Persons"; Chapter XXI, "Guidance of the Individual Child."

Jordan, Part 4, "Testing and Learning."

Morse & Wingo, Chapter XIV, "Evaluating Learning and Teaching."

Mursell, Chapter XVI, "Teaching and Evaluation in Relation to Personality."

Peterson *et al.*, Chapter XIV, "The Measurement of Personality Other Than Intelligence"; Chapter XVI, "The Measurement of Achievement."

Remmers et al., Chapter XI, "Achievement Testing"; Chapter XII, "Constructing Short-Answer Tests"; Chapter XIII, "Interpreting Scores"; Appendix, "Measures of Relationship."

Skinner, Part 4, "Measuremennt and Evaluation."

Witherington, Chapter XIV, "Evaluating Achievement in Learning."

EPILOGUE

As we look back upon our study of human development, learning, and teaching, we become even more convinced of what was said at the outset, namely, that we have provided merely an orientation to a large body of important material. The student should consider this book only a beginning; he must pursue these matters more deeply throughout his professional career. As we have said many times before, teaching stands to profit most from advances in psychology, sociology, and psychotherapy; while these sciences cannot provide the norms for education, they provide indispensable data for the interpretation of child development and learning.

Much remains to be done for the preparation and assistance of Christian teachers. We wish to discuss briefly three such "musts."

First, we need a book on the principles of education. These are not to be confused with the psychological principles presented above. The principles we have in mind are guiding ideals and ideas for a whole mode of activity, in this case education. Every institution devoted to formal education — not only day schools — should be governed by such clearly defined general principles. Our culture is presently embroiled in a near-chaos of competing educational principles; Christian education needs to stand in this chaos with a position based explicitly upon Christian concepts.

Second, we need a guidebook of techniques for Christian teachers. Teachers constantly request practical classroom devices, while at the same time they are bombarded with a multitude of such helps in the name of the latest scientific research. Who will assist the teacher — especially the inexperienced teacher — by providing an authoritative guide to classroom practice?

Finally, there is great need for a systematic exposition of a Christian philosophy of education that takes adequate account of recent developments in educational theory and practice, appraises them, and formulates guiding ideas and ideals in the perspective of a scriptural world-and-life view. It is sometimes said that we have no Christian philosophy of education. The person who says this may not have such a philosophy himself, but by his statement he betrays his ignorance of sources now available. We do need, however, a more systematic exposition than we now possess in printed form.

It is the hope and prayer of the author that this volume may encourage and make a small contribution to the fulfillment of these needs.

Glossary
Bibliography
Index

GLOSSARY OF TECHNICAL TERMS

A

Acculturation — adoption of the cultural traits or patterns of a given group.

Achievement test — test that measures accomplishment in a given area of instruction; e.g., mathematics.

Age norm — average or normal performance for a certain age group.

Anti-theism — the doctrine that denies the existence of a personal God.

Associationist — one who holds the view that behavior can be explained by noting what experiences are related and how they are related; e.g., what ideas or actions are suggested to one by calling a dog.

Appraisal — estimate or guage of the progress in development and learning by various tools available.

Atomism — the belief that behavior and personality are composed of parts that flow together by some external force.

B

Bond theory — the theory that connections established in the nervous system between neurons explain behavior and learning.

Biosocial — in regard to man, pertaining to the view that man is a biological organism capable of conforming his behavior to social or group practices.

C

Canalizing — in reference to behavior, the action of establishing pathways of discharge of energy; also called channeling.

Channeling — as above.

Conduction unit — unit of action in the central nervous system constituted by sensory (affective) and motor (effective) nerves together with connecting nerve (s) and synapse (s) .

Cosmos — the universe in its totality.

Creative expression	— productive communication from the resources of one's own personality, or totality of his experiences.
Culture	— the aggregates of collective attainments characteristic of a group, state, or nation by which it is distinguished from other groups.
Cultural activity	— the use and production of a culture.

D

Decile	— one of the ten equal parts of a distribution of scores; e.g., the first decile would indicate the scores contained in the highest tenth of the group.
Deductive method	— method of reasoning from a general principle, rule, or definition to concrete, specific cases or applications.
Derived score	— a score value obtained by changing a raw score (see below) on a test into its equivalent in a value scale; e.g. a raw score of 65 may have the equivalent value in a given scale of 25th percentile or 3.2 grade level.
Diagnostic test	— a test that seeks to determine the source of difficulties in learning or behavior problems in general.
Discrete	— having no continuity or gradation from one item to another.
Dynamic	— energetic, active, stimulating; the opposite of static.

E

Ego-ideal	— a person conceived of as a standard of one's striving for perfection.
Enculturation	— the act of making the culture a living force for further development and learning.
Experience	— what a person undergoes through interaction with his environment and/or the cumulative effect of the interaction on future behavior.
Experimentation	— investigation by a planned procedure accompanied by control of factors that produce change.

F

| Faculty psychology | — the view that mind or soul as a substance is divided into compartments or categories of power, as knowing, feeling, and willing, each of which can be trained independently. |

Frequency distribution	— a tabulation of values or scores showing the number of each from high to low.

G

Grade norm	— standard for a given grade level.
Group test	— test constructed to measure achievement of individuals as members of a group.

H

Homeostasis	— equilibrium or balance.
Hypothalamus	— a group of nerve cells almost at the center of the base of the brain.
Hypothesis	— a tentative conclusion used to guide further investigation and research.

I

Immanentism	— the view that all of reality is to be seen from a point within the universe; opposite of transcendentalism.
Indigenous motivation	— source of action from within the organism.
Individual test	— a test designed to measure achievement of the individual apart from group attainment.
Individuate	— something of a more general nature which has taken on individual existence.
Inductive method	— method of reasoning from specific cases or concrete items to a general principle, rule, or definition.
In-life relationship	— behavior of the organism in its interaction with its environment.
Inventory test	— a check list of abilities to determine a subject's achievements.

J

James-Lange theory	— a theory independently arrived at by James (U.S.) and Lange (Denmark) which suggests that the bodily response produces the experience rather than being produced by it; e.g., one is afraid because he runs rather than that he runs because he is afraid.

L

Longitudinal	— representing the vertical description of human development from infancy to maturity.

M

Maturation	— changes in the characteristics of an organism resulting from intrinsic development.
Maturity	— stage at which an organism has reached its maximum growth and development; used to indicate the level at which an organism can function independently in a given environment.
Mean (arithmetic mean)	— arithmetic average of all scores on a test; total of all scores divided by the number of scores.
Measure of central tendency	— the score around which all the scores of a test cluster; the central score.
Mechanistic	— pertaining to the doctrine that nature and the processes of life are necessitated machine-like and can be explained according to laws of physics and chemistry.
Median	— the point on a scale below which half the scores fall; the 50th percentile.
Medium for development	— influence or agency in which development takes place and which contributes to development from its own structure.
Metaphysical	— pertaining to the ultimate nature of things.

N

Negative acceleration	— that process whereby progress achieved by practice is leveling off.
Norm	— average performance of a specific reference group.

O

Objective test	— a test that can be scored objectively according to a key.
Observation	— investigation which is purposeful, but does not seek to control the factors involved.
Organic unity	— a wholeness developed and maintained from within capable of reproducing itself.
Organismic	— having inseparable wholeness; no organ functions or develops independently of others
Oriented	— adjusted with relation to; e.g., a physically oriented view of things is a view adjusted to laws of physics and chemistry.
Original nature	— in psychology, man's inherited structure and function.
Original sin	— sin of mankind as transmitted from Adam.

P

Percentile	— one of the ninety-nine parts into which a distribution of scores can be divided; e.g., the 60th percentile represents the score (s) at the 60th part from the bottom.
Perceptual	— pertaining to the act whereby an external situation relates to a person's background of experience.
Phenomenological	— pertaining to interrelatedness on the level of experience with things; e.g., phenomenology explains behavior wholly from observed and recorded data.
Positive acceleration	-- that process whereby improvement resulting from practice continues at steady or increased pace.
Pragmatic bias	— the assumption that practice, behavior, and consequences are primary in development.
Presupposition	— assumption of principle or fact on which one basis subsequent reasoning.
Psychoanalyst	— a psychiatrist who is committed to and practices the psychoanalytic method in therapy; psychoanalysis is the method originated by Sigmund Freud for investigating the deeper areas of the mind by study of normal and abnormal reactions.
Psychogenic	— pertaining to the view that mental behavior is qualitatively to be distinguished from physical activity.

Q

Quartile	— a series of scores is divided into four equal groups from highest to lowest and each group is a quartile; the first quartile is the highest quarter.

R

Raw score	— a score obtained from a test in terms of items right and wrong.
Reinforcement	— the strengthening of learning by practice, rewards, further association, etc.
Reliability	— the accuracy with which a test measures a given achievement; constancy and consistency obtained by repeated measuring.
Religious being	— man in his essence, not merely as an organism that worships; man as of God in creation, image of God, God-like.
Representative expression	— expression that reproduces or reflects a presented structure of fact or ideas.

S

Sampling	— process of selecting a limited number of cases representative of a larger group, people, scores, etc.
Saturation point	— maximum point beyond which further practice does not produce measurable progress.
Scaled test	— a test arranged in order of increasing difficulty.
Self-actualizing	— attaining fulfillment of inherent potential from forces within.
Self-determining	— attaining ends by direction from within.
Self-fulfillment	— attainment of one's potential.
Short-answer test	— a test that calls for brief answers, as marks of true or false, words or phrases, etc. which can be scored by a key.
Soul life	— mental life or non-physical life processes.
Standardized test	— a test characterized by selected content, established norms, and uniform methods of administering and scoring.

T

Theism	— the doctrine that God exists and is personal.
Theory	— a tentative conclusion based on scholarly investigation, more conclusive than a hypothesis and useful as guide in further investigation.
Transactionalism	— the view that development results from an interplay of forces within and without that leave a deposit of behavior patterns in the organism.
Transverse	— a horizontal description of development; e.g., a description of physiological, emotional, social, and cognitive development of early childhood.
Twofold unity	— wholeness of structure and function as it pertains to the person within and to his relationships.

V

Validity of a test	— the extent to which a test measures what it purports to measure; a geography test should measure geographic knowledge, not the ability to interpret long and involved statements.

W

Whole-person-in-action	— wholeness described in terms of behavior.
Whole-person-in-life	— description of wholeness of the personality in terms of human life and its relationships.

BIBLIOGRAPHY

Allen, R., *Education and the Native Church* (London: World Dominion Press, 1928)

Allen, R., *The Spontaneous Expansion of the Church* (London: World Dominion Press, 1956)

Allport, G. W., *Personality: A Psychological Interpretation* (New York: Henry Holt & Co., Inc., 1937)

Augustine, *Confessions*

Beaumont, H., and Macomber, F. G., *Psychological Factors in Education* (New York: McGraw-Hill Book Co., Inc., 1949)

Blair, G. M., Jones, R. S., and Simpson, R. H., *Educational Psychology* (New York: The Macmillan Co., 1954)

Bugelski, B. R., *The Psychology of Learning*

Buros, O. K., ed., *The Fifth Mental Measurements Yearbook* (Highland Park, N. J., The Gryphon Press, 1959)

Burton, W. H., *The Guidance of Learning Activities* (New York: Appleton Century-Crofts, Inc., 1952)

Calvin, John, *Institutes of the Christian Religion*

Chapman, J. C., and Counts, G. S., *Principles of Education* (Boston: Houghton Mifflin Co., 1924)

Coladarci, A. P., ed., *Educational Psychology; A Book of Readings* (New York: The Dryden Press, Inc., 1955)

Cole, L. E., and Bruce, W. F., *Educational Psychology* (Yonkers-on-Hudson, N. Y.: World Book Co., 1950)

Cronbach, L. J., *Educational Psychology* (New York: Harcourt, Brace & Co., Inc., 1954)

Crow, L. D., and Crow, A., *Human Development and Learning* (New York: American Book Co., 1956)

Fullager, W. A., Lewis, H. G., and Cumbee, C. F., *Reading in Educational Psychology* (New York: The Thomas Y. Crowell Co., 1956)

Gates, A. I., Jersild, A. T., McConnel, T. R., and Chillman, R. C., *Educational Psychology*, third ed. (New York: The Macmillan Co., 1949)

Hall, C. S. and Lindzey, G., *Theories of Personality* (New York: John Wiley & Sons, Inc., 1957). A very helpful attempt to bring together in survey existing theories of personality.

Havighurst, R. J., *Human Development and Education* (New York: Longmans, Green and Co., Inc., 1953)

Hebb, D. O., *Organization of Behavior*

Herrick, C. J., *Brains of Rats and Man* (Chicago: The University of Chicago Press, 1926)

Hildreth, G., *Learning the Three R's; A Modern Interpretation*, second ed. (Philadelphia: Educational Publishers, Inc., 1946) first ed. Minneapolis, Nashville, Philadelphia: Educational Publishers, Inc., 1936

Jaarsma, C., *Fundamentals in Christian Education* (Grand Rapids; Wm. B. Eerdmans Publishing Co., 1953)

Jenkins, G. G. *et. al.*, *These Are Your Children*, expanded ed. (Chicago: Scott, Foresman & Co., 1953)

Jersild, A. T., *Child Psychology* (Englewood Cliffs, N. J.: Prentice Hall, Inc., 1954)

Jersild, A. T., *In Search of Self* (New York: Teachers College, Columbia University, 1952)

Jordan, A. M., *Educational Psychology*, fourth ed. (New York: Henry Holt & Co., Inc., 1956)

Kellogg, W. N., and L. A., *The Ape and the Child* (New York: McGraw-Hill Book Co., Inc., 1945)

Kuypers, A., *Inleidung in de Zielkunde* ("Introduction to Psychology"), (Kampen, the Netherlands: J. H. Kok, N. V., 1953)

Lane, H., and Beauchamp, M., *Human Relations in Teaching* (Englewood Cliffs, N. J.: Prentice-Hall, Inc., 1955)

Morse, W. C. and Wingo, G. M., *Psychology and Teaching* (Chicago: Scott, Foresman & Co., 1955)

Mursell, J. L., *Psychology for Modern Education* (New York: W. W. Norton & Co., Inc., 1952)

Olson, W. C., "Redefining the Task of Education," *Educational Leadership*, IX (1952), 219-224

Overstreet, H. A., *The Mature Mind* (New York: W. W. Norton & Co., Inc., 1949). An account of human development based on the maturity concept.

Peterson, H. A., Marzolf, S. S., and Bayley, N., *Educational Psychology* (New York: The Macmillan Co., 1948)

Remmers, H. H., Ryden, E. R., and Morgan, C. L., *Introduction to Educational Psychology* (New York: Harper & Bros., 1954)

Rothney, J. W. M., *The High School Student; A Book of Cases* (New York: The Dryden Press, Inc., 1953)

Schorling, R., and Batchelder, H. T., *Student Teaching in Secondary Schools* (New York: McGraw-Hill Book Co., Inc., 1956)

Skinner, C. E., ed., *Educational Psychology*, third ed., (Englewood Cliffs, N. J.: Prentice-Hall Inc., 1951)

Sorenson, H., *Psychology in Education*, third ed. (New York: McGraw-Hill Book Co., Inc., 1954)

Stephens, J. M., *Educational Psychology;* rev. ed. (New York: Henry Holt & Co., Inc., 1956)

Stoddard, G. D., *The Meaning of Intelligence*, (New York: The Macmillan Co., 1943)

Stroud, J. B., *Psychology in Education* (New York: Longmans, Green & Co., Inc., 1956)

Symonds, P., "Education and Therapy," *Journal of Educational Psychology*, XL (Jan. 1945), 5-20

Thorndike, E. L., *Human Nature and the Social Order* (New York: The Macmillan Co., 1940)

Thorndike, E. L., *The Psychology of Learning* (New York: Teachers College, Columbia University, 1913)

Waterink, J., *Ons Zieleleven* (Wagenningen, the Netherlands: N. V. Gebr. Zomer & Keuning, 1946)

Watson, J. B., *Behaviorism* (New York: The Macmillan Co., 1912)

Witherington, H. C., *Educational Psychology*, rev. ed. (Boston: Ginn & Co., 1952)

Wyngarden, H. R., *Hoofdproblemen der Volwassenheid* ("Major Problems of Maturity"), (Utrecht, the Netherlands: Erven J. Byleveld, 1950)

INDEX